The Cambridge Companion to Molière

A broad and detailed introduction to Molière and his plays, this *Companion* evokes his own theatrical career, his theatres and patrons, the performers and theatre staff with whom he worked and the various publics he and his troupes entertained with such success. It looks at his particular brands of comedy and satire. *L'École des femmes*, *Le Tartuffe*, *Dom Juan*, *Le Misanthrope*, *L'Avare* and *Les Femmes savantes* are examined from a variety of different viewpoints, and through the eyes of different ages and cultures. The *comédies-ballets*, a genre invented by Molière and his collaborators, are reinstated to the central position which they held in his œuvre in Molière's own lifetime; his two masterpieces in this genre, *Le Bourgeois gentilhomme* and *Le Malade imaginaire*, have chapters to themselves. Finally, the *Companion* looks at modern directors' theatre, exploring the central role played by productions of his work in successive 'revolutions' in the dramatic arts in France.

D1388261

THE CAMBRIDGE
COMPANION TO
MOLIERE

EDITED BY
DAVID BRADBY
Royal Holloway, University of London
ANDREW CALDER
University College London

CAMBRIDGE UNIVERSITY PRESS
Cambridge, New York, Melbourne, Madrid, Cape Town, Singapore, São Paulo

Cambridge University Press
The Edinburgh Building, Cambridge CB2 2RU, UK

Published in the United States of America by Cambridge University Press, New York

www.cambridge.org
Information on this title: www.cambridge.org/9780521546652

First published 2006

Printed in the United Kingdom at the University Press, Cambridge

A catalogue record for this publication is available from the British Library

Library of Congress Cataloging in Publication Data

The Cambridge companion to Molière / edited by David Bradby, Andrew Calder. 1st ed.
p.cm. – (Cambridge companions to literature)
Includes bibliographical references and Index.

1. Molière, 1622–1673 – Criticism and interpretation – Handbooks, manuals, etc.
I. Bradby, David. II. Calder, Andrew, 1942– III. Title. IV. Series.
PQ1860.C36 2006
842'.4–dc22

ISBN-13 978-0-521-83759-0 hardback
ISBN-10 0-521-83759-6 hardback
ISBN-13 978-0-521-54665-2 paperback
ISBN-10 0-521-54665-6 paperback

CONTENTS

CONTENTS

LIST OF ILLUSTRATIONS

Chapter 15 – David Whitton

Chapter 16 – David Bradby

NOTES ON CONTRIBUTORS

RALPH ALBANESE, JR, is a Dunvavant Professor of French at the University of Memphis. He is the author of *La Fontaine à l'École républicaine* (2003), *Molière à l'École républicaine* (1992), *Initiation aux problèmes socio-culturels de la France au XVIIème siècle* (1977), *Le Dynamisme de la peur chez Molière* (1976) and of numerous articles on concepts of anomie, criminality, gambling, money, death, critical reception, classical discourse and ideological codes as reflected in the works of seventeenth-century French dramatists, novelists, and poets.

DAVID BRADBY is Professor of Drama and Theatre Studies at Royal Holloway, University of London. He is author of *Modern French Drama 1940–1990* (1991), *The Theater of Michel Vinaver* (1993), *Beckett: Waiting for Godot* (2001) and (with Annie Sparks) *Mise en Scène: French Theatre Now* (1997). With Maria M. Delgado, he edits the *Contemporary Theatre Review* and he is general editor of 'Cambridge Studies in Modern Theatre'.

ANDREW CALDER was formerly Reader in French at University College London. He is author of *Molière: The Theory and Practice of Comedy* (1993), *The Fables of La Fontaine: Wisdom Brought Down to Earth* (2001) and of articles on the history of ideas in writing and painting in the seventeenth century.

MARIE-CLAUDE CANOVA-GREEN is Reader in French at Goldsmiths College, University of London. She is author of *La Politique-spectacle au grand siècle* (1993), *La Comédie* (1993), *Benserade. Ballets pour Louis XIV* (1997), and co-author of *Le Théâtre en France des origines à nos jours* (1997), *Spectaculum Europaeum* (1999) and *Europa triumphans* (2004). She has just completed a monograph on *Les Comédies-ballets de Molière et les débats du temps*.

JIM CARMODY is Associate Professor of Theatre and Dance at the University of California-San Diego, where he was the founding head of the department's doctoral program in theatre. He is the author of *Rereading Molière* (1993), articles on French and American theatre and translations of plays by Molière and Marivaux. He also serves as one of the editors of *TheatreForum*.

JAN CLARKE is Senior Lecturer in French at the University of Durham and has written extensively on all aspects of seventeenth-century French theatre, including architecture, company organisation, the lives of women theatre professionals, and spectacle. She is currently completing the third volume of a series on the Hôtel Guénégaud (1673–80) in which she looks at all aspects of the company's activity, including its establishment, theatre design, financial organisation and production policy, focusing particularly on its spectacular productions.

STEPHEN KNAPPER is Lecturer in Drama at Kingston University. He is author of three articles on the work of the British company Theatre de Complicite and has published three chapters from his doctoral thesis on the mask of Scaramouche. He is now working on a collaborative project with Royal Holloway, University of London exploring the relationships between carnival, mask and *commedia*.

ROXANNE LALANDE is Professor of French at Lafayette College in Pennsylvania. Her research interests lie in the fields of French literature of the *Ancien Régime*, comic and dramatic theory, pre-revolutionary women writers, and the epistolary novel. She is author of *Intruders in the Play World: The Dynamics of Gender in Molière's Comedies* (1996) and editor of *A Labor of Love: Critical Reflections on the Writings of Marie-Catherine Desjardins* (2000); she has also translated Villedieu's *Love Notes and Letters* and *The Letter Case*.

ROBERT MCBRIDE is Professor of French at the University of Ulster, author of *The Sceptical Vision of Molière: A Study in Paradox* (1977), *Aspects of Seventeenth-Century French Drama and Thought* (1979), *The Triumph of Ballet in Molière's Theatre* (1992), *Molière et son premier Tartuffe: genèse d'une pièce à scandale* (2005), editor of La Mothe Le Vayer: *Lettre sur la comédie de L'Imposteur* (1994), *L'Imposteur de 1667 prédécesseur du Tartuffe*, and co-founder and co-editor with Noël Peacock of *Le Nouveau Moliériste*.

CHARLES MAZOUER is Professor of French Literature at the Université Michel de Montaigne Bordeaux III; his theatre history publications, some dozen studies and critical editions of texts, cover French theatre from the Middle Ages to the eighteenth century. They include *Molière et ses comédies-ballets* (1993), *Trois comédies de Molière. Étude sur «Le Misanthrope», «George Dandin», «Le Bourgeois gentilhomme»* (1999) and *Le Théâtre d'Arlequin: Comédies et comédiens italiens en France au XVIIe siècle* (2002). He is currently engaged on a major history of theatre in France.

LARRY F. NORMAN is Associate Professor in Romance Languages and Literatures at the University of Chicago. He is the author of *The Public Mirror: Molière and the Social Commerce of Depiction* (1999) and has edited three volumes on the relation between theatre, book history and the visual arts: *The Theatrical*

Baroque (2001), *The Book in the Age of Theater* (2001) and *Du spectateur au lecteur: imprimer la scène aux XVIe et XVIIe siècles* (2002).

RICHARD PARISH is a Professor of French in the University of Oxford and a Fellow of St Catherine's College. He has written extensively on Pascal, as well as on seventeenth-century French theatre, in which area his writing includes a book on Racine and editions of both Racine and Molière (*Le Tartuffe*).

NOËL PEACOCK holds the Marshall Chair of French, and is Associate Dean (Research) at the University of Glasgow. His publications on Molière include *Molière in Scotland* (1993), *L'École des femmes* (1988), *Les Femmes savantes* (1990) and critical editions of *La Jalousie du Barbouillé et George Dandin* (1984) and *Dépit amoureux* (1989) and many articles. He is co-founder and co-editor with Charles Mazouer of *Le Nouveau Moliériste*.

JOHN S. POWELL is Professor of Musicology at the University of Tulsa and the author of *Music and Theatre in France, 1600–1680* (2000). He has published numerous articles on the Molière-Lully-Charpentier *comédies-ballets* and other works of seventeenth-century musical theatre, as well as a website of musical editions with full-text facsimiles of plays ('Music and Theater in France in the Seventeenth Century': http://www.personal.utulsa.edu/~john-powell/theater/).

JULIA PREST is Assistant Professor of French at Yale University. She wrote her Ph.D. on Molière's *comédie-ballets* and her critical edition of *Le Mariage forcé* was published by Exeter University Press in 1999. She has published articles on *comédies-ballets*, *ballet de cour*, school drama and the court of Louis XIV. Her book on cross-casting and women's roles in seventeenth-century French theatre will be published by Palgrave-Macmillan in 2006.

DAVID WHITTON is Professor of French Theatre at Lancaster University. His publications include *Stage Directors in Modern France* (1987) and *Molière: Don Juan* ('Plays in Performance', 1995). He is currently co-writing with Jan Clarke a history of theatre in France.

PREFACE

Molière is the most companionable of writers. His plays are filled with warmth, generosity, exuberance. In them, the sympathetic, if excessively trusting, young lovers always win out in the end despite the worst efforts of their self-centred and mendacious elders. There is wit and vitality in his dialogue, and a refreshing recognition in the mirror he holds before us that we are all ridiculous enough to be fit material for satire. For all their joyful qualities, however, Molière's plays also demonstrate the darker sides of human relationships. Beyond the happy endings, often contrived to the point of being quite unbelievable, a world of tyrannical power-relationships is revealed. Also, his satire of some aspects of polite society in mid-seventeenth-century France is so accurate that his contemporaries made strenuous efforts to keep some of his plays off the stage altogether.

This *Companion* is offered in the hope that it will assist readers and performers of his plays in exploring for themselves the life-enhancing qualities of this outstanding comic writer. The opening chapters contain a sketch of Molière's life in the theatre, a description of his actual theatres and their day-to-day workings, and a discussion of the acting of his plays – both by Molière himself and by modern troupes; the closing chapters reflect on some of the exciting rebrandings of Molière by modern directors who have found in him and his plays inspiration for their own perpetual rein-ventions of the theatre for their own generations. In the middle of the book, a variety of scholars, using a variety of approaches, look at comedy and satire, at the *comédies-ballets* and at individual comic masterpieces. Of course this is a *Companion*, not a sarcophagus in which we have sought to lodge a complete and embalmed Molière. Many more Molières await rewriting, and both editors and contributors will be pleased if these glimpses of his genius stir others to perform and write new versions of their own.

1622   Birth of Jean-Baptiste Poquelin, baptised 15 January. His family, who live in the Halles district of Paris, are *tapissiers* [tapestry- makers], on both sides and for several generations. He studies humanities (according to La Grange in the *Préface* to the 1682 edition of his plays) at the celebrated Jesuit Collège de Clermont, where the curriculum is grounded on the study of Latin language and literature; the Roman comedies of Terence and the writings of the orator and moralist Cicero are central to the curriculum; the performance of ballets and plays in Latin is part of a Jesuit education.

1631   His father, Jean Poquelin, purchases the office of *tapissier et valet de chambre ordinaire du roi* and, in 1637, obtains the reversion of the office to his fifteen-year-old son.

1632   His mother dies. The inventory of her effects suggests that the family is comfortably off, but not wealthy.

1643–5 After graduating in law and practising for no more than a few months, he receives part of his succession from his father, cedes his right to the office of *tapissier* to his brother and joins with Madeleine Béjart and eight others to found the Illustre Théâtre in the faubourg Saint-Germain. The new troupe spends lavishly on the theatre's furnishings; they appoint four musicians and a dancer. Financial difficulties drive them to move from Saint-Germain to premises in the theatre district on the Right Bank. Jean-Baptiste chooses the stage name of Molière and emerges first as co-leader, with Madeleine Béjart, then as leader of the troupe. Their repertoire is

dominated by tragedies and tragi-comedies written by
fashionable playwrights.

1645–58   Increasing debts lead to Molière's brief imprisonment (not
until 1666 does he finish paying them off). He leaves Paris
and, soon to be followed by the Béjarts, joins the troupe of
Charles Dufresne (belonging to the duc d'Épernon) which,
from a base in the Languedoc, performs mainly in the
southern provinces, both to elite audiences and (less often) to
mixed urban audiences. Molière is leader of the troupe by
around 1650. Surviving documents show him at various
points in Nantes, Toulouse, Albi, Poitiers, Narbonne, Agen,
Pézenas, Bordeaux, Grenoble, Lyon, Montpellier, Béziers,
Dijon and Rouen. The company becomes 'the troupe of
Monseigneur le Prince de Conti' in 1653 (until Conti
withdraws permission to use his name in 1657). Around
1653–4, Molière gives the first performance, in Lyon, of
L'Étourdi (in five acts and in verse), the earliest of his
published plays. This play and another early five-act play in
verse, *Le Dépit amoureux* (1656?), will be revived frequently
after the troupe's move to Paris. Titles of farces from this
period survive, but most are undated, unpublished, and
perhaps only ever existed as rough outlines to be fleshed out
by the actors; texts of two of these, *La Jalousie du Barbouillé*
and *Le Médecin volant*, survive. Fragmentary evidence of the
troupe's repertoire in these years shows that, in addition to
short farces, it includes literary comedy, tragedy, tragi-comedy
and ballet.

1658   Molière's troupe arrives in Paris under the protection of
Monsieur, the King's brother (who does not pay his promised
pension) and performs Corneille's *Nicomède* and a one-act
farce, *Le Docteur amoureux* (now lost), before Louis XIV and
the court. The performance is well received and the troupe is
allotted a share of the Petit-Bourbon, where the Italian
Comedians – including the celebrated Scaramouche (Tiberio
Fiorilli) – are already installed. His repertoire, while continuing throughout the Paris years to include tragedies and
comedies by other authors, is increasingly dominated by
comedies written by Molière himself.

1659   *Les Précieuses ridicules*, a one-act farce and a pointed satire on aspects of contemporary salon life, attracts notoriety, enhancing Molière's reputation while inspiring hostility and jealousy among his rivals and victims.

1660   *Sganarelle ou le Cocu imaginaire* is the most frequently performed of Molière's plays during his lifetime. The Petit-Bourbon is demolished without warning, and the troupe, after three months without a home, moves, in January 1661, to the *salle* built originally by Richelieu in the Palais-Royal.

1661   *Dom Garcie de Navarre*, Molière's only play written in the higher register of tragedy and tragi-comedy, flops. *L'École des maris* is a consistent success. *Les Fâcheux*, his first *comédie-ballet*, is performed at Vaux-le-Vicomte for Fouquet before the King; music and choreography are by Pierre Beauchamp, who will choreograph all of Molière's *comédies-ballets*.

1662   Molière at forty marries the twenty-year-old actress Armande Béjart. *L'École des femmes*, the first of his *grandes comédies*, stirs a major literary quarrel, but establishes Molière's reputation as the leading comic poet of his generation.

1663   *La Critique de l'École des femmes* and *L'Impromptu de Versailles*: two lively one-act plays which discuss the nature of comedy, the theatre and acting.

1664   Molière's son Louis is born (he survives ten months; only his daughter Esprit-Madeleine, born 1665, will outlive him); the King is godfather and Henriette d'Angleterre godmother. Molière turns more and more to the new genre of *comédie-ballet* as his troupe performs with increasing frequency before the King and at court festivals. *Le Mariage forcé*, a *comédie-ballet*, with music by Lully, is performed at the Louvre for the Queen Mother; the King and a number of courtiers take dancing roles. (Lully will compose the music for all of Molière's *comédies-ballets* until 1672.) *La Princesse d'Élide*, a five-act *comédie-ballet*, is performed in the gardens at Versailles, formerly a royal hunting-lodge, as part of *Les Plaisirs de l' Île enchantée*, a festival based on a theme from

Ariosto's *Orlando furioso*. An early version of *Le Tartuffe* (in three acts), the most controversial of all Molière's satires, is performed as part of the same festival. While giving Molière his personal assurance that he sees nothing to censure in this biting satire on religious hypocrisy, the King bans further performances. But private readings in great houses continue.

1665   *Dom Juan*, another controversial play portraying an aristocratic *libertin* and echoing some of the themes from *Le Tartuffe*, is withdrawn by Molière after a brief and successful run. Molière's company becomes 'la Troupe du Roi', and he receives a pension of 6,000 livres. *L'Amour médecin*, a *comédie-ballet* in three acts.

1666   The early months of the year are dominated by Molière's almost fatal illness; he will suffer increasingly frequent ill health for the remaining seven years of his life. *Le Misanthrope*, Molière's fullest portrait of court society and salon life, is performed for the town, but not at court. *Le Médecin malgré lui*, a three-act farce.

1666–7   He collaborates with Benserade, Lully, the Italian Comedians and the troupe of the Hôtel de Bourgogne to create the spectacular *Ballet des Muses*; Molière contributes *Mélicerte*, *La Pastorale comique* and *Le Sicilien*; the ballet is performed for (and by) the King at Saint-Germain-en-Laye. Molière puts on one performance of *L'Imposteur* (a five-act revised version of *Le Tartuffe*) before it is again banned.

1668   Molière presents his version of Plautus' *Amphitryon* as a machine-play. *George Dandin* is performed at Versailles as part of a pastoral entertainment. *L'Avare*: Molière's rewriting of Plautus' *Aulularia* (*Pot of Gold*).

1669   The King gives permission for public performances of *Le Tartuffe*. In terms of gross box-office takings, it is Molière's third most successful play (after *Psyché* and *L'École des femmes*). *Monsieur de Pourceaugnac*, a *comédie-ballet* in three acts, is first performed at Chambord. Molière's father dies.

1670	Appearance of *Élomire hypocondre* (by Le Boulanger de Chalussay), a hostile – but informative – attack on Molière. *Les Amants magnifiques*, a *comédie-ballet*. The King ceases to appear himself in court ballets. *Le Bourgeois gentilhomme*, a *comédie-ballet*, is first performed at Chambord.
1671	*Psyché*, written in collaboration with Corneille and Quinault, a *tragi-comédie et ballet*, and machine-play. *Les Fourberies de Scapin*, a comedy in three acts adapted from Terence's *Phormio*. *La Comtesse d'Escarbagnas*, a one-act play incorporated within a ballet.
1672	*Les Femmes savantes*, a full and polished satire on the world of letters.
1673	*Le Malade imaginaire*, a *comédie-ballet* with music by Marc-Antoine Charpentier. Molière, playing the role of the hypochondriac, falls ill at the fourth performance and dies later that evening. Within a week his troupe, driven no doubt by the need to earn a living, returns to the stage. Four of his actors leave to join the Troupe royale at the Hôtel de Bourgogne. Those that remain, retaining the title of Troupe du Roi, merge with the actors of the Marais theatre and move to the Hôtel Guénégaud on the Left Bank, where they continue to perform Molière's plays.
1680	The Troupe du Roi merges again, at the King's command, with the Troupe royale of the Hôtel de Bourgogne to form the Comédie-Française, also known as La Maison de Molière.

I

MARIE-CLAUDE CANOVA-GREEN

The career strategy of an actor turned playwright: 'de l'audace, encore de l'audace, toujours de l'audace'

On ignore ce grand Homme; & les foibles crayons, qu'on nous en a donnez, sont tous manquez; ou si peu recherchez, qu'ils ne suffisent pas pour le faire connoître tel qu'il étoit. Le Public est rempli d'une infinité de fausses Histoires à son occasion. Il y a peu de personnes de son temps qui, pour se faire honneur d'avoir figuré avec lui, n'inventent des avantures qu'ils prétendent avoir eues ensemble.[1]

[We do not know this great Man, and the feeble sketches we have of him are all wide of the mark, or so lacking in depth that they are not enough to allow us to know him as he was. The general public has heard untold numbers of inaccurate stories about him. There are few among his contemporaries who, in order to enjoy the reflected glory of being associated with him, have not invented adventures that they claim to have shared with him.]

Thus wrote Grimarest in 1705. Three centuries later, we hardly know Molière's life, or his career, any better. We have only a few verifiable facts about his childhood and training. His thirteen years of life in the provinces have left few clues. Even in his last years in Paris, when his career as dramatist is well documented, his private life remains unknown. Moreover, Molière did not talk about himself. Few are the texts where he writes in the first person: a couple of prefaces, petitions and acknowledgements, generally linked to the debates arising from his work, and in the work itself a few passages where he acts out his own role as actor-director-author. Thus we can only get a feel of the man through what his contemporaries said; and their accounts generally take the form of unreliable anecdotes through which either his enemies sought to ridicule him, or else his friends aimed to make him the hero of a golden legend.

Paradoxically, his little-known life continues to fascinate. The time-honoured image of a Molière who lived a life of travail is in fact at odds with his remarkable and obvious success as a dramatist. The death of his mother when he was ten, the conflict with his father, who opposed his choice of career, his marital problems, attacks from enemies, betrayals by friends, sickness, in short everything, even his burial done hastily and by night, seems to point to the difficulties faced by a man who, while inspiring laughter, knew great personal unhappiness. Critics have often imposed a double personality on Molière as playwright too, seeking to distinguish a 'real' Molière, author of *Le Misanthrope* or *Tartuffe*, from a more trivial Molière who, driven by the need for money, sought to please the unenlightened taste of people and court by performing slapstick comedies and *comédies-ballets*. Such critics echo Boileau:

> Dans ce sac ridicule où Scapin s'enveloppe,
> Je ne reconnais plus l'Auteur du Misanthrope.[2]

[In Scapin's clowning with his sack, I do not recognise the author of *Le Misanthrope*.]

It is as if only the serious Molière were worthy of featuring in the myth built up around this poet actor, lauded as a seventeenth-century Terence by his supporters and condemned for the supposed vulgarity and immorality of his work by his enemies. Over the centuries, spreading admiration for this 'universal genius' has made him a symbol of France and a key figure in the history of world drama.

The Early Years

Molière was born Jean-Baptiste Poquelin, and only the 'invincible penchant qu'il se sentoit pour la Comedie' ['overwhelming desire that he felt for the theatre'][3] could make this son of a rich Parisian merchant-class family leave his father's trade of master *tapissier*. However, from these decisive early years, we know only that he was born in January 1622, that his mother died when he was a boy of ten and that in all likelihood he studied until 1639 in the Jesuit Collège de Clermont, the most fashionable school in Paris. While there, according to his first biographers, he met Chapelle, Bernier, future author of the *Abrégé de la vie d'Épicure*, and Cyrano de Bergerac, with whom he attended classes given by the Epicurean philosopher Gassendi. Molière's translation of Lucretius's *De Natura Rerum* possibly dated from this time too. His humanist education, then, was allied to a philosophical training with a libertine flavour.

Evidence on his education, of course, may be flawed: our sources, Donneau de Visé and La Grange, might well have overstated both Molière's philosophical training and his classical learning in order to enhance his theatrical reputation and combat the caricatural image of him as a *farceur* spread by his enemies. For the latter was precisely the image painted by those who evoked a youthful Molière acting on Parisian street corners as assistant to the charlatans Orviétan and Bary, or playing apprentice to the slapstick comic Guillot-Gorju. An interesting implication of these calumnious tales, however, is that they show contemporaries linking Molière with the French comic tradition, calling into question the current view of him as exclusively the pupil of Italian actors: after all, he was not in a position to observe the latter until his return to Paris in 1658, when he shared a theatre with them for several years.

Molière's family, the Poquelins, had connections with court entertainment through their relatives, the Mazuels, a famous family of musicians who undoubtedly helped the playwright gain access to the court. Early biographers also told the story that the child 'avoit un grand-pere, qui l'aimoit éperduëment; & comme ce bon homme avoit de la passion pour la Comédie, il y menoit souvent le petit Pocquelin, à l'Hôtel de Bourgogne' ['had a grandfather, who adored him; and as this man had a great love for the theatre, he often took the little Poquelin to the Hôtel de Bourgogne'].[4] It seems that Molière took up acting no later than January 1643, when he ceded to his brother the rights to the office of *tapissier* to the King, acquired by his father in 1631, and assigned to Molière himself in 1637. On 30 June 1643 Molière entered a contractual partnership with Madeleine Béjart, her brothers and a few friends, to found what was to be the Illustre Théâtre. We cannot be sure whether this was a new company or merely the formal establishment of an already existing group that gave private performances in makeshift settings. Either way, these young people displayed great intrepidity – or rashness – launching such a venture at a time when Richelieu's death threatened the theatre's (if not yet the actors') recent acquisition of respectability.

The Adventure of the Illustre Théâtre

The document drawn up by the solicitor to create the Illustre Théâtre is presented as a '*contrat de solidarité*' between ten signatories (six men and four women). Decisions were to be taken collectively, though three of them were responsible for casting, and Madeleine Béjart was free to choose her own roles. Though a casting director, Molière seems not to have become head of the company until a year later, in June 1644.

The ten-member company had to compete with rivals at the Hôtel de Bourgogne and the Marais, on the Right Bank of the Seine. It was logical for them to seek to avoid direct competition: hence their choice of premises in Saint-Germain-des-Prés, attractive both for its distance from the other theatres and because of the area's growing population, due to the sale in separate lots of Queen Marguerite's private residence and the arrival at the Luxembourg Palace of Gaston, duc d'Orléans, with whom the new company wished to find favour. In autumn 1643, they rented the jeu de paume des Mestayers, which had to be adapted to create a stage, gallery and boxes. Molière and his friends had high ambitions. They had to borrow: to cover the costs of alterations and of recruiting four musicians, followed, in June 1644, by a dancer. Molière's interest in drama combined with music goes back to the very earliest days of the Illustre Théâtre. Indeed, it was with 'deux ou trois entrées de ballet' ['two or three ballet entries'] that the company put on Claude de l'Estoile's *La Belle Esclave* in November 1644. However, financial insecurity was a problem from the start.

The new theatre opened in January 1644. The Marais theatre had just been destroyed by fire, which doubtless made the company's initial successes easier; at least until September 1644 everything went well. This is borne out by the actors' readiness to borrow money, and the ease with which they found lenders. Moreover, the company threw itself into an aggressive commercial policy, playing the latest works of the well-known authors of the time such as du Ryer or Tristan, rather than works already in the public domain. Responding to fashion and taste, they put on several tragedies which showcased Madeleine's talents. Again with an eye to fashion, they adopted a luxurious stage design with sumptuous backdrops and costumes. It is probable that, as part of a broader social strategy, the company performed in the homes of private individuals with the aim of developing a 'special relationship' with members of the Parisian elite. Indeed, by September 1644, the actors could present themselves as 'comédiens associés sous le titre de l'Illustre Théâtre entretenu par son Altesse Royale' ['actors working in a company known as the Illustre Théâtre under the patronage of His Royal Highness'], namely Gaston d'Orléans, the late King's brother.

However, the Marais reopened and competition became more fierce. With rising debts, the company incurred yet more by leaving their premises to settle closer to the other theatres, in the jeu de paume de La Croix-Noire in the Saint-Paul district. Were they fleeing failure or capitalising on early success? We cannot know, but delay opening the redecorated premises at the end of January 1645 and the early closure for Easter, resulting in fewer performances and lower takings, worsened the precarious finances of the Illustre Théâtre. The bailiffs took possession of settings and fittings, and Molière was twice imprisoned for debt in August 1645. In September, the actors were forced to leave and joined various provincial companies. The venture was over. But its collapse was not a result of failure to attract the public, of choosing the wrong plays, or of poor acting. They had held their own professionally against the other companies. Their problems were purely financial. In fact, Molière was not to succeed in getting a foothold in Paris until he could once again take advantage of the fact that the Marais theatre was provisionally closed, and he was only to make a lasting impact once the novelty success of his own plays had made a fashionable playwright of him.

Thirteen Years of Life in the Provinces

Once the Illustre Théâtre had gone and the company had disbanded, Molière, shortly followed by the Béjarts, was welcomed by the duc d'Épernon's company, which was touring in the west of France. Molière would take charge of it only towards 1650. Having become the virtual leader of a Parisian company at the young age of twenty-two, Molière was now to serve a long apprenticeship in the provinces. The sheer daring of this son of a wealthy bourgeois who, as a total novice, had wanted to give Paris a new company, had not paid off. The company started in Guyenne, then went to the Languedoc on the invitation of the comte d'Aubijoux, the King's *lieutenant général*, who procured invitations for them to attend each of the meetings of the province's États Généraux. It was thanks to him that the actors were introduced into the private circle of a privileged class: the social elite of the Languedoc and the whole network of followers of Gaston d'Orléans, the governor of the province. In 1653, they moved over to the service of the prince de Conti, who became patron of the company and allowed them to use his name. The picture painted by Molière's detractors of an assortment of 'caimans vagabonds, morts-de-fain [sic], demi-nuds' ['half-naked, starving lazy beggars and vagabonds'],[5] acting to crowds of illiterate peasants with vulgar tastes, is therefore misleading. On the contrary, the playwright was part of a company enjoying the patronage of a social elite, remunerated by the États Généraux and acting before distinguished gatherings.[6]

Until 1657, the company hardly left the Languedoc except for a few visits to Lyon, where doubtless they had to deal with an audience which consisted of paying commoners, very different from the elite social circle for whom they performed in Montpellier, Pézenas or Béziers. Molière and his fellow actors thus initiated a strategy of playing to different audiences, which they were to stick to later in Paris. There were two main strands to this 'success strategy': gaining the approval of aristocratic, princely circles, and guaranteeing a steadier income from the paying public.[7] It was thanks to their princely contacts in the Languedoc that Molière and his company were immediately presented to the court on their return to Paris in October 1658, under the protection of Monsieur, Louis XIV's only brother.

Not much is known of their provincial repertory, other than that it included 'ces petits divertissemens qui luy avoient acquis quelque reputation, & dont il regaloit les Provinces' ['those little plays which had earned him a good reputation, and which gave great pleasure in the provinces']⁸, namely old farces from the medieval tradition which Molière would rework on his return to the capital. We can assume that the company also put on tragedies, pastoral plays and comedies in five acts, particularly for the États Généraux. It was then that Molière's *L'Étourdi* was first staged, in Lyon from around 1653, and *Le Dépit amoureux*, in Béziers, 1656, both following the Italian model of the *commedia sostenuta*. Again in Lyon in 1653, the company staged *Andromède*, a machine-play by Corneille with music and dancing, displaying once again Molière's taste for spectacle and experiment, a taste no doubt encouraged by the presence of the musician d'Assoucy working with him during those years. It is possible that Molière was the author of the *Ballet des Incompatibles* staged in Montpellier for the Carnival of 1654–5 and in which he performed himself.

The actors' highly successful time in the Languedoc came to an abrupt close at the end of 1656 with the death of the comte d'Aubijoux and the sudden conversion of the prince de Conti, who withdrew his support from his actors. They had to leave a province now hostile to them and seek refuge in Lyon, where the prince 'leur [a] fait dire de quitter [son] nom' ['sent a message to tell them to stop using his name'].⁹ After touring there for a few months, they went to Rouen in the spring of 1658 and prepared for what was to be their permanent return to Paris in the autumn of that year. They returned under the aegis of Philippe, the King's brother, for experience had taught Molière that success was not possible without a patron. On 24 October, the actors performed a Corneille tragedy, followed by a short comedy by Molière, *Le Docteur amoureux*, before the King, in the Louvre.

A Dazzling Rise to Fame

This performance, of which no account survives, was a key event in Molière's career: it allowed him to arrange the loan of the huge *salle* in the Petit-Bourbon from the King, which he was to share with the Italian actors, before being rehoused in the Palais-Royal in 1660. Madeleine Béjart was really the star of this new company. From now on, Molière combined the roles of actor, *orateur* and, above all else, author. He initially sought to win success as much with tragedies as with his own comedies, such as *Les Précieuses ridicules* (1659) or *Sganarelle ou Le Cocu imaginaire* (1660), because he wished to compete with the Hôtel de Bourgogne on its own ground, and not as a company specialising in comedy. But he soon found that the public was more numerous when he put on one of his short plays after a tragedy, or when the programme included *L'Étourdi* or *Le Dépit amoureux*. He responded from 1663 by considerably reducing the number of tragedies performed, though he did not stop altogether until the last seasons at the end of his life. Molière was ambitious, too, to compose tragedies, the highest literary genre after the epic, and certainly the shortest route to attaining the glorious status of true poet and playwright. Thus in 1661 he staged his own *Dom Garcie de Navarre*, his first and last attempt to escape specialisation. Faced with the play's mediocre success, he had to decide to follow the path marked out for him by fashion and by the tastes of the theatre-going public.

Molière's strategy was to recycle the ingredients of his first comedies, turning them into longer plays such as the three-act *L'École des maris* (1661); to ensure the success of these, and so maintain reasonably steady box-office takings, he would put them on with established full-length pieces. Gradually, he moved on to comedies in five acts such as *L'École des femmes* (1662). At the same time, with *Les Fâcheux* (1661), he launched into *comédie-ballet*, a genre combining music, dance and text which, if not completely new, is still associated with his name. Created for the court, these works were afterwards performed in town with just as much success. It was the *comédie-ballet* that especially brought Molière to the King's attention.

This success strategy explains the diversity of Molière's output, in which farces, social satires, character plays and *comédies-ballets* provided a rich array of styles. It also explains the variety within individual plays, where different theatrical genres mingled: he introduced farcical elements into five-act plays in verse (for example in *L'École des femmes* and *Tartuffe*) or blended text, music and dance in multiple configurations. Such aesthetic innovation was possible because the audacity necessary to bring success was matched by the audacity of the playwright's invention. Molière aimed to be at the cutting edge of innovation, raising originality to the level of a literary value. More flexible than tragedy, and still very much in the process of being codified, comedy lent itself to innovation. His inclusion of such a variety of elements, reflecting the 'galant' aesthetics developing in the salons, allowed him to satisfy the expectations of a diverse public, whether at court or in town, whether well-heeled aristocrats in the private boxes or the lower orders standing in the *parterre*. And, for the most part, audiences poured in – and box-office takings. Only the literary establishment and the purists, keen on enforcing compliance with the rules of genre, found fault with his work.

Sure of his talent, Molière used every means to promote the image of actors. He had understood from early in his career the need for a good public-relations network. Hence his private performances in the capital, which became increasingly frequent and ended only when the King took over the company in August 1665. Such performances enhanced Molière's reputation. The status he achieved of 'writer without equal' was converted into social status for, though not ennobled like Corneille, he had the right to come into the presence of the King and his name was on the list of royal *pensions* drawn up by Chapelain in 1662. Recognition, fame and material well-being, Molière knew all of these.

Six Years of Fighting

But all this came at a price. His troubles may often have been exaggerated, but troubles there were: Molière as company director and playwright had to contend continually with the jealousy of rival actors and playwrights, criticisms from purists and above all the hostility of those who clung to a narrow religious and moral conformism, some of whom opposed the very survival of the theatre. In seeking to gain recognition as an author and as an author with ideas, Molière had to take on a society with many entrenched opinions. *L'École des femmes* in December 1662, although a triumph, and an unfinished *Tartuffe* in May 1664 were to plunge him into a period of controversy from which he was to emerge only six years later.

L'École des femmes, a neo-classical comedy in verse in five acts, based upon new aesthetic principles, stirred jealousy among the dramatic poets of his time and was greeted by a barrage of criticisms and libels. Molière responded with two short plays, *La Critique de L'École des femmes* and *L'Impromptu de Versailles*, in which he defended his comedy and caricatured his enemies, especially the Hôtel de Bourgogne actors. He affirmed the paramount importance of remaining faithful to nature, describing his plays as 'miroirs publics' ['public mirrors'] and 'peintures ridicules qu'on expose sur les théâtres' ['ridiculous portraits that are exposed on the stage'].[10] Such mirror-like fidelity was essential if the theatre was to fulfil its pedagogic role; however ridiculous, then, his gallery of portraits was to be seen and enjoyed as part of human nature. Molière also set out his principles as an actor and contrasted his direct style with the turgidity and caricatural affectation with which the Hôtel de Bourgogne actors declaimed their lines. In his desire to imitate natural diction, to search for harmony between subject, style and speech, he chose to move away from the practices of traditional oratory. This went hand in hand with his rejection of the stilted acting style of his rivals, and a preference for the variety and fluidity of movement and gesture which characterised the acting of the Italians. Lastly, by making the plot of *L'Impromptu de Versailles* the representation of the rehearsal of a play by his own company, Molière depicted himself in his own role as director-producer, taking care not to distribute 'ses rolles à des Acteurs qui ne seussent pas les executer' ['his roles to actors who did not know how to play them'], 'ne les pla[cer] point à l'avanture' ['miscast them badly']¹¹ and showing that he directed them with 'honnêteté' and in 'une manière engageante' ['an engaging fashion'].¹²

The *Querelle* of *L'École des femmes* barely over, Molière stirred new controversy with *Tartuffe*, a play in which he mocked sanctimonious hypocrites and argued for open, tolerant morals. He now encountered far more dangerous adversaries. The play was banned following pressure from the devout members of the Compagnie du Saint-Sacrement, who doubtless also saw to it that *Dom Juan*, first performed in February 1665, was swiftly withdrawn. Although the latter, where the provocative element was hidden behind expensive stage sets and machinery, was never staged again in his lifetime, Molière did all he could to get the ban on *Tartuffe* lifted. After the failure to get it performed in 1667 in a rewritten version as *L'Imposteur*, it was only in 1669 that it appeared at the Palais-Royal in its final version. It was a huge success, the more so because of the wait.

Despite everything, the period 1663–9 had been an extremely prosperous one for Molière and his company. In addition to the plays that had pro-voked – or contributed to – literary battles, Molière had been successfully writing different kinds of plays. The neo-classical character comedies, such as *Le Misanthrope* (1666) and *L'Avare* (1668), alternated with revamped farces, *George Dandin* (1668) and *Le Médecin malgré lui* (1666), and the mythological comedy of *Amphitryon* (1668). In the latter, borrowed from Plautus, Molière had a subtle revenge on those who accused him of flouting the classical tradition. No less important were the *comédies-ballets* written for the court, combining burlesque, 'galant' and mythological elements, and showing the full range of the playwright's creative palette: *Le Mariage forcé* (1664), *La Princesse d'Élide* (1664), *Le Sicilien* (1667) and *Monsieur de Pourceaugnac* (1669). If such range and variety are proofs of his talent and strategic skills, they also reveal a Molière writing under the many and varied pressures coming from King and court, from his Parisian public and from the running of his company. Attracting audiences is the aim of every theatre company, and Molière had to renew his repertory rapidly in order to fill his theatre; while satisfying the tastes of the day, he had to take into account his own and his actors' talents, characters and physical appearance, as well as the need to create a role for everybody. As La Grange noted with regret, Molière had also to respond swiftly to the King's wishes and sometimes work on topics not of his own choosing.[13] However, nowhere does one find Molière complaining of this. Was not the King's favour, shown in such commands, the true mark of success? To make life easier, we can be sure Molière reused work from his time in the provinces as well as borrowing freely from classical authors and his own contemporaries.[14]

The company certainly had difficult moments in Paris, especially when, in 1667, *Tartuffe* was banned twice. That year was particularly difficult, the more so because Molière fell ill in the spring and the actress Du Parc defected to the Hôtel de Bourgogne. The season of 1665–6 had had its troubles too: Molière's first illness and then the period of mourning for the Queen Mother, which closed the theatres, brought real hardship. The actors could never be guaranteed a stable income. No longer able to use the wide range of established works originally in their repertoire, the company found itself precariously dependent on new plays and on Molière's own creations. Any flop or ban resulted in serious difficulties.

In the King's Service

Powerful patrons helped Molière to overcome these difficulties. Firstly there was Monsieur, under whose wing the company returned to Paris; then Madame and the prince de Condé, who supported Molière during the *Querelle* of *Tartuffe*, and above all Louis XIV himself, who allocated him a theatre in the Louvre as soon as he returned in 1658, rehoused him in the Palais-Royal after the demolition of the Petit-Bourbon in 1660, took his side during the *Querelle* of *L'École des femmes* by agreeing to act as his son's godfather and by commissioning *L'Impromptu de Versailles* for the court in 1663 and lastly giving him and his company a leading role in the *Plaisirs de l'Île enchantée* in spring 1664. It was the King again who, soon after the ban on *Dom Juan*, adopted the company in August 1665, giving them a *pension* of 6,000 *livres* a year; the King also who, whilst maintaining the ban on *Tartuffe*, let it be known that this was for the sake of keeping peace in the kingdom and then lifted the ban at the first sign of calm. This protection amounted almost to a monopoly: once Louis XIV had become the company's patron, Molière became the named – if not sole – provider of the monarch's entertainment, from light after-dinner distractions during the hunting season to grand festivals in the palace gardens. The company's visits to the court became longer and more frequent, risking loss of support and consequent loss of income from the Parisian public. From 1664 to 1672, out of twenty-one plays written by Molière, fifteen were for the King. This proportion increased: between 1667 and 1672 Molière composed only two plays for the town, *L'Avare* (1668) and *Les Fourberies de Scapin* (1671), compared with seven *comédies-ballets* for the court. This shift in balance, at first evident only in court performances (three *comédies-ballets* to one single comedy), was increasingly found in his work as a whole. However, *Les Femmes savantes* (1672) showed a Molière still determined to be the leading entertainer both at court and in town: while the only dramatic poet to draw together music, dance and drama – of which the principal example was the tragedy-ballet *Psyché* (1671), the greatest success of his career – he composed in *Les Femmes savantes* one of his most polished neo-classical character comedies.

The Last Battles

The beginnings of the breakdown of Molière's partnership with the musician Lully probably dated from *Psyché*. This rupture occurred in the last years of Molière's career. In March 1672 Lully bought for his sole use the privilege granted to Perrin in 1669 which reserved the right to the Académie Royale de Musique to 'représenter et chanter en public des Opéra et Représentations en musique et en vers françois, pareilles et semblables à celles d'Italie' ['to put on and sing in public operas and plays in music and in French verse, as in like manner any from Italy'].[15] The draconian terms of the first draft of Lully's privilege, by limiting the musical accompaniment of plays to 'deux airs et deux instruments' ['two singers and two instrumentalists'][16] would have virtually prevented every theatre, including Molière's, from putting on works containing dancing and singing. Aware of the difficulty of filling the theatre without music, Molière was more disturbed by this restriction than by Lully's monopoly on opera itself. His tastes anyway tended more towards a union of the arts than towards pure opera, and a union in which the spoken text was the dominant element. However, while failing to stop the registration of the privilege, he did succeed in getting the conditions relaxed[17] and continued to stage *Psyché*. Disregarding the royal edict that gave Lully the rights to every text he had set to music, Molière even dared to restage *Monsieur de Pourceaugnac*, *Le Bourgeois gentilhomme*, *Le Mariage forcé* and *La Comtesse d'Escarbagnas*. And in *Le Malade imaginaire*, he put on a new *comédie-ballet* for the winter of 1673 which rivalled the spectacle that Lully and his new collaborator, Quinault, were preparing on the King's orders.

Molière continued his visits to court but only to put on plays. He was not asked to participate in the carnival festivities of 1673. The obvious cooling of relationships between Molière and the court has long been attributed to the split with Lully and a change in the King's tastes, but it can also be explained by the growing value Molière placed on his status as a writer rather than on his role as court poet. His success strategy was to focus increasingly on the publication of his plays and on protecting and profiting from his authorial rights. He had his *comédies-ballets* printed although, as court entertainments, they belonged to the King, and he fought against the illegal appropriation of his first nine plays by Parisian printers and booksellers. He acquired a general privilege in 1671 for his complete works, but the printer's cartel scandalously refused to register it and twice succeeded (in 1670 and 1672) in getting a verdict of exile pronounced against Molière's printer, Ribou.[18]

Whilst the spectacle *Cadmus et Hermione* prepared by Quinault and Lully was staged only in April 1673, Molière played his *Malade imaginaire* as early as February, as if to show that he alone could always be ready on time. It was a triumph, but Molière was ill. Knowing that the play's success rested on his role and his performance, he refused to rest and collapsed on stage during the fourth performance, on 17 February. He died at home that evening, unable to renounce the profession of an actor or receive the last rites. It was only on the intervention of Louis XIV to 'éviter l'éclat & le scandale' ['to avoid the commotion and scandal'][19] that Armande Béjart was able to obtain his burial in the cemetery of the parish of Saint-Eustache. He was buried hastily, and at night.

Epilogue

The rest is history. Not knowing quite what to do, Molière's company continued to stage *Le Malade imaginaire* until the end of the season at Easter. A few months later, on the order of the King, and without the four actors who had joined the Hôtel de Bourgogne, the company merged with the Marais, keeping the title Troupe du Roi, and moved to the Hôtel Guénégaud on the Left Bank. The theatre in the Palais-Royal was handed over to Lully to stage his tragedies set to music. In 1680, the Troupe royale of the Hôtel de Bourgogne merged in its turn with Molière's former company, leaving the Hôtel de Bourgogne to the Italian actors. The Comédie-Française was born.

NOTES

1 Jean Grimarest, *La Vie de Monsieur de Molière* (Paris: Jacques le Febvre, 1705), p. 3.
2 Nicolas Boileau-Despréaux, *Art Poétique*, in *Œuvres complètes*, ed. Françoise Escal (Paris: Gallimard, 1966), III, 399–400, p. 178.

3 Préface, *Les Œuvres de Monsieur de Molière*, ed. La Grange and Vivot (Paris: Denis Thierry, Claude Barbin, Pierre Trabouillet, 1682), I, p. ãiij recto.

4 Grimarest, *Vie*, pp. 6–7.

5 Le Boulanger de Chalussay, *Élomire hypocondre*, reproduced in Molière, *Œuvres complètes*, 2 vols., ed. Georges Couton (Paris: Gallimard, 1971), II, 1,231–86, p. 1,271.

6 See C. E. J. Caldicott, *La Carrière de Molière entre protecteurs et éditeurs* (Amsterdam and Atlanta: Rodopi, 1998).

7 See Alain Viala, *Naissance de l'écrivain* (Paris: Minuit, 1985).

8 La Grange and Vivot, *Œuvres*, préface, p. ãiiij recto and verso.

9 Letter from the prince de Conti to the abbé de Ciron (15 May 1657). Reproduced in Georges Mongrédien, *Recueil des textes et des documents du XVIIe siècle relatifs à Molière*, 2 vols. (Paris: Centre National de la Recherche Scientifique, 1965), I, p. 96.

10 *La Critique de L'École des femmes*, in Couton, *Œuvres complètes*, I, Sc. 6, p. 658.

11 Grimarest, *Vie*, p. 206.

12 Jean Donneau de Visé, *Mercure Galant* (1673), IV, pp. 267–319.

13 La Grange and Vivot, *Œuvres*, preface, p. ãvj verso.

14 See Grimarest, *Vie*, p. 47.

15 Privilege granted to Perrin on 28 June 1669. Reproduced in Charles Nuitter and Ernest Thoinan, *Les Origines de l'Opéra français* (Paris, 1886), p. 98.

16 *Factum de Sablières et Guichard*, in Nuitter and Thoinan, *Les Origines*, pp. 234–5.

17 The final version of the privilege published by royal edict in March 1672 contained no restrictions concerning the number of singers and instrumentalists. Molière also succeeded in getting the severity of the later royal edict of August 1672 relaxed, obtaining the choice of using six singers and twelve musicians.

18 On these questions, see Caldicott, *La Carrière de Molière*.

19 Nicolas Boileau-Despréaux, *Les Œuvres de Mr. Boileau Despréaux*, ed. Claude Brossette (Geneva: Fabri et Barrillot, 1716), I, p. 237. Note by Brossette to Épître VII, verse 19 ff.

2

JAN CLARKE

The material conditions of Molière's stage

Molière's Theatres

On 12 September 1643, the Illustre Théâtre, of which Molière was a member, rented the jeu de paume des Mestayers with the intention of converting it into a theatre.[1] The first building in which Molière performed professionally was, therefore, a former tennis court. *Paume* had been popular since the Middle Ages, but had declined by the seventeenth century, leaving many buildings empty. There was at this time only one purpose-built theatre in Paris: the Hôtel de Bourgogne, constructed by the Confrérie de la Passion in 1548 for the production of mystery plays, on which it held the monopoly in the capital. These were soon banned, and the Confrérie profited from its premises by renting them out to the companies of actors newly circulating in France following the end of the Wars of Religion. Since its monopoly was interpreted as applying to all theatrical activity in the capital, troupes performing elsewhere, in an empty *jeu de paume* for example, were heavily fined. This was the situation until the 1630s, when, gradually, two more or less permanent troupes were established in the capital, one at the Hôtel de Bourgogne and the other in a *jeu de paume* in the Marais district, called simply the Théâtre du Marais. It was with these that the Illustre Théâtre had to compete.

Tennis courts did not make ideal theatres. They were long, narrow buildings (a three-in-one ratio of length to width was standard), and the sightlines from anywhere other than directly in front of the stage were poor. It had been thought that early companies converted these buildings by installing a second gallery opposite the existing spectators' gallery and building a simple trestle stage at one end. However, in all those theatres for which there is evidence, the shell alone was employed, and companies had elaborate arrangements of stage, boxes, *parterre* and *amphithéâtre* constructed from scratch, as it was stipulated that buildings be restored to their original condition on termination of the lease.

1. Frontispiece to the rules of *jeu de paume* (Paris: Charles Hulpeau, 1632).

In a typical installation, the stage occupied the whole width of the building and was approximately six feet high. In front of it was the *parterre*, or pit, for rowdy, male, standing spectators. Running down each long side of the *parterre* were usually two rows of boxes, with the lowest raised six feet above the ground. Sometimes, these were topped by a gallery known as the *paradis*, and sometimes the rows projected over the stage to create stage boxes or *loges d'avant-scène*. Facing the stage were one or two rows of boxes, known as *loges du fond* or *de face*.

Much of the debate on early auditoriums concerns the placing of the *amphithéâtre*, which was a raked seating area opposite the stage. In the

Marais, as it was reconstructed after a fire in 1644, it was above the *loges du fond*,[2] while in later theatres, including Molière's Palais-Royal, it was between the *parterre* and the *loges du fond*. This was no doubt an attempt to provide seating with better sightlines for the privileged members of the audience who could afford to be placed there.

When the Illustre Théâtre leased the Mestayers, it installed the usual stage and boxes with galleries to provide access behind them. The building was located in Saint-Germain-des-Prés, between the rue de Seine and the rue Mazarine, and the company had part of the rue Mazarine paved and earth removed to allow easier passage for spectators and carriages. Thirty years later, it was still the custom for a theatre company to have an employee sweep the street in front of the theatre for the convenience of patrons.[3] We have no information as to the disposition of the Mestayers' auditorium, but the boxes were probably 6 *pieds* (1.95 m) in width. They were equipped with seats (probably benches) and were separated by wooden posts.

The Illustre Théâtre was soon in financial difficulties, which it attempted to resolve by mortgaging the wood and cloth used in the construction of its stage, boxes, galleries and *parterre*. In search of a more profitable location, on 19 December 1644, the company left the Mestayers and took out a lease on a second *jeu de paume*: the Croix-Noire, on the Seine, between what is now the rue de l'Ave-Maria and the quai des Célestins. When reconstructing its stage and auditorium in the new premises, the company's contract with the carpenter specified that there should be two rows of boxes 'like those of the Marais', which was evidently considered the acme of theatre design. Similarly, when the Hôtel de Bourgogne was renovated in 1647, the Marais was again given as a model. Not all the Croix-Noire boxes came direct from the Mestayers. There were six new ones, probably *loges d'avant-scène*, since a contract with a tapestry-maker gives details of their upholstery, together with those for the benches positioned in front of them.[4] In other theatres, privileged spectators sat on chairs at the side of the stage, although these could sometimes be moved, as Molière describes to comic effect in *Les Fâcheux*.

Unfortunately, the Illustre Théâtre was no more successful at the Croix-Noire than it had been at the Mestayers, and Molière left Paris for the provinces. Little is known of the theatres he occupied while on tour, but spaces in which he and his comrades performed included various *jeux de paume* and large rooms in public or private buildings. Not all towns were welcoming, and in 1654 the tennis court owners of Vienne were forbidden to rent their premises to the actors, and an individual who had begun to construct a theatre in a 'little *jeu de paume*' was ordered to destroy it.[5]

2. François Chauveau, frontispiece to *L'École des maris* (Paris: Guillaume de Luyne, 1661).

In 1658, Molière arrived in Rouen with the intention of returning to Paris. Accordingly, Madeleine Béjart took out a lease on the Marais, which was then standing empty while its company toured the provinces. In the event, this lease was not taken up, for, following a performance before the King in the Salle des Gardes in the Louvre, the Troupe de Monsieur was given permission to share the Petit-Bourbon with the *commedia dell'arte* troupe led by Scaramouche (Tiberio Fiorilli) that was already performing there.

The Petit-Bourbon was situated in the Louvre, between what are now the rue du Louvre, the rue des Prêtres-Saint-Germain-l'Auxerrois, the rue de l'Arbre-Sec and the quai du Louvre. It had housed the Estates General in 1614, and had also been used for court ballets and other productions, including *Le Ballet comique de la reine* (1581) and *La Finta Pazza* (1645). It was a large room, 28 by 8 *toises* (54.6 × 15.6 m), with a curved area at one end giving a further 7 *toises* (13.65 m) in depth. It had two balconies, one above the other, along each of its long sides, separated by partitions to form wide, open boxes. Marais-style boxes were probably constructed at some point, perhaps with the original galleries behind them providing access, since Molière's troupe was given permission to remove these boxes when the Petit-Bourbon was demolished in 1660. This was a surprising move: La Grange recounts how, on 11 October 1660, without notice, M. de Ratabon, Superintendent of the King's Buildings, began to demolish the Petit-Bourbon, ostensibly to make way for the Louvre's new colonnade, but perhaps also at the instigation of Molière's enemies.[6] However, the dramatist fought back, and the troupe's patron, Monsieur, obtained from the King that it be awarded the use of Richelieu's former theatre in the Palais-Royal. The troupe was given permission to remove the boxes and anything else it required from the Petit-Bourbon, excepting the decors. These were awarded to the newly arrived Italian stage designer, Carlo Vigarani, who claimed he was going to use them in his new theatre, the Salle des Machines in the Tuileries. Instead, he had them burned so that nothing would remain of his illustrious predecessor, Torelli.

The Grande Salle in the Palais-Royal (formerly the Palais-Cardinal), constructed to provide Richelieu with a hall suitable for spectacle, was inaugurated in 1641 with the production of *Mirame*. It was 18 *toises* (35.1 m) long by 9 (17.55 m) wide, with the stage and the five central steps leading up to it occupying a depth of some 7 or 8 *toises* (13.65 to 15.6 m). The auditorium was original in that it did not have a flat floor. Instead, there was a kind of extended *amphithéâtre* consisting of twenty-seven deep stone steps equipped with benches running across the whole width of the room. To the rear of these steps was a portico, and two gilded balconies ran down each long side. By 1660, when Molière moved in, this hall was sadly

3. Anonymous frontispiece to *Le Misanthrope* (Paris: Ribou, 1667).

dilapidated. Three of its beams were rotten and broken, and the roof had collapsed so that half the auditorium was exposed and in ruins. Ironically, the King ordered Ratabon to make the necessary repairs, but these can hardly have been extensive, since for over ten years the troupe performed beneath 'a large blue cloth suspended by ropes'.

Again treating the building as a shell, the troupe arranged for the construction of two rows of seventeen boxes, one above the other. These ran around the three sides of the auditorium, with five facing the stage and six along each side. The mention of a support rail above the upper row of boxes suggests that the troupe intended to have a *paradis*. But this may not have been installed at this time, since a third row of boxes was constructed in 1671.[7] As with the Petit-Bourbon, the original side balconies may have served as access galleries, with the vestiges overhanging the stage probably forming *loges d'avant-scène*. In its original form, the Palais-Cardinal had no *parterre*. Molière's company could not afford to neglect this influential section of its audience, and so had one constructed, 6 *toises* (11.7 m) wide by 4 (7.8 m) deep, sloping upwards from the stage to meet the remaining stone steps behind. These formed a ready-made ground-level *amphithéâtre*. A new stage floor was also built, 5 *toises* (9.75 m) wide (corresponding to the width of the five *loges du fond*) and 8.5 (16.6 m) deep. This was installed above the original stage, with a partition 6 *pieds* (1.95 m) high closing off the front.

From the conversions of the Petit-Bourbon and the Palais-Royal, we see that, even after they had ceased to perform in *jeux de paume* proper, those companies to which Molière belonged continued, despite its obvious impracticalities, to recreate a *jeu de paume* environment in halls that had been designed for other purposes.

In 1671, with the ever-increasing popularity of spectacle theatre, the troupe renovated its Palais-Royal theatre for the production of *Psyché*, rebuilding the stage and above-stage area to make it suitable for machines, mounting a third row of boxes, repairing and reupholstering the *amphithéâtre*, boxes, stage boxes and benches, and constructing a ceiling over the whole auditorium to replace the old blue cloth. This ceiling was painted, as were all the other fixtures and fittings. Work took from 18 March to 15 April, and cost 1,989 *livres* 10 *sols*, of which the Italians paid half. Less than two years later, following Molière's death, the Palais-Royal was awarded to Jean-Baptiste Lully for the production of his operas, and the remaining members of the troupe were forced to seek premises elsewhere. In the space of a few weeks, they lost their chief dramatist and leading comic actor, and the theatre in which they had recently so heavily invested.

4. Pierre Brissart, frontispiece to *Psyché*, from *Les Œuvres de Monsieur de Molière* (Paris: Denys Thierry, Claude Barbin and Pierre Trabouillet, 1682).

5. Christa Williford, stage view of a model of the Palais-Royal theatre (see also Christa Williford, 'Computer Modelling Classical French Theatre Spaces: Three Reconstructions', *French Classical Theatre Today: Teaching, Research, Performance*, ed. Philip Tomlinson (Amsterdam and Atlanta: Rodopi, 2001), 155–64).

Ticket Prices and Audience Composition

Using the account book for the last year of the troupe's activity in Paris as a guide,[8] it is possible to calculate the capacity of the renovated theatre as follows: stage, 40; first-row boxes, 136; *amphithéâtre*, 120; second-row boxes, 136; third-row boxes, 136; *parterre*, 500.[9] This gives a potential capacity of over 1,000 spectators, although the greatest number of tickets sold on any one occasion was 925 at a performance of *Psyché* on 20 November 1672. Attendances in a given area could vary enormously, largely due to the practice of raising prices for the cheaper areas for the first performances of new plays, known as performances *au double*. Normal prices and prices *au double* are shown in the chart on p. 24.

This was done to maximise income from wealthy spectators wishing to see new plays in an atmosphere of exclusivity. It involved careful calculation, however, to determine when to have more spectators paying less, and when fewer paying more. In the light of his dual reliance on the court and the *parterre*, it is not surprising that Molière took such care to flatter both in

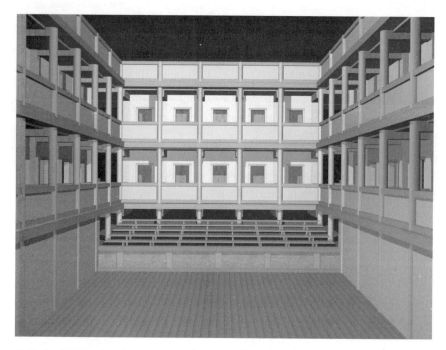

6. Christa Williford, auditorium view of a model of the Palais-Royal theatre (see also Christa Williford, 'Computer Modelling Classical French Theatre Spaces: Three Reconstructions', *French Classical Theatre Today: Teaching, Research, Performance*, ed. Philip Tomlinson (Amsterdam and Atlanta: Rodopi, 2001), 155–64).

Area	Au simple	Au double
Stage	5 *livres* 10 *sols*	5 *livres* 10 *sols*
First-row boxes	5 *livres* 10 *sols*	5 *livres* 10 *sols*
Amphithéâtre	3 *livres*	5 *livres* 10 *sols*
Second-row boxes	1 *livre* 10 *sols*	3 *livres*
Third-row boxes	1 *livre*	2 *livres*
Parterre	15 *sols*	1 *livre* 10 *sols*

La Critique de l'École des femmes (Sc. 5 and 6). In fact, Molière's Parisian audience was probably socially quite mixed, with some plebeian spectators in the *paradis* and the *parterre*, mingling in the latter with those male aristocrats and bourgeois who appreciated its unique atmosphere. The first and second-row boxes were occupied by aristocrats and bourgeois, often women whose male companions were either in the *parterre* or on the stage.

Lighting

The typical seventeenth-century theatre was lit by candlepower.[10] Sconces were attached to walls or beams in the boxes and *amphithéâtre*, and in the access passages and stairways. More sconces were placed around the *parterre*, which also had chandeliers suspended above it. Other chandeliers hung over the stage, which was equipped with footlights, and additional, hidden light sources provided for the illumination of decors and the creation of special effects. We know that the Palais-Royal was equipped with at least ten chandeliers, since the troupe removed them when obliged to leave the theatre after Molière's death.

Conditions in different theatres and different periods varied enormously. For example, in the 1630s and 1640s, when performances started in the early afternoon, some companies relied on natural daylight to illuminate both stage and auditorium. However, by the 1670s, not only did performances start later (at about five o'clock), making artificial light imperative for much of the year, but companies even took steps to exclude natural light, using candles to show off their decors to best advantage and create special lighting effects. This raises the question of whether the auditorium was darkened to make lighting effects more striking, or whether it remained illuminated throughout the performance. Again, it seems that there was an evolution: while early or more rudimentary theatres may not have had this facility, it was certainly possible in some theatres dedicated to spectacle for the auditorium to be plunged into sudden darkness.

Candles were a heavy expense as they were used for performances, rehearsals and to prepare decors. Companies generally used low-grade tallow candles that smoked, gave out heat and made the atmosphere thoroughly unpleasant. They had to be trimmed between acts to reduce smoking and guttering,[11] a duty of one of the stage designers or *décorateurs*, who for their pains were allowed to sell back any stubs to the candle-maker.

Staging

There was evolution too in Molière's staging practices.[12] His early works take place in a conventional farce decor of a street between two houses, providing an ideal environment for the chance encounters with which they abound. Such locations were represented on stage by means of sturdy angle flats, often with practical doors and windows, with a backdrop closing up the rear of the acting area. Decors of this type served for *L'Étourdi*, *L'École des maris* and *L'École des femmes*.[13] However, as contemporary critics noted, by *L'École des femmes*, with its long, personal conversations between Arnolphe and Agnès, the street decor had been stretched to the limits of credibility, causing Molière to move his plays indoors. He had, though, flirted with an indoor decor once before in *Les Précieuses ridicules*, where Mascarille, arriving on stage in a sedan chair, brings the street into the *salle basse* where his two hostesses receive him. These interior settings were represented using an identical arrangement of angle flats and backdrop, only now painted to show a domestic interior. A ceiling cloth enhanced the illusion of a room. Decors of this type were used for *Le Misanthrope* and *Tartuffe*, and the content of these plays, both evoking a struggle for territorial possession, reflects the change in scenic location.

Not all of Molière's plays were main plays, and for those given as afterpieces, the actors preferred not to make the audience wait while the whole set was changed. So, for plays like *La Critique de l'École des femmes* or *L'Impromptu de Versailles*, the rear wall of the 'room' consisted of a shutter or *ferme*, which was drawn aside to reveal the decor of the *petite pièce*: a small box-set placed upstage of the set for the main play. Having appeared against this decor, the actors moved to occupy their normal acting position at the front of the stage, regardless of the fact that the downstage angle flats still represented the setting for the previous work. The box-set thereby operated in a similar way to a mansion on the medieval stage. Similar *fermes* were also later used to represent shifts in location within a single play in works such as *Le Sicilien* or *Le Médecin malgré lui*. The acting area was also sometimes divided up, as for *L'Amour médecin*, where the area between the wings represented the interior of Sganarelle's house; the area downstage of them, a street scene; and the upstage box-set, the garden where Lucinde appears to take the air.

The first play to use such a *ferme* was *Dom Juan*, where it was drawn aside to allow the hero and Sganarelle to enter the Commander's tomb. In fact, this play marked a significant development in the use of decor generally in that, for the first time, Molière abandoned angle flats and employed a more sophisticated system of moveable flats running in grooves parallel to the front of the stage to create a perspective effect. Using cables and pulleys, the onstage flats could simultaneously be pulled aside and new ones substituted to create the highly appreciated effect of a *changement à vue*. Such effects had been a feature of ballet and opera in France and Italy from the sixteenth century onwards; and it is an indication not only of their popularity, but also of the extent to which they were becoming more widespread in the public theatre, that, in 1665, Molière, too, considered it worthwhile investing in spectacle. He was assisted by the fact that the Palais-Royal had been designed for spectacle and was the only theatre of its period to have a proscenium arch. Decors of this type were beyond the capabilities of the company's own *décorateurs*, and specialist painters had to be brought in. For 900 *livres*, Prat and Simon provided flats and shutters to create six decors together with sky bands and ceiling friezes.[14] Unfortunately, the investment did not pay off, and having no doubt offended the authorities, *Dom Juan* was taken off after only fifteen performances.

Molière returned to simple exteriors for *Amphitryon* and *George Dandin*, but now imbuing the decor with the same emblematic value as his previous domestic interiors, since both plays represent the frustrations of men excluded from their property. The *ferme* was used again, though, for *L'Avare* and *Le Bourgeois gentilhomme*: revealing the garden in the first and creating an appropriate space and vista for the Turkish ceremony in the second. In *Les Fourberies de Scapin* and *Les Femmes savantes*, however, he looked backwards, employing a street scene for the first and a domestic interior for the second.

We have seen how the Palais-Royal was renovated before *Psyché* to make it suitable for machines. Though it would not have been staged there with the same pomp as for its premiere in the Salle des Machines, the published version still calls for seven different decors, involving numerous *changements à vue*. The theatre's new technical possibilities were exploited again for *Le Malade imaginaire*, where, for the first time, the scene-changing technology usually associated with spectacular productions was employed to create a domestic interior, which appeared by means of a *changement à vue* after the prologue, changed for the first *intermède* and then changed back again. The cost of producing *Le Malade imaginaire* was high at 2,400 *livres*, and again the company was unable fully to capitalise on its investment. It could hope to pay off its creditors only by continuing to perform its costly new play whatever the conditions, which helps explain the decision, criticised by certain contemporary commentators, to bring back *Le Malade imaginaire* just a week after Molière's death.

Company Organisation

Grimarest describes the dramatist on the evening of his last, fatal performance protesting that that the show must go on because of the numerous employees who depended on him for their livelihood.[15] Samuel Chappuzeau gives us some idea of who they were. His *Théâtre français*, published in 1674, the year after Molière's death, describes theatrical practice from the first establishment of permanent troupes in the capital, showing it had changed very little.

A theatre company consisted of a number of shareholders or *sociétaires*, possessing shares of different values, mostly full or half shares. Chappuzeau vaunts companies' democracy, but their structure was not quite democratic, since those holding full shares had a greater say in the company's affairs than those holding part shares. Even Molière, however, had only one share until 1661, when he was awarded an additional share 'for himself or for his wife should he marry'.[16] He married Armande Béjart in February 1662, and the additional share then passed to her. A shareholder could retire at any time, receiving 1,000 *livres* per annum in lieu of his or her share. For example, Louis Béjart retired in 1670 to join the army, and his pension continued to be paid until his death eight years later.[17] When a current or former company member died, their share or pension was paid to their spouse or heirs until the end of that season. The actors were permanent shareholders in the company, but associates of the troupe could be awarded shares as payment for their services on a particular production. For example, the costumier Baraillon received a share in *Le Malade imaginaire*. This was also one of the ways of remunerating playwrights, though plays were sometimes purchased outright, as when Pierre Corneille received 2,000 *livres* each for *Attila* and *Tite et Bérénice*.

Members of the company congregated after each performance to settle the day's expenses, decide how much to put aside towards paying off debts or production expenses and divide the remainder of the takings according to the value of their shares. Other financial meetings were held to settle the *frais extraordinaires* of spectacular productions, to hear reports on other current spending, or to deal with longstanding debts or obligations. The company met for play-readings and castings and to plan its future repertory. Chappuzeau maintains that sexual equality was the rule at all meetings other than those for play selection, where actresses tended to leave decisions to their male colleagues.

Company affairs were administered by *bas officiers*, paid employees of the troupe, and *hauts officiers*, who were shareholders in the company. Another important company member, considered separately by Chappuzeau, was the Orator. The Orator had two main duties: to address the audience at the end of each day's performance, thank its members for their attention and announce forthcoming attractions; and to compose the posters to be displayed on street corners.[18] There has been debate as to whether the Orator should be considered company leader: the Orator at the Hôtel de Bourgogne received two shares rather than one, and Chappuzeau, noting that the Orator opened company meetings and stated his position, which the company would often adopt, seems to suggest as much. However, the Comédie-Française actors vehemently rejected so much as the existence of the Orator in 1680 (possibly because the post was too closely associated with that of leader), and, though Molière acted as Orator at both the Petit-Bourbon and the Palais-Royal, he handed over this role to La Grange in 1664. This raises the question of whether Molière was, in fact, the recognised leader of the troupe commonly known by his name. La Grange answers this when, in 1661, describing the attempts of rival companies to break up the company, he records the actors' determination to stand fast because they loved their leader, Molière.[19] The sheer multiplicity of Molière's talents placed him at the centre of his troupe.

The Secretary received the day's box-office takings and recorded incomings and outgoings. The Controller was present when the accounts were balanced and recorded them in the account book. Often these posts were combined. The Treasurer received money for the payment of debts or for regular outgoings, as well as income from other sources, such as rent from the refreshment booths.

The *bas officiers* included those involved with theatre maintenance: for example, the concierge responsible for looking after the building and guarding against fire, a permanent danger in a wooden building, with tapestry, painted cloth and naked flame. Barrels of water were kept filled at all times, and regular payments were paid to the order of Capucins, which acted as an unofficial fire brigade.

On arrival at the theatre, the public purchased their tickets from the box-office manager (for many years Mme Provost, née Anne Brillard, who worked with Molière's company and its successor at the Hôtel Guénégaud), who weighed their coins to make sure none were light and handed the day's takings to the Treasurer at the end of the performance. Attenders then moved on to the two door controllers, positioned at the entrance to the boxes and the *parterre*, and received further tickets indicating where they were to sit according to what they had paid. Marie de l'Estang, La Grange's future wife, was at one time employed in this capacity, as indeed was Anne Brillard before her promotion.

The door controllers supervised the porters, and Chappuzeau advises them to ensure the latter are polite and refuse to take bribes. Two porters, stationed near the door controllers, prevented disturbances by those, usually drunken soldiers, entering without paying. Some were injured in the course of their duties, resulting in the hiring of guards, particularly for new productions. Once past the porters, the public were finally shown to their places by the ushers or *ouvreurs de loges*, four or five in number, serving the boxes, the stage and the *amphithéâtre*. At the Petit-Bourbon these included Anne Brillard's parents.

Play Production

Chappuzeau also describes how plays were selected and produced. The author of a new play would approach the actors, who, if they liked it, would arrange a reading. Chappuzeau criticises actresses who, though as able to judge a play as a man, were reluctant to attend such meetings. He felt too that it was useful to hear an author read his work and discuss difficulties with him. Once a play was accepted, the roles were cast. This could present problems, particularly with actresses, since many refused to play women over forty; hence the practice of having older women such as Mme Pernelle, Mme Jourdain or Philaminte played by men, usually by André Hubert, the specialist in such parts. Rivalry could also present problems, and Molière sometimes despaired of satisfying his three leading ladies. Once decided, only death or departure could change the allocation of roles. Mlle De Brie was still playing Agnès to popular acclaim at fifty-five.[20] Such inflexibility and the practice of typecasting more generally were no doubt due to the size of the repertory. Molière's company performed between twelve (1669–70) and twenty-eight (1660–1) plays per season, while the repertory of its successor at the Hôtel Guénégaud rose on occasion as high as forty-nine.[21]

It is a curious feature of seventeenth-century play production that no actor had an overview of the script. The troupe either received a single manuscript of a new play or purchased a published version of an old one. Individual parts were then copied and distributed to the actors by the company's copyist (Lapierre for Molière's troupe), who also acted as prompter for performances and rehearsals.

Rehearsals began only once the actors had mastered their roles. Chappuzeau maintains that most actors could learn a part in a week, with some taking only three mornings. Note, however, that the main complaint of the over-pressed actors in L'Impromptu de Versailles (Sc. 1) is that they need more than a few days to learn their lines. Rehearsals were usually onstage at the theatre; sometimes performances were cancelled to allow for the rehearsal of spectacular productions. Refreshments were provided by the company, especially when large numbers of singers and dancers were involved. On such occasions, a choreographer/ballet master was also required (usually Beauchamp for Molière's troupe), as were the company's musicians.

The author was often present at rehearsals to give direction, assisted by the more experienced actors. Indeed, it seems that the role of director as we understand it today was unknown on the seventeenth-century French stage, with plays being produced as a collective effort. It might be objected that, in *L'Impromptu de Versailles*, Molière is clearly seen in the role of director. However, this play presents a dramatised rehearsal where Molière is both company leader and author of the inner play they are supposedly preparing; this dual function helps explain the pre-eminent role he occupies in this work. A final note on rehearsals is that understudies were not regularly employed.[22] Replacements were occasionally used when the run of a new play was threatened. For example, when La Grange was seriously ill, Du Croisy replaced him in *Les Fâcheux*, and Molière and his wife were both substituted at different times during the run of *Psyché*. More often, when a play could not be performed, the company simply slotted in another one from the repertory. For minor or walk-on roles, or where there were insufficient actors, *assistants* were employed and paid per performance. Most frequently named in this context are Châteauneuf and Prévost, the husband of the box-office manager. Similarly, whenever children were required, for plays such as *Le Bourgeois gentilhomme*, *Monsieur de Pourceaugnac* or *Le Malade imaginaire*, the company called on the offspring of company members and associates, who were also paid per performance.[23]

While rehearsals were going on, backstage staff were preparing decors. Flats consisted of wooden frames covered with cloth coated with size and then painted. This was the responsibility of the company's *décorateurs*: first Mathieu in 1660 then members of the Crosnier family.[24] Actors generally furnished their own costumes, but those for *assistants*, singers and dancers were provided by the company, and properties for spectacular productions were the responsibility of the widow Vaignard.

Performances

The theatrical season ran from Easter to Easter with a short break in between. The theatre week was divided into the *jours ordinaires* (Tuesday, Friday and Sunday) and the *jours extraordinaires* (Monday, Wednesday, Thursday and Saturday), the former being preferred. When Molière's troupe first shared the Petit-Bourbon with the Italians, it performed on the *jours extraordinaires*, but, on transferring to the Palais-Royal, it took advantage of the Italians' temporary absence to seize the more favoured days. The most popular day was Sunday, and new plays or major revivals usually opened on a Friday to create publicity and attract larger audiences the following Sunday. New plays were usually introduced in winter, when noble households were more likely to be in town.

Programming

A company's repertory was changed constantly, with old plays giving way to new ones or to significant revivals. Molière's company gave approximately one hundred performances per season.[25] The repertory varied from twenty-eight plays in 1660–1 to twelve in 1669–70. In general, the repertory grew smaller over the first three-quarters of the troupe's time in Paris, though it increased in the last three seasons. Of the plays given each season, three on average were premieres. A significant proportion of the repertory, therefore, consisted of older works, whether Molière's own plays or those of other authors. These were frequently combined to form double bills, no doubt on the principle that two old plays would prove more popular than one.

On his return from the provinces, Molière's repertory consisted primarily of older works, including tragedies by Pierre Corneille and comedies by Thomas Corneille and Scarron. Their gradual displacement by Molière's own works is one of the most striking patterns to emerge from a study of the company's repertory. When Molière arrived from Rouen with *L'Étourdi*, *Le Dépit amoureux* and a couple of short comedies, his works comprised just 11 per cent of the repertory. By 1669–72, this had risen to 92 per cent, before peaking at 100 per cent in 1671–2.

Another discernible pattern in the programming is what might be called 'weekly rep'. Old and, on occasion, new plays were sometimes rotated on a weekly basis from Friday to Tuesday. Thus, for their first runs, *Le Bourgeois gentilhomme* and Pierre Corneille's *Tite et Bérénice* were performed week and week about. An evening's entertainment could consist of a single play, two plays or (occasionally) a play and a ballet. When two plays were performed together, they could either be a main play (tragedy or comedy) and a *petite pièce*, or two plays of more or less equal length (in any combination, but rarely two tragedies). Some plays were only ever given alone, some at first alone and then with one or a variety of second plays, and others always as second plays. A newly introduced play was generally performed intensively, if not necessarily consecutively, with prices *au double*, until it had exhausted its popularity. The length of this first run was considered an indication of a play's success, and longer works were performed alone until audiences began to flag, when a second play was added. New second plays were combined with first plays during their initial run, although sometimes two new plays could be given together. Thus, Donneau De Visé's *Mère coquette* was premiered part way through the first run of *L'Amour médecin*.

Molière was allowed to re-establish his company in the capital in 1658 at least in part due to royal satisfaction at the performance of the *petite pièce Le*

Docteur amoureux, after a less than pleasing *Nicomède*. Recent critics have argued that Molière reintroduced farce to the Paris stage. It is my view that this development was a by-product of his company's practices in programming, so that *petites pièces* came to be seen as attractions in their own right; flexibility in the creation of varied and complementary programmes was part of a sophisticated strategy to maximise theatre attendances.

Success of Molière's Plays

Using information taken from the account books, the success of Molière's plays can be calculated in a variety of ways. The most frequently performed plays were:

1	*Le Cocu imaginaire*	123
2	*L'École des maris*	106
3	*Les Fâcheux*	100
4	*L'École des femmes*	88
5=	*Tartuffe*	82
5=	*Psyché*	82
7=	*Le Dépit amoureux*	65
7=	*Le Misanthrope*	65
9	*L'Amour médecin*	64
10	*L'Étourdi*	61

The ten plays with the highest box-office takings were:[26]

1	*Psyché*	79,128 *livres* 5 *sols*
2	*L'École des femmes*	65,642 *livres* 5 *sols*
3	*Tartuffe*	61,814 *livres*
4	*Les Fâcheux*	53,349 *livres* 5 *sols*
5	*Le Cocu imaginaire*	43,139 *livres* 5 *sols*
6	*L'École des maris*	42,880 *livres*
7	*Le Bourgeois gentilhomme*	35,694 *livres* 5 *sols*
8	*La Critique de l'École des femmes*	32,037 *livres* 10 *sols*
9	*Le Misanthrope*	31,683 *livres*
10	*Les Précieuses ridicules*	29,796 *livres*

These tables favour plays that were in the repertory longer. A list of plays based on average income per performance gives a different picture:

1	*Le Festin de pierre*	1,341 *livres*
2	*Le Malade imaginaire*	1,317 *livres*
3	*Psyché*	965 *livres*
4	*La Critique de l'École des femmes*	890 *livres*
5	*Les Femmes savantes*	788 *livres*
6	*Tartuffe*	754 *livres*
7	*L'École des femmes*	746 *livres*
8	*Le Bourgeois gentilhomme*	744 *livres*
9	*La Princesse d'Élide*	611 *livres*
10	*L'Impromptu de Versailles*	608 *livres*

Interestingly, in a classification of all plays performed by Molière's troupe, it is only in this last list that plays by other authors would appear in the top ten.[27]

Conclusion

In this brief survey, we have seen the practical circumstances in which Molière operated, in terms not only of theatre architecture and technology, but also of company administration and theatre organisation. In 1954, René Bray first drew our attention to Molière the 'homme de théâtre'. Today it is virtually impossible to contemplate any study of the celebrated dramatist that does not situate him firmly within this social, cultural and even, one might say, political context that necessarily informed every aspect of his artistic activity.

NOTES

1 This section is based on Jan Clarke, 'Les Théâtres de Molière à Paris', *Le Nouveau Moliériste*, 2 (1995), 247–72.
2 According to S. Wilma Deierkauf-Holsboer, the Marais had one row of *loges du fond*, whereas John Golder believes that there were two. See the former's *Le Théâtre du Marais*, 2 vols. (Paris: Nizet, 1954–8), and the latter's 'The Théâtre du Marais in 1644: Another Look at the Old Evidence Concerning France's Second Public Theatre', *Theatre Survey*, 25 (November 1984), 127–52.
3 Samuel Chappuzeau, *Le Théâtre françois* (1674) (Brussels: Merten et Fils, 1867; repr. Plan de la Tour (Var): Éditions d'Aujourd'hui, 1985), p. 122.

4 An arrangement of this type can be seen in an engraving published by Charles Perrault, *Le Cabinet des Beaux-Arts* (Paris: Edelinck, 1690), which has been identified as representing the Hôtel Guénégaud.

5 See Madeleine Jurgens and Elizabeth Maxfield-Miller, *Cent ans de recherches sur Molière, sur sa famille et sur les comédiens de sa troupe* (Paris: Imprimerie Nationale, 1963), pp. 283–328 passim.

6 The actor La Grange recorded these events and many others in the personal account book he kept of the activity of Molière's troupe (Bert Edward and Grace Philputt Young (eds.), *Le Registre de La Grange, 1659–1685*, 2 vols. (Paris: Droz, 1947)). This should not be confused with the official account books in which the company recorded its business.

7 Note, however, that a third-row gallery is often referred to as the 'troisièmes loges' whether or not actual boxes were present.

8 This account book, covering the season 1672–3 and known as the 'Registre d'Hubert', has been published by Sylvie Chevalley in the *Revue d'histoire du théâtre*, 25 (1973), 1–132, with an *étude critique*, 145–95. Two other account books survive for the seasons 1663–4 and 1664–5. See Georges Monval (ed.), *Le Premier Registre de La Thorillière* (Paris: Nouvelle Collection Moliéresque, 1897); and William Leonard Schwarz, 'Light on Molière in 1664 from *Le Second Registre de La Thorillière*', *PMLA*, 53 (1938), 1,054–75.

9 Maximal occupation in this season was actually: stage, 36; first-row boxes, 99; *amphithéâtre*, 124; second-row boxes, 206; third-row boxes, 78; *parterre*, 514. Where ticket sales exceed capacity in a given area, we can assume spectators moved to sit elsewhere.

10 This section is based on Jan Clarke, 'Illuminating the Guénégaud Stage: Some Seventeenth-Century Lighting Effects', *French Studies*, 53 (1999), 1–15.

11 See William Brooks, '*Intervalles*, *Entractes* and *Intermèdes* in the Paris Theatre', *Seventeenth-Century French Studies*, 24 (2002), 107–26.

12 This section is based on Roger Herzel's seminal article, 'The Décor of Molière's Stage: the Testimony of Brissart and Chauveau', *PMLA*, 93 (1978), 925–54.

13 The Chauveau frontispiece of *L'École des maris* is particularly enlightening, for it shows not only the chandeliers suspended above the stage, but also the planks of the stage floor complete with nails.

14 See Christian Delmas, 'Sur un décor de *Dom Juan* (III, 5)', *Littératures classiques*, 5 (1983), 45–73; and '*Dom Juan* et le théâtre à machines', *Littératures classiques*, 6 (1984), 125–38; also Roger Herzel, 'The Scenery for the Original Production of *Dom Juan*', in David Trott and Nicole Boursier (eds.), *The Age of Theater in France* (Edmonton, Alberta: Edmonton Academic, 1988), pp. 247–55.

15 Grimarest, *La Vie de Monsieur de Molière* (1705), ed. Georges Mongrédien (Paris: M. Brient, 1955), p. 120.

16 *Registre*, I, p. 33.

17 See Jan Clarke, *The Guénégaud Theatre in Paris (1673–1680), vol. I: Founding, Design and Production* (Lewiston, NY, Queenston and Lampeter: The Edwin Mellen Press, 1998), p. 120.

18 See William S. Brooks, 'Chappuzeau and the *Orateur*: a Question of Accuracy', *The Modern Language Review*, 81 (April, 1986), 305–17; also Clarke, *The Guénégaud Theatre in Paris*, pp. 5–8, 131–3.

19 *Registre*, I, p. 27.
20 See Jan Clarke, 'In the Eye of the Beholder? The Actress as Beauty in Seventeenth-Century France', *Seventeenth-Century French Studies*, 25 (2003), 111–27.
21 Clarke, *The Guénégaud Theatre in Paris*, p. 209.
22 See Jan Clarke, 'Molière's Actresses: Birth, Death and Other Inconveniences', *Women in Theatre Occasional Papers*, 3 (1996), 1–15.
23 See Jan Clarke, 'De Louison à Fanchon: des enfants-acteurs et leurs costumes chez Molière et à l'Hôtel Guénégaud', *Le Nouveau Moliériste*, 4–5 (1998–99), 171–90.
24 See Jan Clarke, 'The Function of the *Décorateur* and the Association of the Crosnier Family with Molière's Troupe and the Guénégaud Theatre', *French Studies*, 48 (1994), 1–16.
25 Information in this section is taken from Jan Clarke, 'Molière's Double Bills', *Seventeenth-Century French Studies*, 20 (1998), 29–44.
26 When more than one play was performed as part of an evening's entertainment, it is sometimes difficult to say which element constituted the greater draw. The table shows, therefore, the income from all performances at which the plays in question were given, regardless of whether they were performed alone or before or after other plays. For a more detailed discussion and examples of this type of analysis, see Jan Clarke, 'Comment définir mineur/majeur? Une étude du répertoire de la troupe de Molière et de la compagnie de l'Hôtel Guénégaud', *Littératures classiques*, 51 (2004), 186–204.
27 These include the *Bradamante ridicule* by the duc de Saint-Aignan with an average of 818 *livres*, *Alexandre le grand* by Racine (722 *livres*), *Tite et Bérénice* by Pierre Corneille (707 *livres*) and *Huon de Bordeaux* by Gilbert (632 *livres*). Also featuring in this list is *Alcionée* by Du Ryer, which was given a single performance in 1659 where the takings were an astonishing 1,400 *livres*. However, since on that occasion it accompanied the second performance of *Les Précieuses ridicules*, it is probably fair to say that it was the latter play that drew the crowds and not the rather elderly tragedy.

3

STEPHEN KNAPPER

The master and the mirror: Scaramouche and Molière

Qualis erit? tanto docente magistro. What will he be like with such a great master? With hindsight it is difficult to know how seriously to take the question accompanying the frontispiece illustration to Le Boulanger de Chalussay's attack on Molière (fig. 7). Though Weyen's print has been described by the Italian theatre scholar Ferdinando Taviani as perhaps the only image we have of a seventeenth-century actor transmitting his knowledge to another, the same scholar reminds us that, whereas a similar image would not be out of place in an eastern context, or if it had depicted western clowns, acrobats or dancers, this one in particular is a satirical depiction of two actors, and therefore its overriding intention is the denigration of its target, Molière.[1]

If this is so, then presumably the satire is intended to function by the association of the French actor/author with the great Neapolitan actor/ clown Tiberio Fiorilli, studying his comic grimaces with the aid of a mirror and under the threat of an eel-skin whip. This chapter will examine the extent to which we can trace this relationship and the effect it has had upon both Molière's own acting and the acting of Molière in France and Italy at the close of the twentieth century. Starting with seventeenth-century eye-witness accounts, I will concentrate particularly upon the implications of Molière's relationship with Scaramouche for his *jeu* or style of playing. Developing positions put forward by H. Gaston Hall, I will consider the interplay between the French farce tradition, the Italian comic actors' reliance on physicality and the relationship of mask to seventeenth-century theories of physiognomy. I shall then analyse the possible effects of this acting relationship on his dramatic output as actor/author particularly in the characterisation of Sganarelle and the inspiration it gave Dario Fo and Jean-Pierre Vincent in their respective productions of *Le Médecin volant, Le Médecin malgré lui* and *Les Fourberies de Scapin* in 1990. I shall conclude with some thoughts on the effects this relationship has had upon the work of the Neapolitan total theatre practitioner, Leo de

7. L. Weyen, Scaramouche teaching Élomire his student (1670), Paris BnF.

Berardinis, offering a possible template for the acting of Molière in the future.

Although published in 1670, Weyen's engraving represents the culmination of similar attacks on Molière throughout the 1660s. These years saw the consolidation of his troupe's success and the playwright's confrontations with the targets of his satires at the court of Louis XIV, after being granted the use in 1660 of the theatre in the Palais-Royal, formerly known as the Palais-Cardinal, as it had been built by Richelieu, where it was joined by the returning Italians, led by Tiberio Fiorilli in January 1662. The first extant records of Molière's meeting with Scaramouche date from 1658. This encounter, movingly depicted by Philippe Caubère and Mario Gonzalèz in Ariane Mnouchkine's film *Molière*,[2] has been interpreted as having had a decisive influence on the subsequent development of his career.[3]

The charge that Molière had plagiarised Scaramouche was echoed in the so-called *guerre comique* [comic war], after performances of *L'École des femmes* in 1662 and the ensuing publication of his *Critique de l'École des femmes*. Many references were made to Molière having copied his costume, his facial appearance, his acting style and even the composition of his comedies from Scaramouche.[4] These are summed up by Le Boulanger de Chalussay in an oft-cited passage from his *Élomire hypocondre*, in which he describes the actor Élomire (i.e. Molière), mirror in hand, mimicking every 'contortion, posture and grimace of the great Scaramouche'.[5]

Many scholars have accepted that there is an underlying truth in this denigrating attack; Bernadette Rey-Flaud, for example, in one of the most recent studies on Molière and the tradition of farce acting, sees the first documented contact with the Italians in Paris as the final stage of Molière's theatrical apprenticeship. Far from serving their original derogatory purpose, these attacks reflect a predominance of physical characterisation and visceral energy in Molière's own playing that moved through a *jeu bouffon* or comic register to a *naturel* style of playing. Jocelyn Powell has seen this description as primary evidence of the remarkable shifts in emotion that Molière was able to communicate through both facial play and physical movement.[6]

Indeed if we were to look at Scene 17 from *Sganarelle ou le Cocu imaginaire*, the most played of Molière's comedies throughout his career, it is possible to discern the violent physical contortions in his acting complained of by his contemporaries, particularly in his changes of mood. Oscillating between rage and fear after his opening declaration of a desire for revenge, we are told that Sganarelle turns back, after making three or four steps, to reconsider the wisdom of attacking his presumed rival.[7] Similarly, later on in the speech, he clutches his stomach while girding his resolve to announce his wife's infidelity. There is clear evidence here to echo the 'denigratory' accounts of a physical and facial style of acting relying upon extreme shifts of mood and grotesque contortion of the face and body for comic effect.

In a detailed examination of the composition of Molière's company, Roger Herzel has argued that the central reason behind the transition from a *jeu bouffon* to a *jeu naturel* is to be found in the interludic distribution of roles in the troupe; Molière's revolutionary[8] acting style is to be understood in the context of the juxtaposition of the grotesque style of a Gros-René and the heroic style of a La Grange.[9] Herzel's observations are echoed by Samuel Taylor in the same collection of essays, when the latter underlines the importance of gesture in the cross-fertilisation of the Italians' style with Molière's innovations on the neo-classical stage. Gesture underpinned both tragic and comic registers of acting styles; however, the difference between the Italians and the French tragedians of the Hôtel de Bourgogne was in the attention the former placed on the syntax, rhythm, design and arrangement of their simple vocabulary into a spatial dialogue. The immobility and reduced place of physical gesture for rhetorical effect in tragedy was opened up by the physical brio of the Italians' pantomime, and the hegemony of the word over the body was directly challenged in a moment that was to have lasting repercussions for acting styles in Western Europe from then onwards. The actor's body was liberated and placed at the centre of theatrical action.[10]

Indeed, if we compare the above cited 'satirical' evidence with La Neufvillenaine's description of Molière's playing of Sganarelle in *Le Cocu imaginaire*, we find some remarkable coincidences in the description of his mime:

> Il n'est jamais rien vu de si agréable que les postures de Sganarelle, quand il est derrière sa femme: son visage et ses gestes expriment si bien la jalousie, qu'il ne serait pas nécessaire qu'il parlât pour paraître le plus jaloux des hommes ... [11]

> [There's never been anything so pleasing as Sganarelle's postures when he is behind his wife: his face and gestures express jealousy so well that there's no need for him to speak to appear the most jealous of men ...]

Le Boulanger de Chalussay's attack on Molière was probably written originally in 1664 and then expanded upon in 1666, before being sent to the publishers at the end of 1669, after the reopening of the medicine debate with performances of *Monsieur de Pourceaugnac* in that year. John Cairncross has suggested that much of Le Boulanger de Chalussay's biographical account of Molière's disputes with prominent members of the medical profession is based on fact, and, if this is to be accepted, then more credence can be deductively given to the evidence of the actor's debt to

Tiberio Fiorilli.[12] Certainly it was good enough for René Bray in the 1950s, who was sufficiently convinced by the testimonies of both La Neufvillenaine and Donneau de Visé to conclude that Molière trained as a 'bouffon à l'école de Scaramouche'.[13] For H. Gaston Hall, however, such direct derivation is to be viewed with suspicion. Dismissing earlier conclusions of moliéristes such as Will Moore, and repeated by Bray, that Molière owed his mime skills to having been trained in the mask technique of the commedia dell'arte (which also led to the profusion and development of fixed character types in his plays), Hall points out that Fiorilli's great innovation to the commedia dell'arte was to play unmasked, enfariné [his face whitened with flour] in the tradition of the great French farce actors such as Jodelet (whom Molière had engaged to perform in the productions of the Docteur amoureux at court on 24 October 1658 and in Les Précieuses ridicules the following year, and whom Hall also identifies as an influence upon him). Hall's argument is that Fiorilli was also influenced by the traditions of French farce and that Molière's debt to him has to be explained within a longstanding tradition of cross-fertilisation of an Italianate influence on court entertainments naturalised in France.[14]

Such an observation would help to explain this engraving from the 1640s (fig. 8), which is linked to a mazarinade published between 1640 and 1645 entitled Dialogue burlesque de Gille le Niais et du Capitan Spacamon and shows an athletic captain with the same physiognomic attributes and black costume of Tiberio Fiorilli's Scaramouche also dressed as the French farceur Gille le Niais.[15] Renzo Guardenti wonders whether the engraving may be a depiction of Fiorilli, citing the performance of May 1659 at the French court in which Scaramouche played alongside Jodelet as evidence of the cross-fertilisation of French farce and the commedia dell'arte.[16] It would seem that the conditions for the joint influence of the farceur tradition and of the Italians were indeed present in Paris when Molière began to play there in 1658. Hall, however, argues that the most discernible influence Fiorilli (and Jodelet) had upon Molière was in the transition of his style of acting from an essentially tragic register to a comic, even bouffon-esque, one which he dates from his interpretation of Sganarelle in Le Cocu imaginaire, first performed at the Petit-Bourbon on 28 May 1660. Hall argues that Molière's skill as a mime had led him to perform unmasked and suggests that the innovations Molière brought to the roles he wrote for himself (e.g. Arnolphe, Orgon, Harpagon, Monsieur Jourdain) were due to the influence on his playing of the expressive style of Fiorilli.[17] Hall's emphasis on the naturel quality of Molière's acting style is supported by Nicolas Du Tralage's testimony: 'Molière aimait fort Scaramouche pour ses manières naturelles; il le voyait jouer fort souvent, et il lui a servi à former

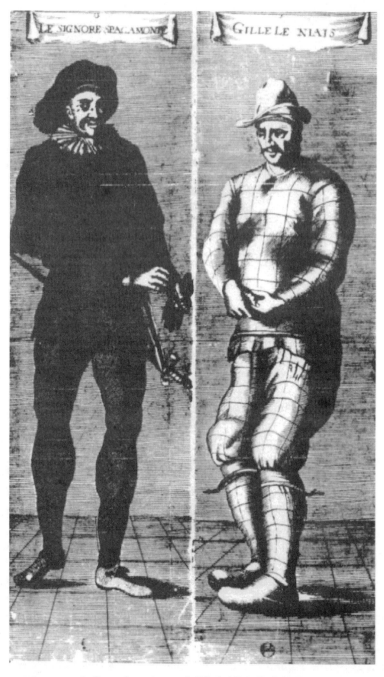

8. Signor Spacamon and Gille le Niais, Paris BnF.

les meilleurs acteurs de sa troupe' ['Molière liked Scaramouche so much for his natural style; he saw him play a lot, and used him to train the best actors of his troupe'].[18]

A quotation from Fiorilli's fellow player and biographer Angelo Costantini's *La Vie de Scaramouche* echoes this point: 'Il fut le maître de Molière / Et la Nature fut le sien' ['He was Molière's master and Nature was his own']. After a description of Scaramouche's physical attributes, the same biographer tells us that:

> la nature l'avoit doué d'un talent merveilleux, qui étoit de figurer par les postures de son corps, et par les grimaces de son visage, tout ce qu'il vouloit, et cela d'une manière si originale, que le célèbre Molière après l'avoir étudié long temps avoua ingénuement qu'il luy devoit toute la beauté de son action.[19]

> [nature had given him a wondrous talent, which was to represent through the postures of his body, and through facial grimaces, whatever he wished, and that in a manner so original that the famous Molière, having studied him for a long time, confessed ingenuously that he owed him all the beauty of his action.]

Again there is an emphasis on the *naturel* quality of Scaramouche's acting providing its appeal for Molière. We are specifically informed that it was his postures and his grimaces that Molière imitated, and striking iconographical evidence of this has already been pointed out in a comparison of two independent portraits of the two actors (figs. 9 and 10). Here we see Molière as Sganarelle with a very similar facial expression to Scaramouche and, as Marco De Marinis has observed, the posture of both actors owes much to the feet positions of courtly dance.[20]

Recently discovered iconographical evidence of Tiberio Fiorilli at a much earlier stage in his career has also concentrated on the importance of his facial expression. This Caravaggesque painting (fig. 11), that has been attributed to either Pietro Paolini (1603–81) or his Roman master Angelo Caroselli (1585–1652), and dated circa 1630, shows a weeping Scaramouche flanked and being consoled by a masked *zanni* and a sumptuously dressed serving woman. Maria Inès Aliverti, who discovered the painting in a private collection, attaches great significance to his facial depiction of sorrow, contrasting its vivacity with the 'still life rigidity of the *Zanni*'s mask', and links it to the visual representations of the passions that had interested artists, art theorists and philosophers since the end of the fifteenth century.[21]

Within this context she invokes the Neapolitan G. B. Della Porta's study of physiognomy,[22] and in her fascinating interpretation there is much that

9. Molière as Sganarelle, Paris BnF.

can be applied to the artistic and intellectual climate in which commentators saw Molière's changes in a style of acting, in imitation of Scaramouche, predating by a little less than a century Goldoni's much-heralded reforms of the codified style of acting he termed the *commedia dell'arte* in Italy. In 1649 Descartes had published his *Traité des passions de l'âme*, which had a great influence upon the court painter Charles Le Brun, who himself wrote a treatise around 1670, published in 1698, entitled *A Method to Learn to Design the Passions* in its English translation of 1734. Descartes's theory prescribed a physical manifestation for simple and complex passions originating in the soul located within the pituitary gland, and these were famously sketched by Le Brun.[23] This area of Molière's performance has been thoroughly explored by Jocelyn Powell, who concludes his study of Molière's art of grimacing with detailed reference to the plays, and suggests that Charlie Chaplin might serve as a modern model for this physical style of playing.[24]

Scaramouche entrant au Theatre.

10. Nicolas Bonnart, Scaramouche coming on stage, Rome, Biblioteca e Raccolta Teatrale del Burcardo.

David Wiles has situated this neo-classical theory as the basis for the eighteenth-century theatre of the passions leading to nineteenth-century naturalism. There is evidence, he suggests, of a western 'mask' tradition based upon the facial representation of the passions and motions of the soul, a tradition which is echoed, albeit with substantial modifications, through the influence of Freud, in the work of Stanislavsky, which was, perversely, to be rejected by the Russian actor's contemporaries such as Vakhtangov, Meyerhold and Copeau in their call for a return to the masked performance of the *commedia dell'arte*. Strange then that the origin of this process of 'unmasked' performance in neo-classical comic theatre probably lies in the depiction of the passions and postures Molière may have learned

11. Caroselli/Paolini, a weeping Scaramouche, Private Collection.

from Scaramouche. As La Neufvillenaine observed:

> Il faudrait avoir le pinceau de Poussin, Le Brun ou Mignard pour vous représenter avec quelle posture Sganarelle se fait admirer dans cette scène où il paraît avec un parent de sa femme.[25]

> [The brush of Poussin, Le Brun or Mignard would be needed to show you with what posture Sganarelle makes himself admired in the scene where he appears with his wife's relative.]

Unfortunately, those artists have left no visual testimony of the relationship between Fiorilli and Molière. However, by situating the influence of Le Brun's theories of artistic composition in the context of what we can glean of both actors' technique from extant iconographical and textual sources, it is perhaps possible to identify the significance of that relationship for the history of Western European acting.

As we have seen, there is ample iconographical and documentary evidence to suggest that Scaramouche was indeed the Italian counterpart of Sganarelle, at least for the manner in which he was played. It is however difficult, in the absence of a tangible text or primary evidence of the performance, to argue convincingly a direct derivation for the Sganarelle of *Le Médecin volant* from a similar role Fiorilli may have played as

12. Dario Fo, Sganarelle in Jean-Loup Rivière, *Farcir la Farce* in *Molière – Dario Fo, Le Médecin malgré lui et Le Médecin volant*, illustrations by Dario Fo (Paris: Imprimerie Nationale, 1991), 7–9.

Scaramouche in 1647. Yet the premise served as a particularly inspiring departure for Dario Fo's vibrant production of the play at the Comédie-Française in 1990 on the invitation of its then director, Antoine Vitez.[26] Here the recognition of Scaramouche as the *'père' de Sganarelle* provided a springboard for a host of acrobatic *lazzi*, musical interludes and improvised additions to Molière's text based upon archival research in what has been termed 'l'invention d'une tradition'.[27] In the published diagrams Fo used as directorial notes, Sganarelle can be seen in the black costume of Scaramouche (fig. 12). Fo alluded to his consultation of a Neapolitan scenario,[28] probably the *Medico volante* of the Casamarciano collection, and of Biancolelli's notes on the 1667 performance to fill in the many gaps in Molière's text with physical business.[29]

Fo's production of the farce was accompanied by a similar treatment of *Le Médecin malgré lui*,[30] and the spectator was struck by the affinities the two plays share, principally the disguise Sganarelle adopts as a doctor, albeit under different circumstances, in order to dupe a reluctant but gullible father out of marrying off his daughter against her will. Fo's direction was to create a visual, physical, musical and improvised performance text which not only delighted audiences with its rhythmically paced comedy but also illustrated something of the performance techniques of comedy-ballet Molière himself would have used following examples from the Italians.[31] One instance of this was the chorus of acrobats employed in scene changes and choreographed dance interludes in both plays, some of them dressed as Scaramouches and thus echoing the second *entr'acte* of *L'Amour médecin*: 'Plusieurs Trivelins et Scaramouches, valets de l'opérateur, se réjouissent en dansant' ['Several Trivelins and Scaramouches, servants of the Operator, rejoice by dancing'].[32] Whereas Molière gratuitously incorporated his dancing Trivelins and Scaramouches into the action of *L'Amour médecin* by making them servants of the singing charlatan, *L'Opérateur*, from whom Sganarelle buys the antidote *l'orviétan*, Fo's innovation is to make his dancing acrobats facilitators of the dramatic action by their assistance in scene changes and by using them to reinforce key moments in the action in both plays. For instance the jubilation they show in the *farandole* dance during the duping of Gorgibus in Scene 15 of *Le Médecin volant*, when Sganarelle swings from one house to another, provides a popular, carnivalesque background for the trickery of the master.

Indeed, it has been remarked that there is a subtle but distinct political agenda to these additions, stressing a community working against the *ancien régime*, with a flavour of Robin Hood and contemporary references to police clampdowns on street performance in Paris.[33] The chorus was also involved in other dance and acrobatic *lazzi* in the same play: most notably in the substitution of a doll for a lover in a musical interjection in Scene 3 between Gorgibus and Gros-René; in the carrying of Sganarelle's long train when disguised as the doctor on his entrance in Scene 4; and in assisting in the passing of Sabine's urine to Sganarelle by standing on each other's shoulders in the same scene. It is in the creation of these *lazzi* that Fo is described as inventing a tradition by developing elements from the commedia dell'arte scenarios he drew upon in his production. Perhaps the most brilliant is one without precedent, the disguising of a dog as a sheep, which betrayed its real nature every time it barked! (fig. 13)

13. Dario Fo, *Le Médecin volant*, Paris, Comédie-Française, Roger Viollet.

Fo recommended a similar style to Jean-Pierre Vincent, who directed Molière's later farce *Les Fourberies de Scapin* in the Cour d'Honneur at the Avignon Festival in the same year:

> La pièce a été construite avec subtilté et un immense talent, mais Molière ne s'est pas soucié d'écrire ou d'indiquer le contrepoint mimique, il n'a pas décrit les points d'appui ni les solutions gestuelles. En somme, la pièce est un texte dépouillé, un texte nu. Alors il faut l'habiller, et qui n'est pas couturier, lui aussi, reste nu.[34]

> [The play was constructed with subtlety and an immense talent, but Molière didn't bother to write down or indicate the mimic counterpoint; he described neither the fixed points nor the gestural solutions. In short, the play is a stripped down text, a naked text. So it needs to be dressed, and if you're not a tailor, then you'll remain naked too.]

Vincent appeared to heed this advice, for his production of the play that Molière wrote in admiration of Scaramouche's success at the Palais-Royal was replete with bravura performances.[35] He openly recognised Molière's debt to Scaramouche in creating the wily protagonist servant, the Neapolitan Scapin, attracted by his sense of trickery, his clowning and his acting ability which moves effortlessly from laughter to tears.[36]

The title role was given to Daniel Auteuil and the play set on the rooftops of Naples, under *le soleil de Scaramouche* with Scapin as a *Dom Juan des quartiers* [a downmarket Don Juan]. Unlike Fo's production, which used actors from the Comédie-Française untrained in the *commedia* techniques of maskwork and improvisation (who adapted marvellously to their material under his direction), Vincent's *Fourberies* employed an expert in mask technique, Mario Gonzalès, as Géronte. A former actor with the Théâtre du Soleil (Scaramouche in *Molière*), Gonzalèz brought with him memories of his role as Pantalone in that company's attempt to modernise the *commedia dell'arte* in 1975 with *L'Âge d'or*.

The idea of Scaramouche as Dom Juan served as a fruitful point of departure for Leo De Berardinis, a stalwart of the present Italian avant-garde. Before going into rehearsals of his *Il ritorno di Scaramouche di Jean Baptiste Poquelin e Leon de Berardin* in 1994 he started with the premise that Tiberio Fiorilli playing Dom Juan goes to hell. The performance echoed the protean role of the Scaramouche of the scenarios with a poly-valent protagonist representing Molière/Fiorilli/De Berardinis in the pros-cenium and auditorium donning the mask of Pantalone on the trestle stage. There are echoes here, albeit unconscious, not only of the Théâtre du Soleil's choice of portraying Scaramouche through the mask of Pantalone in Mario Gonzalèz's interpretation in *Molière*, but also of the biographical picture we have of an avaricious, lascivious *pater familias* from both Angelo Costantini's biography and documentary accounts of Fiorilli's life held in archives in Paris and Florence. Indeed, there is also evidence from the scenarios Fiorilli played in Paris to justify De Berardinis' choice of a mask which mirrors Molière's own transition from playing the duping servant to the solipsistic master.

The political force of the Molière and Scaramouche axis was potently observed in reviews of the production on its opening in the Teatro Mercadante in Naples, coinciding with the fall of the first Berlusconi gov-ernment.[37] In particular, the foregrounding of the exchange with Sganarelle in the hypocrisy speech from the last act of *Dom Juan* reinforces this political element.[38] Similar quotations are taken from *Le Misanthrope* and *L'Avare*,[39] but De Berardinis also highlights the issue of economic migration from the South to the North through the example of the Italian players and their use of dialect and anachronistic reference to contemporary Naples. In a manner predating The Wooster Group's 2001 treatment of Racine in *To You, the Birdie* (*Phèdre*), the 'classical' text is framed in a ludic *mise en scène* by an actor/director eager to impose his own aesthetic and his own message emphasising the importance of *commedia* for cultural politics, symbolised in the show by the utopian space of the trestle stage on the proscenium. The result is a palimpsest mixture of text, improvisation, dance, music, mask and *mise en scène* which privileges the physical being of the actor and underlines once again Fiorilli's legacy to Molière. As an actor himself, De Berardinis wanted to return to the relationship between Scaramouche and Molière in order to highlight the primacy of the actor over the written text and thus confront the literary bias of much of the study of not only Molière but written texts for theatre in general which, in Italy, he attributes to the influence of Benedetto Croce.[40] Just as Sganarelle castigates Dom Juan for speaking like a book, De Berardinis' production echoes the main argument of this chapter, which is to emphasise the importance of the physical underpinning of the comic acting style Molière inherited from his Neapolitan master.

In conclusion, it ought to be kept in mind it was just after the Italians' performance of *Il Convitato di pietra* at the Petit-Bourbon that Molière began to share the same theatre with them, playing on the *jours extra-ordinaires* – Mondays, Wednesdays, Thursdays and Saturdays – and paying them 1,500 *livres*. By January 1662 the situation had been reversed with the new Italian troupe Fiorilli had brought to Paris – which included Domenico Biancolelli as Arlequin – paying Molière's company 2,000 *livres* for the same *jours extraordinaires*.[41] It is interesting that during this period there was a court case in which various *valets de chambre* were prosecuted for forced entry to one of the Italians' performances without paying; the indictment, lodged in the French national archives, is the only extant document signed by both Fiorilli and Molière.[42] This close proximity surely provided Molière with the opportunity to closely observe Scaramouche's acting and to adapt it for his varied portrayals of Sganarelle, making the latter's influence upon him 'more of a commonplace than a point of contention', in the words of one English scholar.[43] The way Sganarelle moves between duper and duped mirrors not only Molière's choice of playing solipsistic, misanthropic, miserly bourgeois as objects of laughter in the *grandes comédies* but also the transition in Fiorilli's own career from playing the servant to playing the *senex* [old man] duped by Arlequin.[44] It is of course ironic that many of the lascivious and avaricious characteristics of that part were mirrored in Fiorilli's own life. The relationship between the two thus served as a potent source of inspiration for productions in the late twentieth century, highlighting contemporary political issues; this lasting legacy of Molière is perhaps most eloquently expressed in recent years by the investigation of Islamic religious fundamentalism in the Théâtre du Soleil's *Tartuffe* (1995). This has been echoed recently by references to Islam in a production of *Tartuffe* set in Turkey at the Arcola Theatre in Dalston, North London (2004/5), which seems to have gone unnoticed in the climate of religious vigilance in the British theatre at the time of writing, which witnessed the withdrawal of

Behzti from the Birmingham Rep (2004) following riots led by elements of the Sikh community and the evangelical Christian protests over the broadcasting of the Battersea Arts Centre/National Theatre's production of *Jerry Springer, The Opera* on BBC 2 (2005). For the actor Marcello Magni, cofounder of Complicite, who played Scapin in Theatre Clwyd's *Wise Guy Scapin* in 1993, the subtleties of *Tartuffe* make it the play for these religiously obsessed times.[45] On a humbler level, after a lecture on Molière, I gave the theme of hypocrisy in modern-day life to my second-year drama undergraduates at Kingston University to investigate for practical performance of *commedia* today; their response was to produce caricatures of Blair on weapons of mass destruction in Iraq and on tuition fees in British universities. Their class work was witnessed by the University Chancellor, Sir Peter Hall, and he described it as fundamental to the training of any young actor today. Perhaps this persistent political charge is best expressed by the anecdote reported by Molière himself in the preface to the 1669 edition of *Tartuffe*, where he reports a conversation between Louis XIV and the Prince de Condé:

> 'Je voudrais savoir pourquoi les gens qui se scandalisent si fort de la comédie de Molière ne disent mot de celle de Scaramouche?'; à quoi le prince répondit: 'La raison de cela, c'est que la comédie de Scaramouche joue le ciel et la religion, dont ces messieurs-là ne se soucient point; celle de Molière les joue eux-mêmes; c'est ce qu'ils ne peuvent souffrir.'[46]

> ['I would like to know why the people so greatly scandalised by Molière's play don't say a word about Scaramouche's.' To which the prince answered, 'The reason for that is that Scaramouche's play mocks heaven and religion which these gentlemen care nothing of; Molière mocks them themselves, that's what they can't bear.']

Though Molière's complaint is that his satire is perceived to be too direct by its targets, it is interesting that the parody of his work in *Scaramouche ermite* is seen by him to escape censure through those same targets' dismissal of the higher plains of heaven and religion, where Fiorilli, operating as a representative of a wider carnivalesque culture, is allowed free rein. Similar arguments have of course been put forward to explain the durability of Molière's own work – albeit in the context of classical theory – through the movement between the universal and the particular in his comic characterisation.[47]

Richard Andrews cites the engraving with which we began this discussion as evidence of the Italian influence on Molière.[48] The actor/author is seen there holding a mirror, which is rich in metaphorical significance: it can be seen in the light of the reflective satire alluded to above, but we could also reverse the motto on the engraving and imagine Scaramouche holding up a mirror to Molière; in the scenario of *L'Addition au triomphe de la médecine*, performed in 1674, Scaramouche is recorded as playing the role of a hypochondriac duped by the medical profession into becoming one of their members – a plot heavily influenced by Molière's last performance of *Le Malade imaginaire*.[49] The straight answer to the satirical question in the engraving with which this essay began seems to be that the student became equal to, if not greater than, his master, which has undoubtedly been the judgement of posterity. Would it have been possible for him to have become so without him? On the basis of the accumulated evidence the answer is surely no.

NOTES

1 Ferdinando Taviani, 'Un vivo contrasto. Seminario su attrici e attori della commedia dell'arte', *Teatro e Storia*, 1 (October 1986), 25–75, p. 59.

2 The film (1977–8) also showed a fictional performance by a masked Scaramouche (Gonzalèz) and La Mort (Caubère) on the Pont Neuf, watched by the young Molière on his grandfather's shoulders, to underscore the influence of the Italians on him. A remastered version of this film was released on DVD by Belair classiques in December 2004.

3 See Bernadette Rey-Flaud, *Molière et la farce* (Geneva: Droz, 1996), p. 65.

4 See for example Jean Donneau de Visé, *Zelinde, Comédie ou la véritable critique de l'escole des femmes et la critique de la critique* (Paris: Guillame de Luyne, 1663), pp. 90–91.

5 Le Boulanger de Chalussay, *Élomire c'est à dire Molière, Hypocondre ou Les Médecins vengez. Comedie* (Paris, 1671), I, 3, pp. 16–17 (1st edn 1670).

6 Jocelyn Powell, 'Making Faces: Character and Physiognomy in *L'École des femmes* and *L'Avare*', *Seventeenth-Century French Studies*, 9 (1987), 94–112, p. 107.

7 Molière, *Sganarelle ou Le Cocu imaginaire, avec les arguments de chaque scène* (Paris: Jean Ribou, 1660), p. 41.

8 Molière has been seen as 'conducting a revolution in acting style on two fronts. For the tragic genre he advocated a natural style; and for the comic genre he himself adopted a mixture of clowning, stylised acting, and naturalness'; see David Maskell, *Racine: A Theatrical Reading* (Oxford: Clarendon, 1991), p. 116. See also p. 117.

9 Roger Herzel, 'Le Jeu "naturel" de Molière et de sa troupe', *XVIIe siècle*, 132 (1981), 279–83.

10 Samuel S. Taylor, 'Le Geste chez les "Maîtres italiens de Molière"', *XVIIe siècle*, 132 (1981), 285–301.

11 La Neufvillenaine, *Arguments du Cocu imaginaire* (Paris, 1660), quoted in W. D. Howarth, *Molière: A Playwright and His Audience* (Cambridge: Cambridge University Press, 1982), p. 17. La Neufvillenaine was a pseudonym for the publisher Jean Ribou, whose pirated editions of Molière's plays played their part in prompting the actor/author to seek royal privileges to protect his works and their revenue. See Joan DeJean, *The Reinvention of Obscenity, Sex, Lies and*

Tabloids in Early Modern France (Chicago and London: University of Chicago Press, 2002), pp. 92–3, 167 and notes 22–3.

12 See John Cairncross, *New Light on Molière, Tartuffe; Élomire Hypocondre* (Geneva: Droz, and Paris: Minard, 1956).

13 René Bray, *Molière, homme de théâtre* (Paris: Mercure de France, 1954), p. 152.

14 H. Gaston Hall, 'Ce que Molière doit à Scaramouche', in *Comedy in Context: Essays on Molière* (Jackson, MI: University Press of Mississippi, 1984), 36–55, p. 44.

15 See my article, 'The Shifting Political Significance of Scaramouche in Mazarin's France', *Théâtre et Drame musical / Theatre & Musical Drama*, Bilingual European Review published by the Société internationale d'histoire comparée du théâtre, de l'opéra et du ballet, Paris, 2 (2003), 23–46.

16 Renzo Guardenti, *Gli Italiani a Parigi. La Comédie Italienne (1660–1697). Storia, pratica scenica, iconografia*, 2 vols. (Rome: Bulzoni, 1990), I, p. 50.

17 Hall, 'Ce que Molière doit à Scaramouche', p. 54.

18 See Howarth, *Molière. A Playwright and his Audience*, p. 16.

19 Angelo Costantini, *La Vie de Scaramouche* (Paris: Barbin, 1695), p. 101.

20 Marco De Marinis, *Capire il teatro. Lineamenti di una nuova teatrologia* (Florence: La Casa Usher, 1988), p. 161.

21 Maria Inès Aliverti, 'An Unknown Portrait of Tiberio Fiorilli', *Theatre Research International*, 23 (1998), 127–32.

22 To see the extent to which the observations of Della Porta with their accompanying illustrations, later developed by Le Brun, have influenced mid-twentieth century reconstructions of masked acting technique, see the *Glossarietto fisiognomico* in Donato Sartori and Bruno Laneta, *Maschera e Maschere. Storia, morfologia, tecnica* (Florence: La Casa Usher, 1984), pp. 31–9.

23 David Wiles, *The Masks of Menander: Signs and Meaning in Greek and Roman Performance* (Cambridge: Cambridge University Press, 1991), pp. 116–17.

24 See Powell, 'Making Faces'.

25 La Neufvillenaine, *Arguments* ..., Sc. 12, in Hall, 'Ce que Molière doit à Scaramouche', p. 50.

26 For a detailed analysis of the production, see Christopher Cairns, *Dario Fo e la 'Pittura scenica'. Arte Teatro Regie 1977–1997* (Naples: Edizioni Scientifiche Italiane, 2000), pp. 153–72.

27 Jean-Loup Rivière, 'Farcir la Farce', in *Molière – Dario Fo, Le Médecin malgré lui et Le Médecin volant*, illustrations by Dario Fo (Paris: Imprimerie Nationale, 1991), pp. 7–9, p. 8.

28 *Agence France Presse*, 27 May 1990.

29 As well as providing a comprehensive summary on the scholarship treating the derivation of *Le Médecin volant* from Italian sources, Delia Gambelli notes how Fo has shed light on the interpretation of the drinking of urine. See Delia Gambelli, *Arlecchino a Parigi. Lo Scenario di Domenico Biancolelli*, 2 vols. (Rome: Bulzoni, 1997), I, pp. 203–10, p. 206.

30 See Cairns, *Dario Fo e la 'Pittura scenica'*, pp. 172–80.

31 The closing act of Lully's comedy ballet *L'Amor malato* of 1657 has the composer dressed as Scaramouche and surrounded by doctors as he grants a

mock doctorate to an ass whose theses are dedicated to Scaramouche. See H. Prunières, *L'Opéra Italien avant Lulli* (Paris: Champion, 1975), p. 200.

32 Molière, *Théâtre complet*, ed. Robert Jouanny, 2 vols. (Paris: Garnier, 1962), I, p. 799.

33 John Towsen, 'Molière "à l'italienne":' Dario Fo at the Comédie Française', *Theatre*, 23 (Summer/Fall, 1992), 52–61.

34 Dario Fo, 'Jouer dans la Cour d'Honneur' in *Le Monde*, numéro spécial, 5 July 1990.

35 Compare Rey-Flaud, *Molière et la farce*, p. 202.

36 It is surely significant that variations of this Neapolitan *fourbe* character also appear in Sbrigani in *Monsieur de Pourceaugnac* and Covielle in *Le Bourgeois gentilhomme*.

37 Franco Cardelli, *L'Europeo*, 51, 28 December 1994.

38 Leo De Berardinis, *Il Ritorno di Scaramouche di Jean-Baptiste Poquelin e Leon de Berardin* (Bologna: Fuori THEMA, 1995), pp. 33–4.

39 Ibid., pp. 63–5.

40 De Bernardinis (ibid., p. 5) sees Croce as being responsible for the continuing paradox in which the theatre is not only identified with the written text but the act of reading is seen as being preferable to the theatrical event itself.

41 Bert Edward and Grace Philputt Young (eds.), *Le Registre de La Grange, 1659–1685*, 2 vols. (Paris: Droz, 1947), I, p. 42.

42 1662, 25–26 février. *Plainte et informations pour les comédiens italiens et français contre plusieurs valets de chambre*. Archives Nationales Y 13858 (Musée AE II 854 bis, réserve de la section ancienne), cited in Madeleine Jurgens and Elizabeth Maxfield-Miller, *Cent ans de recherches sur Molière, sur sa famille et sur les comédiens de sa troupe* (Paris: Imprimerie Nationale, 1963), p. 370.

43 Richard Andrews, 'Arte Dialogue Structures in the Comedies of Molière', in Christopher Cairns (ed.), *The Commedia Dell'Arte from the Renaissance to Dario Fo* (Lewiston, NY, Queenston and Lampeter: Edwin Mellen, 1989), p. 142.

44 Delia Gambelli notes how in the second part of Biancolelli's *Scenario* Fiorilli oscillates between humble and powerful roles but is always the butt of the wily *zanni*. See Gambelli, *Arlecchino a Parigi*, II, p. 545. For Renzo Guardenti the records suggest that the years following 1680 represent the decline of Fiorilli, eclipsed by Biancolelli at court, with the exception of his bravura appearance in Nolant de Fatouville's *Colombine, avocat pour et contre* (1685). See Guardenti, *Gli Italiani a Parigi*, I, pp. 65–82.

45 Interview with Marcello Magni on 20 October 2004. Magni talked of the joy and difficulty of playing Scapin. It was physically exhausting to maintain energy on stage but intensely pleasurable, particularly in acting out what for him was the *leitmotif* of the play, the victory of the servant over the master in the *lazzi* of the sack.

46 See Preface to *Le Tartuffe*, in Molière, *Œuvres complètes*, 2 vols, ed. G. Couton (Paris: Gallimard, 1971), I, pp. 883–8, p. 888.

47 See Andrew Calder, *Molière: The Theory and Practice of Comedy* (London and Atlantic Highlands, NJ: Athlone Press, 1993), pp. 16–17.

48 See Andrews, 'Arte Dialogue Structures in the Comedies of Molière', p. 142.

49 Stefania Spada, *Domenico Biancolelli ou l'art d'improviser. Textes, Documents, Introduction, Notes* (Naples: Istituto Universitario Orientale, 1969), pp. 147–50.

4

LARRY F. NORMAN

Molière as satirist

Miroirs dans les logis, miroirs chez les marchands,
  Miroirs aux poches des galands,
  Miroirs aux ceintures des femmes ...

[Mirrors in the houses, mirrors in the shops,
  Mirrors in the pockets of the fops,
  Mirrors on the belts of the ladies ...]
                    La Fontaine, 'L'Homme et son image', *Fables* I, xi

In rewriting the myth of Narcissus, La Fontaine reminds us that nothing
was so hard to avoid in seventeenth-century France as were mirrors. It is a
statement both literally and figuratively true. In concrete terms, the Hall of
Mirrors at Versailles is the most famous example of a rage for reflective
glass that produced, among other crazes, the explosion of miniature mirror
fashion-accessories described by La Fontaine. More broadly speaking, the
ubiquitous mirror was perfectly indicative of a powerful collective obsession with individual reputation: that is, with the reflection of personal
honour, wit and respectability displayed in the mirror of others' opinions.
The birth of a new leisured class under absolute monarchy – characterised
by an increasingly powerless aristocracy seeking what distinction it could
find in personal cultivation and charm (and from a bourgeoisie emulating
its glamour) – created a world in which personal worth was determined less
by political or economic power than by the value of one's stock in the social
exchange. Both nobles and the rich bourgeoisie played their role in the
social comedy of court or town before an audience of critical and ever-
gossiping peers, and they carefully gauged their image as reflected in
their aristocratic circles, their literary salons or, more mundanely, their
neighbouring bourgeois homes.

Such was the world that Molière found on his return to Paris in 1658,
after thirteen years of provincial touring with his troupe. The playwright
adapted quickly to circumstances. Molière knew nothing better than how

to satisfy his audience's desires (even while slyly challenging them) and he immediately began work on a string of satirical comedies that he branded his *miroirs publics*, or 'public mirrors'. From his first play depicting the affectations of contemporary literary fashion (*Les Précieuses ridicules*), through his biting portraits of court aristocracy (*Les Fâcheux*), bourgeois husbands and fathers (*Sganarelle, L'École des maris, L'École des femmes*), scholars (*Le Mariage forcé*), doctors (*L'Amour médecin*) and religious extremists (*Tartuffe*), Molière had, in six years or so, pretty well pointed his satiric mirror at the full gamut of contemporary society (excepting, of course, the untouchable monarch and royal family). The playwright was quickly celebrated as the 'Painter' of the 'portrait of his own time' ['portrait du siècle'].[1] The resemblance of his satiric depictions to contemporary life was so striking that some accused him of moving through the streets and salons of Paris with a hidden notepad in which he transcribed overheard conversations and drew sketches of his contemporaries for future replication in the dialogues and performances of his plays.[2] Audiences guessed as to the 'originals' in real life who inspired the 'copies' that his troupe played on stage; recognising the ridiculed person in Molière's mirror became a popular sport. In short, a public endlessly fascinated with its own image adored his plays.

And detested them. For satire rarely pleases its targets. Molière may rightly claim that 'on veut que ces portraits ressemblent; et vous n'avez rien fait si vous n'y faites reconnaître les gens de votre siècle' ['one wants these portraits to be lifelike, and you haven't accomplished a thing if you don't make the audience recognise the people of your time'] (*La Critique de L'École des femmes*, Sc. 6, p. 661). However, 'the people' that the audience wants to recognise are, as a general rule, *other* people. Few are those who go to the theatre to see themselves personally mocked. Fortunately for satirists, there seems to be a providential myopia that frequently impedes this disturbing self-recognition. As Jonathan Swift remarked in his preface to the *Battle of the Books*, 'satire is a sort of glass wherein beholders do generally discover everybody's face but their own'. Satirists cannot, however, always count on such vain self-blindness. Given the wide range of society mocked by Molière, he inevitably had to confront the wrath of some of the satirised.

This historical contextualisation of Molière's intense exchange with a narcissistic public may surprise today. After all, we often think of Molière's satires as broad commentaries on large moral or social issues like religion and feminism. His audience, though, viewed them in much more intimate terms. For example, readers today may debate whether *Tartuffe* represents an attack primarily on religious hypocrisy, or more generally on religious extremism or even on religion itself. We may see the temporary censoring of the play (from its premiere at Versailles in 1664 until its successful Paris run in 1669) in terms of large historic movements concerning the political role of the Church or the broader public attitudes toward morality. We have every right to do so. But Molière himself framed the question in much different terms. In his preface to the play's first edition, the playwright insisted that the controversy over *Tartuffe* was provoked not by such grand issues, but instead by the play's very concrete satire of a certain, specific kind of person. It was about individuals, not ideas.

Of course, there was nothing new here. Molière had created many such satiric plays without incurring sustained official censorship. Why, then, had *Tartuffe*, unlike his other satires, been suppressed? The difference, according to Molière, is that this time his targets were both more hypersensitive and more powerful.

> Voici une comédie dont on a fait beaucoup de bruit, qui a été longtemps persécutée; et les gens qu'elle joue ont bien fait voir qu'ils étaient plus puissants en France que tous ceux que j'ai joués jusques ici. Les marquis, les précieuses, les cocus et les médecins ont souffert doucement qu'on les ait représentés, et ils ont fait semblant de se divertir, avec tout le monde, des peintures que l'on a faites d'eux; mais les hypocrites n'ont point entendu raillerie. (p. 883)

> [Here is a play that has created quite a stir and that has been persecuted for some time; the people it portrays have shown themselves to be more powerful in France than all those I have portrayed hitherto. The *marquis*, the *précieuses*, the cuckolds, and the doctors have all peacefully endured being represented on stage and have pretended to be amused with everyone else by the portraits that have been made of them; but the hypocrites will not stand to be mocked.]

At the end of the preface, Molière goes in for the kill. In fact, the targets of his satire care not at all for religion, but instead only for their own personal reputation, which they see threatened by the playwright's public mirror. Molière makes the point by quoting a powerful nobleman on the subject of why another religious satire of the day, *Scaramouche ermite*, was not censored, while Molière's play was: 'La raison de cela, c'est que la comédie de *Scaramouche* joue le ciel et la religion, dont ces messieurs-là ne se soucient point; mais celle de Molière les joue eux-mêmes; c'est ce qu'ils ne peuvent souffrir' ['The reason is that the comedy *Scaramouche* mocks heaven and religion, about which these (so-called devout) men don't care a bit; but Molière's comedy mocks them themselves, and that they cannot bear'] (p. 888).

The passage reminds us just how strongly Molière viewed his plays not as moral treatises, but instead as character-based satires, as what he called, in a passage I will examine later, 'ridiculous portraits exhibited on stage'. He was a dramatic painter of his contemporaries, and he knew this meant that he was involved in a tricky dialogue with his audience, one in which he constantly negotiated the pleasure and pain provoked by their recognition of the models he satirised. In doing so, he crafted what was quickly viewed as a new kind of comedy, one that provided a much more keen and biting portrait of contemporary life than any that had come before in France, and one that would immediately make its mark on European theatre – helping to mould, for example, the Restoration comedy of manners as it took form in the hands of a Molière-reader like Wycherley.

We see thus how a moment in the history of what Norbert Elias has called the 'civilisation of manners' favoured Molière's practice of satire.[3] Yet, something seems missing here. This vision of a playwright firmly imbedded in his historic moment fails, on first sight, to account fully for Molière's true genius. If he indeed aimed so singularly to depict 'the people of his time', what explains his universal appeal for readers and spectators through the ages – and to this very day? Why are his plays so much more than a simple note for the literary scholar or a curious document for the social historian?

To explain Molière's remarkable posterity, we may first be tempted to look beyond satire. We can, for example, as other chapters in this Companion do, see instead in the playwright the master artisan of comic mechanisms, plot development and dramatic irony. That he certainly is. However, it is also certain, I believe, that Molière's innovative satire, and even his desire to satisfy the audience of his day, also explain his universal appeal. How? In the following pages I want to suggest two ways that Molière transforms contemporary satire into timeless theatre. First, Molière's shrewd manipulation of the audience's sense of self-recognition led him to develop a satire that deftly mixed the particular and the general, the individual and the universal. This adroit mixture is, after all, essential to satire's continuing success. A too contemporary and individualised portrayal quickly loses its appeal as time passes and as people and manners change. On the other hand, a satire too general and too universal proves a flabby and dull affair, lacking the spice of keen characterisation and lifelike detail. Molière's genius lies in the adroit blending of the two. Secondly, and most importantly, Molière transforms this same tension between direct and indirect satire into a motor for dramatic action. Perhaps more than any other playwright before or after, Molière turns an often purely discursive and prescriptive literary form, satire, into an essentially dramatic and theatrical machine.

Direct and Indirect Satire

From his opening gambit in contemporary satire, the 1659 *Les Précieuses ridicules*, Molière had to confront accusations of slanderously personal depictions. One account from the day even suggested that a nameless powerful literary figure, feeling his circle defamed by the comedy, succeeded in having *Les Précieuses* banned for a few days.[4] This was only the beginning of a career filled with such controversy. Rumours flew as to the models for Molière's fops, doctors, prudes and pretentious poets. Some of the talk about Molière was juicy indeed. One anecdote, for example, concerning his penultimate play, *Les Femmes savantes* (1672), recounts that Molière actually managed to obtain the old clothes of one of his satiric targets, the contemporary man of letters Cotin, and used them to costume the actor who played him on stage – under the thinly veiled name of Trissotin (meaning, literally, 'three times a fool').[5] Spectators would thus recognise not only the affected manners and speech of the poet, but his very ribbons!

Such curious, if at times apocryphal, tales aside, there is no doubt that direct satire was risky business at the time. The statutes of the kingdom did, after all, include an explicit prohibition against 'comic actors naming known or unknown people on stage'.[6] More broadly, direct satire had a bad reputation in French classical thought, generally reminding critics of Aristophanes' infamous satire of Socrates in *The Clouds* – and with the kind of social and cultural disorders perceived to be associated with satiric licence. Furthermore, if direct satires of fellow literary figures could raise nasty polemical storms, and even a possible lawsuit, doing the same to a powerful nobleman could lead to much more dire results. According to one anecdote of the day, for example, a powerful nobleman who felt targeted as the model for Molière's ridiculous Marquis in *La Critique de L'École des femmes* (hereafter *La Critique*), took the playwright by the head, and, while mocking a line spoken by the character whom he thought modelled on himself, inflicted bloody wounds on Molière's face by forcibly rubbing it against his sharp buttons.[7]

And yet even while Molière's critics denounced the supposedly slanderous directness of his plays, his admirers, as we have seen, loved the thrilling appearance of individual detail. Indeed, by the time of his death, it seemed to be his defining quality. The famous letter-writer Mme de Sévigné mourned Molière above all because no one was left to depict the current events of Paris life, remarking, for example, about one scandal of the time, 'it is too bad Molière is dead, he would make a good farce out of what is happening at the Bellièvre's town house'.[8] And Molière's own troupe only encouraged this perspective. Indeed, it paid homage to the playwright a few months after his death by creating a one-act comedy set in an Elysian underworld, *L'Ombre de Molière* [*Molière's Shade*],[9] in which the phantoms of those formerly mocked by Molière charge him with slander before the court of Pluto and Minos. Far from denying the charges, this playlet simply mocks the touchiness of the satirised, and urges everyone to learn to be a good sport and bear a little mockery.

The perception of direct satire thus brought both applause and danger. What to do? Molière's strategy in response to his critics was, from the beginning, clear and consistent: unflinching ambiguity. His motto might be: keep them guessing. To keep the laughers laughing, and to keep the disturbed disarmed, the playwright continually shifted his satiric focus from the particular to the general, from the individual to the collective. And he did so in a dizzying ballet full of dramatic leaps and swirls.

To understand the cat and mouse game that Molière played with his audience, let us consider the very scene in which his principle of the public mirror is stated. The scene is from *La Critique*, a play that Molière wrote in the wake of controversy over his previous play, *L'École des femmes*. *La Critique* is set in a largely aristocratic salon where the characters debate the merits of *L'École*, and where much of the dispute rages over the playwright's satire of bourgeois morals and gender roles. As one might guess, Molière's critics are portrayed as ridiculously hypocritical and pedantic, while his defenders are likeable and reasonable. In a crucial passage, Climène, a prudish (yet coquettish) critic of Molière, attacks the playwright for his 'unkind satires' ['satires désobligeantes'] of women, no doubt feeling that she is herself targeted. (And rightly so, given that, even before appearing on stage, Climène has been accurately identified by another character as one of Molière's favourite targets, that is, as 'what's called a *précieuse*, in the worst sense of the word' ['ce qu'on appelle précieuse, à prendre le mot dans sa plus mauvaise signification'] (Sc. 2).) The defender of Molière, the shrewd Uranie, senses in Climène's voice a personal wound, and responds by remarking that the satire is entirely general and impersonal.

CLIMÈNE: ... vous ne me persuaderez point de souffrir les immodesties de cette pièce, non plus que les satires désobligeantes qu'on y voit contre les femmes.

URANIE: Pour moi, je me garderai bien de m'en offenser et de prendre rien sur mon compte de tout ce qui s'y dit. Ces sortes de satires tombent directement sur les mœurs, et ne frappent les personnes que par réflexion. N'allons point nous appliquer nous-mêmes les traits d'une censure générale; et profitons de la leçon, si nous pouvons, sans faire semblant qu'on parle à nous. Toutes les peintures ridicules qu'on expose sur les théâtres doivent être regardées sans chagrin de tout le monde. Ce sont miroirs publics, où il ne faut jamais témoigner qu'on se voie; et c'est se taxer hautement d'un défaut, que se scandaliser qu'on le reprenne. (Sc. 6, p. 658)

[CLIMÈNE: ... you will not persuade me to suffer the indecency of this play nor the unkind satires it presents of women.

URANIE: As for myself, I'm careful not to be offended by them and to take anything personally that is said there. These kinds of satire target manners directly and strike people only by reflection. Let us not apply to ourselves the strokes of a general censure; and let us profit from the lesson, if we can, without seeming as if we were spoken to. All the ridiculous portraits exposed on the stage ought to be seen by all without distress. They are public mirrors, where one should never admit to seeing oneself; to be offended by the reproof of a fault is to accuse oneself openly of it.]

Uranie's reply beautifully exemplifies Molière's rich ambiguity. She begins by stating that all of Molière's satires are general ones of manners, and not specific ones of individuals. So far, so good. But her remarks then veer in a very different direction. The emphasis shifts from the object in question (Molière's satires) to the subject's response to them (the audience's reaction). Suddenly, Uranie no longer states that Molière's satires are not aimed at us, but instead simply that we should not 'seem' to feel that they are. In other words, one might, in fact, be targeted by Molière, but one should not 'admit to seeing oneself'. Why? The end is the clincher: to be personally offended by Molière's satire is to admit to the vice satirised. Self-recognition is self-incrimination. The satirist thus blackmails the satirised: Accuse me of mocking you, and you thereby mock yourself.

If only life – and satire – were so neat and clean. In reality, the Climènes of the world are not so easily hushed. Thus the contentious dialogue continues. By accusing Climène of recognising herself in Molière's satire, Uranie has indeed landed a sharp blow. Climène knows it too well, and responds indignantly, 'je pense que je vis d'un air dans le monde à ne pas craindre d'être cherchée dans les peintures qu'on fait là des femmes qui se gouvernent mal' ['I think my life is such that I need not fear being sought in those portraits of women of ill conduct']. But, of course, everything in La Critique tells us that Climène is just the sort of hypocritical prude who is not above indulging in a little of the 'ill conduct' that she so vociferously deplores. In this vein, the dialogue follows with an acidly sarcastic remark (by Uranie's sister Élise) concerning Climène's doubtful 'conduct'. The conversation proves thus deliciously witty and cruel. It is also, however, quite dangerous: to imply that Climène leads an disrespectable life shatters the decorum of a polite salon. Scandal threatens to erupt. Uranie thus must immediately smooth over the offence. She quickly retreats by saying that she meant nothing personal. But she does so with biting irony: 'Aussi, Madame, n'ai-je rien dit qui aille à vous; et mes paroles, comme les satires de la comédie, demeurent dans la thèse générale' ['Thus, Madam, I say nothing that regards you; my words, like the satires of the comedy, are in the bounds of a general thesis']. But haven't we just seen that Uranie's 'general thesis' concerning audience reaction actually had an acidly personal application to one audience member – Climène? And must we not conclude that Molière's own 'general theses' have pointed personal application as well?

The answer, of course, is that Molière, like Uranie, can elaborate a general thesis while still painting an individual portrait. And like Uranie, he knows how to keep a delightfully acid dialogue going with his public. By handling his brush with surgical precision, Molière manages to suggest to his audience a perfect resemblance with contemporary individuals, while adroitly blurring and budging the edges of his portraits. It is Climène, it is not Climène, he seems to be saying. To gauge Molière's genius in this regard, consider again the example of *Tartuffe*. Molière claims, as we have seen, that he has riled his enemies by a keen satire of his contemporaries, and not by some 'general thesis' regarding religion. But just which of his contemporaries has he satirised? Molière paints a multitude of details and, accordingly, a multitude of people feel painted. With respect to his own day, the models seem to be at times the accommodating Jesuits and at times the rigorous Jansenists – two opposing religious camps with contradictory characteristics nearly impossible to render in one portrait. Yet it seems that Molière did. And audiences today can recognise, through this same cocktail of individual detail and universal qualities, a variety of types: played in period costumes we recognise seventeenth-century *dévots*; set in Modern Islam or America (as has been done in Parisian and New York productions), we recognise the fundamentalist or televangelist. In short, Tartuffe is a remarkably 'real' character with an unreal mutability, a sharply drawn figure with confoundedly fluid outlines.

Satire as Dramatic Action

Uranie's exchange with Climène thus helps explain how Molière's own dialogue with his public moulded plays whose mixture of lifelike detail and universal breadth still creates today the thrill of recognition. But the scene also illuminates, as a gemlike example, Molière's genius for comic situations and dramatic structure. Uranie compares her words, that is, her verbal depiction of Climène, with the satires of Molière. She is more right to say so than she knows. For Molière's satire operates almost entirely through the 'words' of his characters – and through their effect on other characters. It is a matter of dramatic dialogue, not authorial discourse. Indeed, Molière's silence within the comedies is deafening. He included very few stage directions in his published plays, and almost none serve to describe the characters or their motivations. Of course, Molière's spectators also witnessed an extra layer of satiric depiction in the actors' costumes, movements and voice. However, Molière, like all classical playwrights, tried to put as much information regarding these performative aspects into the dialogue of his plays, where characters describe each other down to the colour of the ribbons they wear.

This does not mean that critics have not sought the authority of Molière's voice inside his plays. It has been argued that those sensible characters delivering philosophical speeches promoting moderation and reason – characters like Cléante in *Tartuffe*, labelled by critics as *raisonneurs* – are effective spokespersons for the author's viewpoint. That may be so, but such admirable speeches tell us nothing about satire itself, as defined by Molière. As we have seen, powerful and entertaining satire results not from such philosophical discourses, but instead from keen and recognisable depiction. Satire is a portrait, not a treatise. Molière is clear on that point: 'Les plus beaux traits d'une sérieuse morale sont moins puissants, le plus souvent, que ceux de la satire; et rien ne reprend mieux la plupart des hommes que la peinture de leurs défauts' ['The finest strokes of high moral philosophy are generally less powerful than those of satire; and nothing reproaches most men more effectively than a painting of their faults'] (Preface to *Le Tartuffe*, p. 885).

As the scene between Uranie and Climène demonstrates, to render vibrantly dramatic the 'painting' of 'faults' on stage, you have only to place the brush in the hands of the characters. Let one character paint another, and the game of depiction and recognition begins. It should be noted that, in this regard, Molière's plays perfectly reflect the social life of the time. The obsession with social self-presentation produced not only the age of the mirror, but also the age of the portrait. At the same time that the Holland of Rembrandt and Franz Hals gave rise to the golden age of the oil portrait, French high society saw a rage for the word-portrait, a kind of literary salon game where peers produced short verbal descriptions of one another.[10] Though these portraits often tended toward the flattering, the social creatures of town and court naturally also enjoyed far more acid descriptions – generally delivered, for obvious reasons of polite decorum, in the absence of the subject targeted. Indeed, 'satire' was considered at the time as much an amateur conversational practice as a literary genre. Consider this seventeenth-century dictionary definition of the verb *satyriser*: 'to mock someone in a piquant and satiric fashion. *He is a man who satirises his best friends: all he does is satirise* ' ['railler quelqu'un d'une manière piquante et satyrique: *C'est un homme qui satyrise ses meilleurs amis: il ne fait autre chose que satyriser*'].[11]

'All he does is satirise': the phrase effectively describes a panoply of Molière's characters who do nothing so well as mock each other. Consider the following carrousel of basic types drawn from three key satires: *Les Précieuses ridicules*, *L'École des femmes* and *Le Misanthrope*. The *précieuses* (e.g., Cathos and Magdelon) decry the ignorance of the unrefined, conservative bourgeois; the conservative bourgeois (e.g. Arnolphe), in his turn, recounts in horror the scandals of coquettes; the coquette (e.g. Célimène) regales her company with descriptions of the dullness and vanity of the fops around her; and these fops (e.g. Acaste and Clitandre), in a final turn, unconsciously satirise *themselves* by proudly describing their own silly ribbons and sillier wit. And such descriptions are not simply satiric interludes or embellishments. No, they also structure and drive the action of the plays.

To understand how Molière effectively harnesses dramatic structure to characters' verbal satires, let us briefly consider the early evolution of the great five-act verse comedies (traditionally labelled in Molière criticism the *grandes comédies)* that date from his first masterwork in 1662, *L'École des femmes*, to the arguable perfection of the form in 1666 with *Le Misanthrope*. In each case, the play begins with a series of satiric descriptions whose complex and ironic applications will proceed to structure the action, shape dramatic conflict and define the resolution. *L'École des femmes* opens with Arnolphe's own laughing descriptions of the infidelity of the town's wives and the foolishness of their cuckolded husbands. He does so with a supreme confidence in his satiric role: 'Enfin, ce sont partout des sujets de satire; / Et comme spectateur ne puis-je pas en rire?' ['Thus everywhere one finds subjects for satire; and, as a spectator, can I not jest?'] (I, 1, 43–4). But of course, as his friend Chrysalde forewarns, the future holds 'un revers de satire' ['a reversal of satire'] for Arnolphe, who risks becoming the cuckold he mocks (line 56). And indeed, through the traditional devices of mistaken identity and backfiring schemes, each act (except the second) produces a delicious scene in which Arnolphe is elaborately tortured with a cruel satire of his own behaviour, delivered from the mouth of the unwary Horace (I, 4; III, 4; IV, 6; V, 2).

Molière's second *grande comédie*, *Tartuffe*, opens with an equally rich and perverse play of satiric dialogue. The enraged grandmother of the family, Mme Pernelle, dominates the opening dialogue by drawing cruel portraits of each member of the sociable family – excepting, of course, her two allies in moralising zeal: the tyrannical father Orgon and his spiritual adviser, Tartuffe. In doing so, though, she effectively paints her own portrait as the kind of reactionary killjoy that fun-loving theatre audiences naturally abhor. She is not, however, the only portraitist on stage. Her arch-enemy, Dorine, responds with her own series of counter-portraits of Tartuffe-like neighbours and effectively unmasks their hypocrisy and prudery. So begins a five-act battle of verbal portraiture – including, for example, Dorine's famously detailed description of Tartuffe's gluttony to an obsessive Orgon, who can only imagine the hypocrite as a 'poor man' ['pauvre homme'] (I, 4). It is a battle that only ends once Orgon finally recognises his folly upon hearing Tartuffe – unaware that Orgon is hiding under the table – draw a biting portrait of Orgon's gullibility (IV, 5).

Le Misanthrope, Molière's third five-act verse comedy, represents the culmination of this satiric dramaturgy. Again, the comedy begins with a character, Alceste, describing the folly of others. Of course, in keeping with Alceste's eponymous misanthropy, his portrait is a general one of contemporary mankind. But the second scene of the act makes his 'general thesis' against society a very personal – and thrillingly dramatic – one. Alceste is confronted with a character, the amateur poet Oronte, who perfectly incarnates the false politeness and vain refinement that he has just denounced. When forced to appraise one of Oronte's poems, Alceste – not unlike the more canny Uranie – tries to hide his disdain by couching his critique in general terms, pretending to be describing not Oronte, but instead a nameless bad poet. However, just as with the Climène–Uranie dialogue, the pretence to generality quickly collapses, Oronte recognises himself in Alceste's satire of poetasters, and conflict is unleashed. Of course, Alceste is not the sole keen painter of others' foibles in the play. In contrast to Alceste's broad moralising, Célimène, the object of his affections, is defined as a sharp-witted *médisante*, that is, as one who loves to speak ill of her individual peers – providing that they do not know it. Her own attempts to prevent her admirers from recognising that they too are the models of her acid portraits frame the action of the play, which concludes when her satiric game is exposed by the public reading of her letters.

Le Misanthrope is thus largely a satire about satire, a play where satiric utterances – and the recognitions they provoke in fellow characters – not only propel the action, but also pose difficult questions for the readers and spectators. The exchange between Alceste and Oronte seems to ask us whether satire can ever be truly moral and general in nature, or if personal applications always lie at its heart. Likewise, Célimène's sad fate, rejected by her admirers when they realise they are the sources of her comic material, reminds us that the fun of satire is risky stuff – if not just plain poison. It has been suggested that in so unmercifully interrogating satire in *Le Misanthrope*, Molière was expressing his doubts about a dramatic form that had caused him so much grief, in particular with the censorship of *Tartuffe* in 1664 and of *Dom Juan* in 1665. According to this perspective, Molière dramatised his artistic self-crisis with *Le Misanthrope*, before largely abandoning the satiric comedy of manners in favour of *comédies-ballets* and farces like *Le Bourgeois gentilhomme* and *Scapin*.[12] There is probably some truth to this theory, though it can be replied that these later plays continue to amply exploit the kind of satiric dramatic mechanisms we have seen, and that his penultimate play, *Les Femmes savantes*, was a classic satire of contemporary life.

Whatever the consequences for his later career, the question remains a valid one. Does *Le Misanthrope* put in doubt the beneficial power of satire to reform its audience? Molière certainly did make such prescriptive claims for satire in his preface to *Tartuffe*, where he states that the 'object of comedy is to correct the vices of men' ['l'emploi de la comédie est de corriger les vices des hommes'] (p. 885). And yet, if we look at the results of satire among the characters in his plays, it is difficult to find evidence of any satiric redemption. When Cathos and Magdelon of *Les Précieuses* realise that they have been successfully mocked by valets mimicking their manners, they promise revenge against the mockers, but certainly not self-reform. When Arnolphe finally understands that he has become the object of his own earlier satire, he learns no lesson, but instead first persists in his folly and then finally flees the world with an inarticulate 'Oh!' (V, 9, 1,764). It appears that the angry and incorrigible Climène is typical of all those who recognise themselves in the public mirror.

Is there, then, nothing to learn from Molière's satire? Are we simply to admire its dramatic dexterity and enjoy its bitter, if hilarious, bite? Molière's comedies, after all, have been staged for over 300 years, yet the world has seen precious little reduction of religious hypocrisy, intellectual pretentiousness or medical fraud. Perhaps, then, we need to look elsewhere for the lessons that Molière teaches us. These lessons, I believe, often lie more in Molière's depiction of satiric dramatic exchange than in a single moral truth to be pulled from the play. They lie, that is, more in process than result. To explain, let me provisionally entertain an autobiographical reading of the comedies. It has been said that the cuckold-fearing Arnolphe is something of a self-portrait by Molière, who also took a much younger, and independent, bride. Likewise, Alceste, in his desire to expose openly the faults of society, has been compared to the playwright who staged contemporary vices. If this is the case, we might ask this simple question: did the plays cure Molière of his own follies? Did he cease fearing cuck-oldry? Did he learn placidly to accept society as it was? Unlikely, since if it were so, he would probably have lost the creative drive that kept him furiously writing comedies about the same subjects until his untimely death.

But if we pursue this autobiographical hypothesis, what we can confidently say is this. Even if his plays did not rid him of his demons, he must have learned much about them by depicting them. Now, one does not have particularly to subscribe to such an autobiographical reading (and I do not), to conclude that each reader or spectator can, like our hypothetically autobiographical Molière, see some of themselves in the playwright's characters. The reader and spectator are no more likely to reform themselves than was our autobiographical playwright, but they may come to a better understanding of how their 'vices' appear to others. Molière's comedies teach the dynamics of satire as it is practised every day in every social situation. From them we learn that even the most vicious – and funniest – portrait cannot be easily dismissed; that those who wish to flee the judgements of others are doomed not only to endlessly repeat their follies, but also to live in profound ignorance of themselves. Such is the sad case of an Arnolphe or an Alceste. Solitary contemplation proves less fruitful than social exchange – even if it is punctuated by cruel, yet delectable, laughter. It is a profoundly pertinent lesson from a dramatic author whose sole art was putting people together on stage and making them interact.

NOTES

1 From Donneau de Visé's preface ('Lettre sur le Misanthrope') to the first edition (1667) of *Le Misanthrope*. See Georges Couton's edition of Molière, *Œuvres complètes*, 2 vols., ed. George Couton (Paris: Gallimard, 1971), II, p. 132. All page numbers for Molière's works throughout will refer to volume I (unless noted as vol. II).

2 Recounted in Donneau de Visé's *Zélinde* (1663), excerpted in Molière, *Œuvres complètes*, ed. Couton, p. 1,032.

3 See Norbert Elias, *The Civilizing Process*, trans. Edmund Jephcott (Oxford: Blackwell, 1994).

4 On the question of contemporary reaction to the *Précieuses*, see *Œuvres complètes*, ed. Couton, pp. 254–62.

5 See ibid., II, p. 978.

6 In 'L'Ordonnance du Parlement sur la Requête de Boileau contre Boursault', cited in Pierre Mélèse, *Le Théâtre et le public à Paris sous Louis XIV, 1659–1715* (Paris: Droz, 1934), pp. 423–4.

7 See *Œuvres complètes*, ed. Couton, p. 1,290.

8 'C'est dommage que Molière soit mort. Il ferait une très-bonne farce de ce qui se passe à l'hotel de Bellièvre', in *Correspondance*, ed. Roger Duchêne, 3 vols. (Paris: Gallimard, 1972–8), 10 July 1675.

9 See Guillaume Marcoureau de Brécourt, *L'Ombre de Molière, comédie* (1673) (Paris: Librairie des Bibliophiles, 1880).

10 See Jacqueline Plantié, *La Mode du portrait littéraire en France, 1641–81* (Paris: Champion, 1994).

11 'Satyre' in the 1694 *Dictionnaire de l'Académie*.

12 This is the central thesis elaborated by Gérard Defaux in his *Molière ou les métamorphoses du comique: de la comédie morale au triomphe de la folie* (Lexington, KY: French Forum, 1980). Patrick Dandrey argues against the idea of a break in Molière's career in *Molière ou l'esthétique du ridicule* (Paris: Klincksieck, 1992) pp. 8–10, 272–81.

5

RICHARD PARISH

How (and why) not to take
Molière too seriously

The difficulty no doubt arises in part from Molière himself. If a writer of comedies writes in addition about the nature and purpose of comedy, we are likely to attend to what he says; and Molière does this both in a range of liminary pieces and, most engagingly, in two metatheatrical plays, *La Critique de L'École des femmes* and *L'Impromptu de Versailles*. The status of utterance in the two types of text is clearly subtly different, and it should certainly not be assumed that everything spoken by Molière's apparent mouthpieces can be taken at face value. But then, it is not clear that everything written by Molière can either.

La Critique de L'École des femmes (hereafter *La Critique*) is a one-act play, in which certain of the objections to, amongst other things, the use of sexual innuendo in the play it defends (*L'École des femmes*) are addressed and ridiculed by the urbane and discriminating figures of Dorante and Uranie. One of the episodes at issue concerns the young and naive Agnès's confession to her possessive guardian and would-be husband Arnolphe that her clandestine suitor Horace, in the course of a previous encounter, had stolen her ribbon (II, 5). This confession scene is exploited comically, how- ever, by Agnès holding back the crucial noun which will reveal what it was that was taken from her. The fact, therefore, that the masculine definite article, *le*, is left hanging over several exchanges, allows both her incensed interlocutor and, crucially, the audience to assume that what was indeed lost was not 'le ruban' ['my ribbon'] but another masculine noun, almost certainly 'le pucelage' ['my virginity']. You do not need to have an especially smutty disposition to finish the hesitantly articulated sentence: 'Il m'a pris le ...' ['He took my ...'] with a less than innocent grammatical object. And yet the commentator in a twentieth-century scholarly edition[1] assures the reader in a footnote that 'it could be argued that [Molière] does not here exploit innuendo for its own sake'. The process of sanitising Molière is at work.[2]

When the passage is discussed in *La Critique* (Sc. 3), the prudish Climène is not so easily fooled: after one of the play's (and by extension Molière's) defenders, Uranie, assures her that 'si vous voulez entendre dessous quelque autre chose, c'est vous qui faites l'ordure, et non pas elle, puisqu'elle parle seulement d'un ruban qu'on lui a pris' ['if you want to understand something else behind this, it is you who create the smut, and not she, since she is only talking about a ribbon that has been stolen from her'], Climène remarks (entirely correctly in essence if not in tone): 'Il vient sur ce *le* d'étranges pensées. Ce *le* scandalise furieusement' ['Strange thoughts occur about this 'le'. This 'le' is wildly shocking']. On this occasion, however, the same commentator spots the game that is being played and informs us, of Uranie's disingenuous profession of the fundamentally innocent nature of the scene, that 'Molière se moque de nous' ['Molière is having us on'].[3] Exactly.

Two points arise from this simple example. First, that Molière, whether or not disguised as Uranie, may well on occasion have his tongue in his cheek; and, second, that the attempt to clean up Molière may, of itself, become a comic spectacle. As Dorante says in the same play of the experience of watching a disapproving *marquis* at a performance of *L'École des femmes*, 'ce fut une seconde comédie, que le chagrin de notre ami' ['our friend's discomfiture was like a second comedy']. It is armed with such a perspective that we may now scrutinise three of Molière's sententious utterances, and test them against the reader's or spectator's likely responses to works in the corpus.

(1) 'Si le devoir de la comédie est de corriger les vices des hommes en les divertissant, je ne vois pas par quelle raison il y en aura de privilégiés' ['If the business of comedy is to correct the vices of men by entertaining them, I don't see why there should be any exceptions'] (Preface to *Le Tartuffe*).

If we begin by assessing how far the first hypothesis holds its ground, we might initially ask how far Molière's monomaniacs are corrected, and if so, to what effect in comedic terms.[4] The answer is very few, if any. The monstrous old tyrants who stand in the way of the fulfilment of young love are neutralised, either by virtue of their machinations being thwarted (Harpagon, for example, in *L'Avare*) or by their aberrant obsessions being indulged (Argan, in *Le Malade imaginaire*). Yet, even if they are frustrated rather than accommodated, we are still given to understand that the future potential for further obsessive departures remains intact: thus Harpagon runs back to his money, Orgon (*Le Tartuffe*) swears to turn from being a religious fanatic into being an irreligious one, and even Alceste (*Le Misanthrope*), as he storms out to seek solitude, does nothing thereby to persuade us that this stage exit will prove any more definitive than his previous ultimata.[5] Only in *L'École des femmes* might we feel that no such potential exists, necessitating, as Molière realises, the rapid departure from the stage of the defeated Arnolphe, before we are able to see him as pathetic: '(*S'en allant tout transporté, et ne pouvant parler*)' ['(*Leaving the stage, beside himself, and unable to speak*)'].[6]

So is Molière showing us nothing to suggest that his hypothetical dictum holds true? Is there no moralistic purpose behind comedy, undertaken in the interests of establishing a moderate and well-balanced society? Or should we rather infer, as his near-contemporary Boileau was to assert, that: 'Tous les hommes sont fous et, malgré tous leurs soins, / Ne diffèrent entre eux que du plus ou du moins' ['All men are mad, and, despite their best efforts, only differ by virtue of degree']?[7] Certainly there is much more in Molière's corpus to favour the latter position. He brings onto his stage a whole gamut of variously deranged protagonists; and indeed one of his earliest plays, *Les Fâcheux*, simply and microcosmically involves a procession of what Molière himself described as 'importuns' ['nuisances']. Nor, in so doing, does he even exhaust the category, and asks, in the guise of 'Molière' in *L'Impromptu de Versailles*: 'Crois-tu qu'il [Molière] ait épuisé dans ses comédies tout le ridicule des hommes?' ['Do you think that he [Molière] has exhausted in his comedies all the absurdity of men?']. Far from society changing as a result of his efforts, it seems rather to produce an endlessly fertile sequence of comedic targets.[8]

If Molière is not a moralist, however, in the modern, normative sense, he is unquestionably a *moraliste*, defined by the *Grand Robert* dictionary as 'a writer who observes and paints manners'.[9] As Uranie cynically recognises of his plays: 'Ce sont miroirs publics, où il ne faut jamais témoigner qu'on se voie' ['They are public mirrors, in which you should never admit that you recognise yourself'].[10] If we do not wish to see ourselves in such 'public mirrors', it is of course because we are dealing with a comic *moraliste*, so that our image will be deformed by the reflection. But it is at our own peril that we dissociate ourselves from the broader human picture. As Ariste advises in *L'École des maris*, in a warning against a self-righteous standing apart from society, of the kind which will be later incarnated in Alceste (*Le Misanthrope*): '[...] il vaut mieux souffrir d'être au nombre des fous, / Que du sage parti se voir seul contre tous' (53–4) ['It is better to count yourself among the madmen than to see yourself as alone being wise'].

So, if there are no corrections, are there equally no exceptions? The young lovers, whose happy union so often seals the denouement, seem to be exempt from blame if not, on occasion, from gentle ridicule. Often the plain-speaking and cunning servants elicit our endorsement. Yet it is a third category, that of the *raisonneurs*, that has caused some of the most consistent moralising about Molière, as we see glaringly illustrated in the long-term *vade mecum* of French secondary education, Lagarde et Michard, where, in a section subtitled 'On the side of good sense', we are assured that 'the couple of young lovers are happily supported by reasonable people, whose sensible if sometimes monotonous speeches have earned them the title of *raisonneurs*'.[11] To see the flaw in this statement, we have only to look at a few of the occurrences of the word in the plays themselves, such as Harpagon's furious riposte to Cléante's valet, La Flèche, in *L'Avare*, as the miser threatens to box his ears: 'Tu fais le raisonneur' (I, 3). ['You're being a *raisonneur*']. Of what does La Flèche find himself accused? Of arguing; because that is precisely what the *raisonneur* does. Of course, he may talk sense in the process, but that is not definitionally the case – thus the intellectually challenged Sganarelle, failing to convince his atheistic master Dom Juan (*Dom Juan*) of the cosmological argument for the existence of God, is reduced to parroting philosophy that he does not understand, and ends up falling flat on his face; yet that does not make him any less a *raisonneur*. Like all arguers, in addition, *raisonneurs* can go on for too long, and Cléante provides an onstage exemplum of such pontificating in *Le Tartuffe* (no doubt with the purpose of reiterating some of Molière's unconvincing self-defence strategies within the text of the previously banned play). But *raisonneurs* are essentially comic foils, nowhere more evidently so than in one of their most-quoted number, Philinte in *Le Misanthrope*. Philinte suffers from the complementary temperamental indisposition to his most frequent interlocutor, Alceste, the bilious lover of the play's title and subtitle (*L'Atrabilaire amoureux*), as he is the first to acknowledge: 'Mon flegme est philosophe autant que votre bile' ['My phlegm is as judicious as your bile'] (166).[12] 'As judicious as', be it noted, not 'more judicious than'. Far from articulating a golden mean, therefore, he opposes to the man for whom everything is a matter of principle the conviction that nothing is really worth fighting for. In the interstices between the two there lies, not the *via media*, but the comedic opportunity.

Some of what has preceded gives to understand a fairly basic theatrical premise: that the reader/spectator identifies *qua* human being with stage protagonists, whilst acknowledging, or at least wishing to acknowledge, what differentiates him/her from the image in the fairground mirror; and one assumption underlying a more high-minded view of Molière is that he/she might pass a favourable moral judgement on a stage counterpart who is either pitiable or admirable in his or her moderation. This is certainly implied in Molière's tacit acknowledgement in *La Critique* (with regard to Arnolphe) that 'il n'est pas incompatible qu'une personne soit ridicule en de certaines choses, et honnête homme en d'autres' ['It is not incompatible for a person to be ridiculous in certain things and a decent man in others']. In other words, in a theatrical medium which aims for some degree of naturalism – a definition that would apply to the majority of Molière's five-act verse comedies – some element of shared human decency within a common recognition of fallibility is conceded. The reader/spectator is receptive to a communality of experience with the *dramatis personae* and likes, dislikes, feels sorry for or despises those dramatic figures whose interaction he or she witnesses – or indeed moves between these responses. But that is not the end of the story, since there is a further opportunity for an associative focus, above all present in farce, in the figure of the *fourbe* or trickster; and that relationship resides in the potential for complicity. If in this light, following the model of *L'École des maris*, we ally ourselves with the *fous*, might we nonetheless ally ourselves with the clever *fous*? If we are all reduced to a common game of folly, can we not at least try to be caught on the winning side?

The evidence of Molière's archetypal *fourbe* in *Les Fourberies de Scapin* gives us an affirmative reply. Scapin, derived from the tradition of the *commedia dell'arte*, manipulates others towards the achievement of his self-imposed goal, to bring to fruition what is described in *L'École des maris* as 'le stratagème adroit d'une innocente amour' ['the ingenious working-out of an innocent love affair'] (362). And what he demonstrates in the process is the simple fact that, whatever his (non-existent) social status or moral integrity, he is born with the wit to carry it off. As he brags in the play's opening scene: 'J'ai sans doute reçu du Ciel un génie assez beau pour toutes les fabriques de ces gentillesses d'esprit, de ces galanteries ingénieuses à qui le vulgaire ignorant donne le nom de fourberies' ['I've no doubt received from Heaven a rather fine gift for all these little kindnesses, these clever initiatives, to which the common herd gives the name of *fourberies*']. And so we side with him. But in order for this to happen, some part of us that we may find less than morally praiseworthy will have to take over. Of course, in an ideal world, we would side with the downtrodden and the misunderstood; but comedy allows us to opt for the clever and the attractive, either as incarnated in a single figure, or as complemented by other dimensions in the more complex comedic psychologies.

At an innocent level, therefore, we applaud the stratagems of a Scapin, the *meneur de jeu* [manipulator of the action], directed against a whole gamut of caricatural opponents; and the same is true in the case of a cunning servant, such as Toinette in *Le Malade imaginaire*. But, in a more complex domain, we have also to examine our attitude towards, for example, the witty, fickle but ultimately seductive Célimène in *Le Misanthrope*, adored for all the wrong reasons by the shallow *habitués* of her salon, since she too, for the time being at least, wins. (Whether she does so in the long term remains as open to question as the post-dramatic uncertainty over the return of Alceste to her salon.) Her defeat is only apparent, as she tantalisingly invites her bilious suitor to hate her, in the smirking hemistich which clinches a long and over-egged speech of self-inculpation: 'Faites-le, j'y consens' ['Fine, go ahead'] (1,747).[13] Célimène has, in addition, previously served as a guide to all the various *fâcheux* of her world, enumerating them in her portrait scene (II, 4), and including Alceste in the list. But that is double-edged, because the company of laughing fawns that she entertains are both laughing with her, and yet ignorant of their own risibility. We may well at this juncture seek to ally ourselves with Célimène; but we also, in so doing, place ourselves at risk of being fellow victims in a category from which even, or especially, the assumption of exemption irrevocably places us. The common state of folly is once again the strongest inference.

(2) 'Si l'on prend la peine d'examiner de bonne foi ma comédie, on verra sans doute que mes intentions y sont partout innocentes, et qu'elle ne tend nullement à jouer les choses que l'on doit révérer' ['If you take the trouble to look at my play in good faith, you will see that my intentions are entirely innocent, and that it nowhere seeks to send up those things that are worthy of respect'] (Preface to *Le Tartuffe*).

Laughing at people rather than with them is not a generous pastime. In Henri Bergson's memorable phrase, it requires 'a momentary anaesthesia of the heart';[14] it presupposes a position of advantage and identifies victims who are deemed to 'merit' such treatment. The Greek origins of comedy furthermore identify it as a genre which celebrates youth and renewal,[15] and the fact that a defeated character in two of Moliere's plays is called Géronte (*Les Fourberies de Scapin* and *Le Médecin malgré lui*) is not a coincidence. Alongside the old come the ill, and we might cite in corroboration Philinte's hardly politically correct rhyme in *Le Misanthrope* as he chastens Alceste for his obsessive behaviour: 'Je vous dirai tout franc que cette maladie / Partout où vous allez, donne la comédie' ['I'll tell you straight that your malady, wherever you go, gives rise to comedy'] (105–6).[16] In Molière's more naturalistic plays, as we have noted, a more complex psychology may be accorded to the protagonists; but satire is nonetheless about laughing at misfortune.

Satire is also applied comedy (in the same way that farce might be termed pure comedy), susceptible of being actualised within a given historical context. The most extreme forms of such actualisation (*clés* [real-life models]) are disingenuously denied, once again, by Uranie in *La Critique*, and they are also the dimension to satire which most obviously becomes dated. Footnotes to explain that the portrayal of Trissotin in *Les Femmes savantes* is an indirect attack on the abbé Cotin (a piece of information for which the majority of readers will require a further footnote) do nothing to promote its universality. But they do tell us something about satire, and show how broader themes, whilst still informed by a degree of historical specificity, may succeed in carrying comic conviction in a different age. Satire, parasitically, lives off its contemporary victims, and yet must also be grafted on to sufficiently universal archetypes in order convincingly to survive, thus *Le Bourgeois gentilhomme* (social climbing), *Les Femmes savantes* (ostentatious female learning) or the various anti-medical pieces. To say nothing of the whole pack of stage lawyers, cuckolds and prudes.

So far, in a way, so innocuous. But where satire most of all comes into its own is in those areas where it is conventionally seen to have no place. Satire loves taboos, because taboos enable and invite iconoclasm, and any domain from which it is definitionally excluded immediately becomes a challenge for it to occupy.[17] Furthermore, it is indiscriminate, and there is nothing remarkable in noting that a satirist will be equally inclined to attack (say) the oppressors of women's rights (Arnolphe in *L'École des femmes*) and the abusers of women's rights (in *Les Précieuses ridicules* or *Les Femmes savantes*).[18] It is a waste of time, and once again a misjudgement of purpose, to seek to build a positive philosophy out of the plethora of negative attacks.

But there was one institution in the period to which the theatre above all related conflictually, and that was the Church. It was not that the Church particularly disliked comedy; the major ecclesiastical writers of the later seventeenth century were opposed to the theatre *tout court*, tragedy included. So that, when Molière wrote *Le Tartuffe*, he did not upset an existing equilibrium; rather, relations were already hostile, and *Le Tartuffe* was the last straw. Furthermore, in this play, no party in the Church survives unscathed – critics have variously seen it as an attack on the rigorous Jansenist movement, the (allegedly) laxist Society of Jesus, the piously intrusive *Compagnie du Saint-Sacrement* or indeed all three. I have argued elsewhere[19] too that elements of biblical parody occur in the play; but also that, more seriously – because more visibly to a contemporary audience – Tartuffe himself deploys a parody of the *Salve Regina* for the purposes of seducing Elmire. To show in this way how easily a prayer to the Virgin can be transformed into an appeal for sexual favours is, of course, also to indicate the degree of semantic overlap that exists between the two discourses and so, crucially, to foreground that potential.

So if *Le Tartuffe* is an attack on the Church, how do we interpret Molière's disclaimers? When he invites us to take a closer look at his comedy in order to discern its innocence, we soon come to realise that it is the non-innocence of his intentions that in fact begins to emerge more clearly and that, once again, we may suspect that 'Molière se moque de nous'. A sizable dose of Uranie-like disingenuousness must be in play; and if he writes in the same Preface that 'l'on doit approuver la comédie du *Tartuffe*, ou condamner généralement toutes les comédies' ['you have either to approve of the comedy of *Le Tartuffe*, or generally condemn all comedies'], the logical inference, for the contemporary Church at least, is to endorse the latter, rather than the former, part of the proposition. There are 'privilégiés'; but those 'privilégiés' are the sitting targets of satire, primarily because they believe themselves to be exempt from it.

One way in which Molière seeks to deflect this criticism, both here and in the Preface to *Les Précieuses ridicules*, is to claim that he is attacking the *faux* and not the *vrai* – and this occurs too within the texts: thus, for example, Cléante, in *Le Tartuffe*, dutifully invites us to 'Du faux avec le vrai faire la différence' ['distinguish between the true and the fake'] (354). But this again smacks of false ingenuousness (or real ingeniousness) for three related reasons. First, the question of potential comes back into focus: here, we are given to understand, are the abuses of which *précieuses* or doctors or Christians are inherently capable. Because, secondly, the *faux* and the *vrai* exist in a relationship that is not one of opposition but of continuum; they occur at two extreme points, but those points are situated on the same spectrum. And thirdly, and most fundamentally for my argument, the places where satire achieves its fullest impact are precisely the places where, conventionally, it may not go. That is the point of the exercise, and that is the point of *Le Tartuffe*, and it only needs Uranie to remind us of the harmlessness of satire to be fully convinced of its venom: 'Toutes les peintures ridicules qu'on expose sur les théâtres doivent être regardées sans chagrin de tout le monde' ['All the absurd portrayals which are put on stage should be viewed with equanimity by everybody who sees them'].

(3) 'Les comédies ne sont faites que pour être jouées, et je ne conseille de lire celle-ci qu'à ceux qui ont des yeux pour découvrir dans la lecture tout le jeu du théâtre' ['Plays are written to be acted, and I only advise people to read this one if they have the eyes required to read all its theatrical dimensions into the text'] ('Au lecteur' to *L'Amour médecin*).

As a final constituent of this argument, we must attend to the stage, since the one liminary text of Molière that seems capable of an uncomplicated reading is the 'Au Lecteur' (a title unique to this piece, incidentally) to the three-act farce-ballet *L'Amour médecin*. In it, he reminds the reader, explicitly, that we have to be able to 'read' the whole range of didascalia that is present, the more often implicitly in the case of Molière; and thereby to be sensitive to the myriad ways in which dress, gesture, facial expression and delivery can be harnessed to heighten the comic impact of a speech or scene. Thus, for example, there are clear guidelines as to the degree of modish exaggeration involved in the *marquis* Clitandre, one of the denizens of Célimène's salon, with 'l'ongle long qu'il porte au petit doigt' ['the long nail on his little finger'], his 'perruque blonde' ['blond wig'] and 'l'amas de ses rubans' ['his mass of ribbons'] (*Le Misanthrope*, 479–84), and, of the speech of such effete aristocrats: we are told in *L'Impromptu de Versailles* that 'la plupart de ces Messieurs affectent une manière de parler particulière, pour se distinguer du commun' ['most of these gentlemen affect a particular manner of speaking, in order to distinguish themselves from the majority'] (Sc. 3). In *Le Malade imaginaire*, we must envisage the gauche etiquette of the younger Diafoirus, characterised as '*un grand benêt ... qui fait toutes choses de mauvaise grâce et à contre-temps*' ['*a big booby ... who does everything awkwardly and inappropriately*'] (II, 5), as he opens his maladroit courtship by addressing, in error, the words prepared for her stepmother to his intended conquest. We might imagine too the expression on the face of Orgon in *Le Tartuffe* as, from under the table, he watches the seduction of his wife by the eponymous impostor (an expression to which the audience alone is privy) – and this in one of Molière's high comedies; or the love declaration of Arnolphe in *L'École des femmes* (a part played by Molière himself), characterised, on the evidence of its companion piece, by '[des] roulements d'yeux extravagants, [des] soupirs ridicules, et [des] larmes niaises qui font rire tout le monde' ['extravagant rolling of the eyes, ridiculous sighs, and idiotic tears which make everybody laugh'] (*La Critique*, Sc. 6). To these may be added explicitly farcical devices such as beatings (*Les Fourberies de Scapin*), jumping in and out of windows (*Le Médecin volant*), or nocturnal non-recognition and the ensuing same-sex gallantries (*George Dandin*).

Perhaps more surprising again is the discovery that several of Molière's female roles were premiered by cross-dressed male actors, such as Madame Jourdain (*Le Bourgeois gentilhomme*), Madame de Sotenville (*George Dandin*) or, most crucially of all, the dominating Philaminte of *Les Femmes savantes*.[20] Thus, to the ample comedy afforded by verbal parody and character interaction in this play is added the far more unsophisticated feature of a man in a dress (unsophisticated, that is, in its immediate impact; intriguingly ambiguous in the confusion of gender roles in the economy of the satire).

Where the disparity between register and delivery is most problematic, however, and where it affords the greatest opportunity for the sobering of Molière, is in the realm of the pseudo-tragic. It is first of all worth underlining the fundamental generic divide that existed in the seventeenth century (as explicitly evoked in *La Critique*, Sc. 6), with the writing of comedy identified as the harder task. The incorporation of an elevated register within the comedic idiom is therefore indicative of a misappropriation of that register, present to a minor extent in Arnolphe (*L'École des femmes*), but definitionally central to the protagonist of *Le Misanthrope*. Alceste, temperamentally melancholic, frustrated in love and incensed at the behaviour of all who surround him, decides that his dilemma is worthy of that of a tragic hero, and thus adopts the discourse and (we infer) gestures of one such. But the risk here of reading as tragic what is in fact mock-tragic is one of the major pitfalls in the interpretation of this piece, and to misjudge the disparity between context and register is to take the play dangerously close to a sentimental drama. Failing to see that the man who *thinks* he is a tragic hero is different from the man who *is* a tragic hero is not just to underestimate the linguistic parody within this play but, more problematic again, to blur the relatively clear contemporary boundaries between genres.[21]

'Jamais on n'a rien vu de si plaisant que la diversité des jugements qui se font là-dessus' ['You have never seen anything as entertaining as the range of opinions which are expressed about it'] (*La Critique*, Sc. 5).

Nothing of what I have been arguing prevents us from thinking hard about the implications and interpretations of comedy or comedies, since reflecting on all these questions is, of itself, an exercise worthy of a *moraliste*. If we laugh at others, we implicitly laugh at our common folly; but we perhaps also, in so doing, recognise that laughter is a gift unique to humankind, and one whose intrinsic value should not be subverted by a surfeit of high-mindedness. Nonetheless, the business of making people laugh is, as Molière writes, 'une étrange entreprise' ['a strange undertaking'], an awareness that is particularly true of the precariously hybrid genre within which he works. He knows he is experimenting with the manifold dimensions of his art, and indeed invites us to be complicit in the experiment, nowhere more directly than in *La Critique*.

What that play, and in particular its self-conscious denouement, tacitly recognises is that, in real life, things don't get resolved, even though in comedies they do. But what is equally foregrounded thereby, is that the situations that are resolved are themselves comedic deformations, and not mimetic reflections, so that a stylised departure from order is either defused by a stylised return to it, or ratified by an equally stylised intensification of it. Of course questions may thereby be asked about human nature, but it is important to distinguish between the theatrical experience and the post-dramatic ruminations about what might have happened in Act VI. Failure to respond spontaneously to the former places us at the risk of being perceived like the deliberately unamused *marquis* in *La Critique*, and worthy of the same reproach: 'Ce fut une seconde comédie'. That comedies feed on the flaws in human nature is indisputable, and can be seen as inherently pessimistic; but the question that ensues concerns our response to that realisation, and the only correction may lie in learning to take on board, lucidly, the implications of universal folly.

Yet even viewed in this light, comedy may still be therapeutic; and it is indeed in Molière's last play, *Le Malade imaginaire*, that such a conclusion is made explicit, as Béralde teases the titular hypochondriac:

> J'aurais souhaité de pouvoir, ... pour vous divertir, vous mener voir sur ce chapitre quelqu'une des comédies de Molière. (III, 3)

> [I should have liked, ... in order to entertain you, to take you to see one of Molière's comedies cn this subject.]

If it is not by one of Molière's plays that Argan is cured, it is nonetheless by a staged comedic fiction that his dreams are fulfilled.[22] But the only person who doesn't see that it is a comedic fiction is Argan. We must be careful not to fall into the same trap.

NOTES

1 Molière, *Œuvres complètes*, ed. Robert Jouanny, 2 vols. (Paris: Garnier frères, 1962), I, p. 909, n. 555.
2 It is hardly as if sexual innuendo or scatology are absent elsewhere; we only have to recall the breast-fondling episodes of *Le Médecin malgré lui*, or the urine drinking of *Le Médecin volant*.
3 *Œuvres complètes*, ed. Jouanny, I, p. 912, n. 601.
4 In the course of this chapter, I shall use 'comedic' to serve as the adjective to designate the theatrical genre of comedy.
5 On such a simple premise is predicated the modern sub-genre of the sitcom: each episode brings a moment of stasis or at least hiatus to the fundamentally unchanging and comedy-provoking mix of characters and situations; but it also vitally allows us to envisage the potential for its perpetuation.
6 This imperative was wilfully ignored at a London production at the Almeida in 1993, in which Arnolphe remained present and downcast on stage at the end of the play, and the onset of a rainstorm accorded him further pathos. Any chance of a comic impact was thereby excluded from the denouement.
7 Boileau, *Satire IV*.
8 As the narrator of Voltaire's *L'Ingénu* remarks of his hero's discovery of the Paris theatre: 'Molière l'enchanta. Il lui faisait connaître les mœurs de Paris et du genre humain' ['Molière delighted him. He taught him about the manners of Paris and of humankind'] (Voltaire, *L'Ingénu*, Ch. 12).
9 The definition is based on Furetière, *Dictionnaire universel* (1690).
10 This image is explored at greater length in Larry Norman, *The Public Mirror: Molière and the Social Commerce of Depiction* (Chicago: University of Chicago Press, 1999).

11 A. Lagarde et L. Michard, *XVIIe siècle* (Paris: Bordas, 1966), p. 191.

12 Robert Jouanny, quoting the sixteenth-century doctor Ambroise Paré, notes that this indisposition makes its victim 'sleepy, lazy and obese' (Molière, *Œuvres complètes*, ed. Jouanny, I, p. 936, n. 999).

13 Robert Jouanny helpfully notes that Mlle Mars (active in the first quarter of the nineteenth century) left the stage, defiantly, with a flick of her fan; but equally records that some modern Célimènes (he does not specify which) have remained on stage, once again in direct disobedience of Molière's explicit stage direction (Molière, *Œuvres complètes*, I, p. 942, n. 1,064; cf n. 6, above).

14 See H. Bergson, *Le rire: essai sur la signification du comique* (Paris: Presses Universitaires de France, 1969), p. 4.

15 See in particular on this question the first chapter of Francis Lawrence, *Molière: the Comedy of Unreason* (New Orleans: Tulane University Press, 1968), pp. 13–22.

16 Arnolphe and Chrysalde in *L'École des femmes* both consider each other mad (I, 1), and 'blessé' ['wounded'] is again the metaphor used by Arnolphe (l. 196).

17 One has only to think of the outcry caused by *Private Eye*'s coverage of the aftermath of the death of the Princess of Wales.

18 To say nothing of what has subsequently become taboo, thus Cléante's question, for example, in *L'Avare*, about a hard money-lender: 'Quel Juif, quel Arabe est-ce là?' (II, 1) ['What kind of Jew or Arab do we have here?'].

19 See my edition of *Le Tartuffe* (Bristol: Bristol Classical Press, 1994), pp. xviii–xxii.

20 See my article in *Nottingham French Studies*, 33, 1 (Spring, 1994), 53–8.

21 Thus, as Alceste prepares for his final epic sulk, Robert Jouanny glosses his couplet (583–4): 'Night has fallen. The salon is half-lit. The atmosphere in the following scenes will be sombre' (Molière, *Œuvres complètes*, I, p. 942, n. 1,058). And Lagarde et Michard evoke 'Molière on the tragic frontier' (*XVIIe siècle*, p. 199).

22 One of the most persuasive readings of Molière's evolution is afforded by Gérard Defaux in *Molière, ou les métamorphoses du comique* (Lexington, KY: French Forum Monographs, 1980) the subtitle of which describes the development 'from moral comedy to the triumph of folly'. Without adhering as closely to such a chronological sequence, I would nonetheless entirely endorse Defaux's view of the celebratory, carnivalesque conclusion to Molière's career.

6

ROBERT MCBRIDE

L'Avare or Harpagon's masterclass in comedy

One of the most striking features of *L'Avare* is the fact that Harpagon bestrides the stage like a colossus, present in twenty-three out of thirty-two scenes, with his dominant presence bearing down even more heavily on the final two acts. At first sight, from a structural point of view, the play seems at best nothing but a series of hastily assembled sketches on avarice, with an inconsequential, meandering plot, at worst simply unbalanced with insufficient counterweight to Harpagon.[1] To many critics, the play ushers into the Molière canon a new disturbing note of bitter cynicism in relationships between the characters.[2] Finally, and most persistently, the familiar accusation of plagiarism levelled against Molière by his contemporaries seems documented to an overwhelming extent. The charge of Riccoboni, to the effect that it would be an achievement to find four scenes of the playwright's own devising, seems self-evident. Yet the view of Molière's friend, the poet Boileau, that *L'Avare* is one of his best plays, is borne out by its perennial popularity with theatre audiences.[3] This chapter seeks to investigate some of the ways in which Molière's stagecraft enables him to theatricalise an old theme through the creation of a multi-dimensional character of comedy, with appropriate references to sources deemed 'major'.

Whenever Molière's legion of contemporary critics questioned the originality of his plays, usually out of well-grounded reasons of professional jealousy, they arrived at the answer implicit in their question. Looking for originality of theme and plot, they concluded predictably that neither was to be found. As a general rule, dramatic and comic unity in the plays is located in the central character, and *L'Avare* is no exception. Beyond the romantic motif of the young people affirming their love against cantankerous old age lies the real love story of the comedy. If a plot is to be discovered, it must be connected with Harpagon's obsession, consisting in his relationship with his *cassette* [money-box], which determines the fate of every other character in the play. The presence of the miser is ubiquitous.

Even when physically absent, he bears down oppressively on other characters. His unseen presence permeates the scenes preceding his entry (I, 3), forcing all the characters to assume a role, the only conceivable way of circumventing his monomania. Thus Valère is reduced to acting out the part of sycophant to win the miser's daughter, Élise, the latter to quivering passivity by the spectre of paternal ire, Cléante to the emboldened lover determined to withstand a father who happens to hold all the cards, in this instance money. The delayed entrance of the principal character, rather than being a dramaturgical error as has sometimes been assumed, heightens the sense of expectancy on the part of the spectators by allowing us to measure the paralysis induced in family life by his fixation. Harpagon enters not with magisterial gesture, but as a whirlwind almost literally sweeping all before him. For the actor of the role there is no warming-up period and its physical demands are prodigious. Its 46-year-old creator, Molière, had to disguise his own persistent cough by making it part of Harpagon's role. In the play by Plautus which serves as Molière's principal literary source, *Aulularia (The Pot of Gold)*, the play's action begins with Euclio, the miser, venting verbal and physical abuse on his elderly housekeeper, Staphyla. At first glance, the resemblance between the Latin source and the French play may be striking, but Molière reworks the subject on his own theatrical terms. The opening verbal salvos of Euclio give way to frenetic movement, the passivity of the servant to spirited defence and counter-attack. Molière's scene is conceived in terms of retort and riposte, action and counteraction. The sequence proceeds in three stages: it begins with the paranoiac miser's self-betrayal as he accuses the valet of telling the world about his master's hidden wealth, is sustained by the servant's questions and *sotto voce* comments about misers and ends in verbal and physical attack from Harpagon. A repeated demand in Plautus that the slave present his hands for searching becomes the pretext in Molière for an extended search of hands, breeches, jacket, to the accompaniment of verbal warfare as La Flèche disparages misers in general and Harpagon responds with a derogatory comment about the valet's ungainly movements.[4] The result is a circular verbal and gestural ballet, expanded and contracted at will, a first sample in concentrated form of fathomless obsession to be exploited subsequently for its comic possibilities. Harpagon's costume, consisting of a coat, breeches, black satin doublet with black silk lace edging (see Mongrédien, I, p. 317), underscores visually La Flèche's hurried aside, given under his master's nose, that he has the very devil in his body. This observation from an expert watcher of Harpagon provides at the outset a barometer and index to the range of hypertrophied behaviour we are about to witness: whether hyperacuity of hearing and vision as he reveals in this scene, hearing and seeing the unsaid and unseen, or loss of hearing and vision in II, 5, with Frosine, all are resources brought into play as appropriate to avoid all expenditure. In his opening scene, we have a graphic picture of Harpagon in unique avaricious mode.[5] He traverses the stage with a greater degree of hyperactivity than any other Molière character, as the first scene illustrates. In truth, it is not so much blood that runs in his veins as mercury or potentised liquid gold.

The rhythm of the Latin model is less frenetic, with Plautus diffusing the miser's activity throughout between the street, house and shrine where his gold is hidden. By contrast, Harpagon's movements are accelerated and focused, as he races between the interior of his sparsely furnished house (Mongrédien, I, p. 317), where potential thieves and suspects lurk (initially this means every character except himself, but by the end of Act IV he will have included himself in this goodly number), and his garden, the locus chosen to protect his *cassette* from prying eyes. His ultra-rapid exits to the garden are used strategically to give dramatic and comic relief from his monomaniac intensity.[6] Thus his wish to impose an ailing and rich husband on his daughter must give way to the higher imperative of overseeing his treasure buried in his garden (I, 5). An unexpected re-entrance obliges Valère to change the subject of conversation with Élise from elopement to filial obedience in mid-sentence (I, 5). The garden becomes a useful stratagem to escape from the wiles of the scheming Frosine (II, 3), or to elude a potential creditor. To a servant announcing an important visitor he cancels the meeting on the pretext of more urgent business (III, 8). In his moment of great prescience he fears the worst, sets up the panic-stricken cry of 'thief' (IV, 7) and at the end of the play takes his leave of the company to be reunited with his *cassette* (V, 6).

The first appearance of the central character in a Molière play is of seminal importance, and Harpagon is no exception. He gives us an overpowering example of his monomania, to be distilled throughout into a range of virtuoso variations on a theme, his fixation with money. Yet his obsession is not at all monolithic or static, as it would easily have become in the hands of a lesser dramatist. It is multi-faceted and forever mobile, necessitating the seemingly arbitrary introduction of episodes and characters to illustrate its depth and scope. All introductions are directly attributable to the effects of his avarice on the family. Arbitrators such as Valère and Maître Jacques intervene to 'resolve' such difficulties, advisers like Frosine and Le Commissaire appear to service the needs of his obsession. Infallibly, they are drawn into the vortex of his obsessiveness.

A major example of his magnetic power is provided by the series of clashes between father and son which runs through the comedy like a continuo accompaniment. The opposition of romantic youth and stern old age has been a stock theme of comedy since time immemorial, prominent in Greek Old and New Comedy as well as in the Roman dramatists Plautus and Terence. The rivalry between the uncle and nephew in Plautus' *Aulularia* becomes that of father and son in Molière. It is sometimes suggested that the prominence given to their conflict undermines paternal authority. Rousseau went so far as to state that the play was a school for corruption (*Lettre à M. d'Alembert*, p. 47). The clashes though are so structured and patterned that they point up the primacy of comic movement over morality. Molière gives them a fresh twist by ensuring that agility of mind and body is not the prerogative of youth, just as inertia is not that of age. When Harpagon takes the initiative in I, 4, by asking Cléante for his opinion of Mariane, he sets in motion a series of parallel questions and answers structured to raise the son's expectation of marrying her. Beguiled by the harmonious pattern of Harpagon's queries, the father's abrupt announcement that he is to marry Mariane himself wrong-foots both son and spectator. His undeviating obsession draws their rivalry as father and son into open competition for Mariane as well as into unromantic and tawdry settings: witness their meeting as usurer and borrower (II, 1 and 2). The interminable list of unsellable bric-à-brac forming part of the loan constitutes an admirable counterpoint to the elegant symmetry of the inevitable subsequent clash of father and son (II, 2). Accusation from one is paralleled in form and content by that of the other, pointed up by contrastive use of the formal 'vous ' and the familiar 'tu' forms of address, making a circular dance pattern in which paternal wrath and youthful rebelliousness swirl around each other. A measure of revenge comes to Cléante in III, 7, as he uses the presence of Mariane and his father to gain the upper hand in their rivalry for her. The Achilles heel of Harpagon is his dread of money being spent: La Flèche, intimating that he can be mortally wounded at this point (II, 4), already foreshadows the only possible key to the denouement. In fact the comedy consists essentially of the miser's responses to a series of challenges to his hermetically sealed obsessiveness. In a gesture which again foreshadows the denouement, Cléante organises an exotic collation to be given in honour of Mariane (III, 7). With the miser thus destabilised, he mounts a romantic ballet, in which he snatches his father's diamond ring to place it on the girl's finger, gyrating around both, simultaneously to prevent her from giving, and Harpagon from taking, it back. Harpagon flounders here as a helpless pantomimist who has strayed onto the stage of a romantic ballet: unable to find either elegant word or gesture, but reduced to his standard fulminatory mode which can only be expressed – torture of tortures for him – *sotto voce*.

The master of elusion is suddenly and uncharacteristically immobilised in helpless rage, for once unable to respond to the challenge of disbursing money.

The triumph of romance is short-lived. The third meeting of father and son in IV, 3 looks for all the world like a simple repetition of their joust in the first act. In fact it contains a variation on a familiar theme, designed to take us into uncharted comic territory. Asked for his opinion of Mariane, Cléante now hedges his replies. Harpagon the attorney uses two series of questions, the first apparently oblique, to ascertain the son's feelings for Mariane, the second forensic, to gauge the depth of their mutual commitment, before imposing his fiat: the opening words of the second series, with its abrupt change from *tutoiement* to *vouvoiement*, ought to have alerted the son and the spectators to the imminent storm. As each emulates the insults of the other with ever-shortening temper and accelerating tempo, enter Maître Jacques, the self-appointed arbitrator.

He offers us an entr'acte in which, as improvised impresario, he stages a microcomedy as revenge on the master who beats him for his plain-spokenness. Separating the adversaries, his lengthy long-distance shuttle diplomacy assures each one that the other complies fully with his wishes, all the while ensuring an ever more explosive outcome. The stylised reconciliation (IV, 5) comprises three movements: the first slow, with deferential apologies by Cléante, paralleled by gracious acceptance by Harpagon, ending with the son's warm appreciation of the giving to him of Mariane in marriage. The second is fractured and abrupt, full of questions, exclamations, as both work through the misunderstanding, and begins with Harpagon's shell-shocked reaction 'Comment?' ['What?']. For we have it on the authority of La Flèche that the verb to give does not figure in the miser's vocabulary and that even his greetings are issued on mere loan (II, 4). The concluding movement is the most violent crescendo of all, the momentum having been generated by long-drawn-out mutual self-deception. Both protagonists are drawn by gradations into the familiar sequence of verbal abuse by father, studied nonchalance by son, to play out the eternal circular conflict of the generations, heightened by the alternating *tutoiement/vouvoiement*, with an economy and symmetry of word and gesture belonging not to life but to art:

a) HARPAGON: Laisse-moi faire, traître.
   CLÉante: Faites tout ce qu'il vous plaira.
b) HARPAGON: Je te défends de me jamais voir.
   CLÉANTE: À la bonne heure.
c) HARPAGON: Je t'abandonne.
   CLÉANTE: Abandonnez.

d) HARPAGON: Je te renonce pour mon fils.
   CLÉANTE: Soit.
e) HARPAGON: Je te déshérite.
   CLÉANTE: Tout ce que vous voudrez.
f) HARPAGON: Et je te donne ma malédiction.
   CLÉANTE: Je n'ai que faire de vos dons.
[a) HARPAGON: Don't stand in my way, you traitor.
   CLÉANTE: Do whatever you like.
b) HARPAGON: I forbid you ever to set eyes on me again.
   CLÉANTE: So much the better.
c) HARPAGON: I'm leaving you to your own devices.
   CLÉANTE: Leave me, then.
d) HARPAGON: I'm disowning you as my son.
   CLÉANTE: Very well.
e) HARPAGON: I'm cutting you out of my will.
   CLÉANTE: Do anything you like.
f) HARPAGON: All I have to give you is my curse.
   CLÉANTE: I don't need you to give me anything.]

The clashes, like the play of which they form a microcosm, are structured around one of the oldest stock-in-trade comic devices known, pointing up the vast disparity between effort expended and result obtained. Henri Bergson describes the process neatly: 'Faire beaucoup de chemin pour revenir, sans le savoir, au point de départ, c'est fournir un grand effort pour un résultat nul' ['Covering a lot of ground only to come back unwittingly to the point of departure means that much effort has been expended without anything to show for it'].[7]

The cycle illustrates the immense range of attitudes and tones which the role requires: by turns, and sometimes almost simultaneously, vituperative and conciliatory, despotic and benevolent, but always paranoiac, perverse and unpredictable – Harpagon plays many parts, speaks many languages. He embodies on stage the maxim of La Rochefoucauld, that self-interest speaks all kinds of languages, plays all kinds of roles, even that of a disinterested person.[8] His protean polyglot roles owe everything to Molière's extraordinary talent for mimicry and role-playing, as glimpsed in *L'Impromptu de Versailles* (1663), where we see his troupe of actors at rehearsal. There he takes off in rapid succession voices and gestures of both male and female actors of his prestigious rivals at the Hôtel de Bourgogne. Endowed with an unusually expressive and mobile face, he is described by a contemporary as a complete actor from head to toe, having many voices, able to speak volumes with a wink, a smile, a mere inclination of the head.[9] All these gifts are brought into play as Molière delights to confront

Harpagon's adamantine refusal to part with the smallest coin with three challenges greater by far than the subjugation of family to his will, namely the redoubtable professional schemer Frosine (II, 5), the reception for his young bride to be (III, 1) and the loss of his money (IV, 7). Frosine may be seen as a more cunning variation on the role of the comic arbitrator, brought in by Harpagon as a 'fixer' of suitable lucrative marriages for his children. Their titanic struggle is built up for the audience by her pro- claimed confidence in her ability to extract money from men. It is heralded by a prologue in which La Flèche observes to her that Harpagon is 'le mortel de tous les mortels le plus dur et le plus serré' ['of all mortal beings, he is the hardest and the tightest where money is concerned'] (II, 4). Her enraged frustration at the end of the struggle provides a fitting epilogue on it and the miser. Although she seizes the initiative throughout, it is Har- pagon who impresses his rhythm on the episode, as he oscillates from mistrust to credulity in response to her advances. The promise of a mar- vellous dowry composed of negative equity (his bride-to-be spending as little on food, clothes and pleasures as a self-respecting miser could desire, according to Frosine) sees him revert to his familiar metallic register: 'ce compte-là n'est rien de réel … et il faut bien que je touche quelque chose' ['that's just an imaginary sum of money … and I need to have something to hold in my hand'] (II, 5). As he warms to her blandishments that he will outlive his children and shows off his profile under her admiring gaze, he touchingly solicits her reassurance: 'Tu me trouves bien ?' ['Do you think I look good?']. Both mistrust and credulity find almost simultaneous expression in voice and gesture through his virtuoso performance, part pantomimic, part balletic: '*Il prend un air sévère*' ['*looking serious*'] as she presses him for money; '*Il reprend un air gai*' ['*looking jovial again*'] as she switches back to flattery. The movement is repeated, before he settles back into mistrustful mode to repel her rapier-like attacks: '*Il reprend son air sérieux*' ['*looking serious again*']. Deaf to her entreaties, yet contriving to hear an unspoken summons (no doubt from his buried *cassette*) he exits in triumph – that is to say, not out of pocket.

The despatch of Frosine is achieved effortlessly, as La Flèche predicted. A more daunting challenge awaits Harpagon in III, 1, with the preparation of the reception for his bride-to-be. The greater the challenge for the virtuoso, the greater the opportunity for deployment of the panoply of his talents, and the greater his confidence in his ability to conquer his audience by the force of his performance. Harpagon faces up to this fresh challenge to his avarice by summoning his household in order to place them on a war footing. The objective is precise: to host a reception for his bride-to-be without incurring expenditure. The weapons mobilised are the same as those used to repel Frosine, but more sophisticated and deadly in range: substitution of gesture for deed, word for substance, doctrine for fact. The enemies to be repulsed at all costs: guests and expenditure.

The imposition of form and gesture on his army requires detailed briefing. If the strategy consists of entertaining without expenditure, the tactics comprise total obedience by his army to the general's battle plan to subjugate all guests. Like all great generals, Harpagon has paid meticulous attention to detail to achieve the desired outcome. Furniture is to be cleaned without being overly rubbed, the purpose of refreshments is not at all that they should be served, rather that they serve as background unattainable decorative accessories, to be used only in *extreme* emergency, that is, when repeatedly requested, and even then they are to be heavily diluted, and the menu is to be composed of cheap, inedible ingredients. Even the certainty of mathematics cannot withstand his battle calculations, since ten guests are calculated to consume as much as eight. And if ten guests are served with eight cheap, inedible portions, the result is a net expenditure of nil pence. Game, set and match to Harpagon.

Several unsolicited objections however arise from the conscripts: what is to be done with a stain on the front of a valet's doublet, a rent in the seat of another's trousers? The objection is easily answered and found, as are all his solutions, in the domain of theatre, as the master of appearances demonstrates how to make proper use of props, however unpromising: position oneself near to the wall, taking care to serve with hat strategically covering the blemish in question. Maître Jacques inadvertently points to the way in which the battle will be won: through ceremonial gesture. When Harpagon wishes to give his cook orders, the servant insists on donning his chef's hat; when the master wishes to address his coachman, he puts on the appropriate headgear. The formal importance with which the chef invests his function merely undergoes refinement and extension in a reception based on gestures; the pre-eminence accorded to the coachman's uniform blends perfectly with Harpagon's insistence that horses whose function is ceremonial do not need to eat, any more than do guests. Mobility of gesture is the weapon which saves Harpagon from a fate worse than death: when the cook mounts a fearsome challenge to Harpagon's reductionist cuisine, by enumerating the list of courses normally served ('potage', 'entrée', 'entremets' ...), Harpagon is galvanised into prompt action to stifle such subversion: *'en lui mettant la main sur la bouche'* [*'placing his hand over the servant's mouth'*]. Maître Jacques is slow to learn from the master's workshop on gesture, as he reveals here when inveigled into giving the miser a glimpse of how others see him. But the lesson from the resultant drubbing from the master actor, a drubbing emulated by his pupil Valère (III, 2) – that performance is the key to self-preservation – is not lost on him as he mounts his own comedies of revenge at their expense (IV, 4–5 and V, 2–3).[10]

The episode of the stolen gold and the miser's distraught monologue (IV, 7) are borrowed from Plautus. The monologue was imitated by Pierre de Larivey in *Les Esprits* (1579). In the original, Euclio arrives in a state of panic, sees the audience laughing at him, then turns to them for help before lapsing into a desolate vision of the future without his treasure. It is likely that Molière knew the French play, a close imitation of the original, but his own source most probably remains the Latin play. Harpagon's monologue differs both quantitatively and qualitatively from the Plautine play. Although it retains roughly the same structure, it is almost twice as long as that in Plautus and Larivey. Euclio's is elegiac, pathetic and in part a lament for his lost treasure. Whilst such elements may be found in Molière, his main focus is radically different from both plays. It is above all a dramatic focus. This is the first appearance of Harpagon alone on stage, and it is the most dramatically charged one. We know from previous scenes that what happens to him is not only lived with seismographic intensity: his perversity ensures that it is experienced as such by other characters. Everything about Harpagon is hypertrophied in comparison to Euclio, a gruff but essentially genial character made miserable by money until he rids himself of it. Harpagon does not at all possess his money – it possesses and transmogrifies him. Hence the frenzied cries as, ravaged and dispossessed, he emerges from his garden. One of his distinguishing marks here is his hypermobility: ten staccato questions are uttered as he rushes from side to side of the stage in pursuit of the thief, only coming to an abrupt halt as he arrests himself. When he cries that without his *cassette* he has no *raison d'être*, that he is dead and buried, and would like someone in the audience to resurrect him by restoring it, that he will have everyone arrested and himself hanged should he not find it, his gestures and words carry conviction in a way that Euclio's cannot. Molière has imbued his character with such a *vis comica* that Harpagon is perfectly capable of any action however egregious – *in extremis veritas*.

In both Plautus and Molière the theft of the miser's hoard leads to the denouement. In the former, Lyconides' slave steals the gold from its cache, and is persuaded to give it to his master in return for his freedom. Lyconides duly restores it to Euclio, who in gratitude gives his daughter in marriage to him. No discovery, however serendipitous, is likely to exert the smallest degree of influence over the fixation of Molière's monomaniac. The theft of the *cassette* therefore becomes the only stratagem to make him agree to the marriages of his children. But the resolution of the impasse is secondary to the comic exploitation of Harpagon's avarice. Molière utilises the theft as a device whereby comic confusion is allowed to snowball as it embraces the commissaire, Maître Jacques, Valère, Élise and finally every character in the wake of the miser's paranoiac reactions. The prolonged misunderstanding between Valère and Harpagon (V, 3), the servant's revenge over the intendant, centring on confusion between Élise and the *cassette*, is an extensive reworking of the quickly resolved confusion between Lyconides and Euclio. With its carefully worked-out progression in ambiguity, proceeding from the purely abstract to the intimate, it exploits one of the oldest sources of comedy: simultaneous, consistent but divergent interpretations of a single event (Bergson, pp. 73–4). The ultra-rapid resolution of the situation by the intervention of the fairy godfather Anselme, who happens conveniently to be the long-lost father of Valère and Mariane, is another variation on the age-old comic process involving disparity between effort expended and result achieved. The resolution must take place around the immovable fixture that is Harpagon. In truth, there is a fixed gulf between his interest and that of his family. Molière squares the circle ingeniously by presenting us with two independent denouements, which at no point intersect.[11] The conventional ending characteristic of comedy, replete here with double marriages and general euphoria, leaves everyone except Harpagon happy. His 'custombuilt' denouement supersedes all else, as do his actions during the play, conforming as it does to the only law by which he lives, that of undeviating devotion to his god Mammon. Thus it is that by majestic legerdemain the great escape artist disengages himself from all familial relationships and attendant responsibilities involving legal fees, dowry and wedding expenses, to devote himself without let or hindrance to its worship. The outfit which he manages to cadge from Anselme is less for the family weddings than for the consummation of the only relationship which matters to him, that with his *cassette*. Those whom Mammon hath joined together, let no familial affection put asunder. In *L'Avare* we have, *pace* Rousseau, the double triumph of comedy: at once over the tentacular clutches of life-denying avarice, and in the celebration of its truly epic progenitor, Harpagon.

NOTES

1 The producer Roger Planchon came to revise such a view of the comedy. See *L'Avare* (Paris: Livre de Poche, 1986), p. 8.

2 J.–J. Rousseau, *Lettre à M. d'Alembert sur les spectacles*, ed. M. Fuchs (Lille-Geneva: Giard-Droz, 1948), p. 47 ; J. P. Eckermann, *Gespräche mit Goethe in den letzten Jahren seines Lebens*, ed. O. Schönberger (Stuttgart: Philipp Reclam Jun., 1994), p. 166; A. Adam, *Histoire de la littérature française au XVIIe siècle*, 5 vols. (Paris: Del Duca, 1964), III, pp. 374–5; *Œuvres complètes de Molière*, ed. G. Couton, 2 vols. (Paris: Gallimard, 1971), from which all quotations are taken.

3 G. Mongrédien, *Recueil des textes et des documents du XVIIe siècle relatifs à Molière*, 2 vols. (Paris: Centre National de la Recherche Scientifique, 1973), I, p. 318.

4 The role was created for Louis Béjart, who had a limp and had been a member of Molière's troupe since 1652.

5 Molière found the name 'harpago' (grappling-iron, by extension a rapacious person) in the supplement added by Urceus Codrus to the incomplete Latin play and translated into French by the abbé de Marolles in 1658.

6 For similar hasty exits on the hero's part, see *Le Misanthrope*, II, 6; IV, 4, and *Le Malade imaginaire*, I, 3.

7 *Essai sur la signification du comique* (Paris: Presses Universitaires de France, 1962), p. 65. *Le Rire* first appeared as three separate articles in the *Revue de Paris*, 1899.

8 François de la Rochefoucauld, *Maximes*, ed. J. Truchet (Paris: Garnier, 1965), no. 39 (p. 48).

9 Donneau de Visé, in R. Bray, *Molière, homme de théâtre* (Paris: Mercure de France, 1954), pp. 185–6.

10 Sganarelle, in *Le Médecin malgré lui*, I, 5, and Sosie, in *Amphitryon*, I, 2, learn the same lesson by the same means.

11 An inevitable solution, in view of the intransigent nature of Molière's comic heroes. See the endings of *Le Bourgeois gentilhomme* and *Le Malade imaginaire*.

7

ANDREW CALDER

Laughter and irony in
Le Misanthrope

Le Misanthrope, written in 1666 at the height of his career, is perhaps the most polished and thoughtful of Molière's plays. It offers us 1,800 or so alexandrines of conversation between elegant figures in a Parisian literary salon on the fringes of the court. It stands in counterpoint to the richly staged *comédies-ballets* and machine-plays, written initially for the court, which dominated Molière's output in the mid-to-late 1660s. *Le Misanthrope* was never performed at court. The play is difficult to place; it does not follow the conventions of literary or erudite comedy which dominated the comic stages of Italy, Spain and France in the Renaissance and seventeenth century. These, though immensely varied, followed more or less loosely the patterns of the Roman or New Comedy tradition of Plautus and Terence, in which complex plots contained tales of romance that, after many twists and turns, ended in universal rejoicing. Corneille's *Le Menteur* (1643) was one of the most elegant examples of the genre. Surprisingly perhaps, for all its polish and its focus on court circles, *Le Misanthrope* owed more to the traditions of French farce: as in *La Jalousie du Barbouillé*, probably the earliest of Molière's surviving one-act farces, the play portrays a battle of the sexes, a row between a would-be tyrant and a clever woman who deceives him; other smaller quarrels in *Le Misanthrope* echo the central one, each in turn imparting its vigour to the play's progress, none ending in reconciliation. *Le Misanthrope* also has features of the *comédie-ballet*. Key encounters in the play are expanded into elegant set-piece performances designed to entertain both the audience and other characters on stage. Two of these are paired readings, one of a sonnet and a popular song (I, 2) and another of two letters (V, 4). The portrait scene orchestrated by Célimène also imitates the structure of a salon entertainment (II, 4). These scenes function like comic *lazzi* in farce, or like the music and dancing tableaux laid on to entertain Monsieur Jourdain in *Le Bourgeois gentilhomme*; though self-contained, they form high points in the action of *Le Misanthrope*. Characterisation in the play also owes much to farce. The caricatural role of Alceste in particular demands a richness of action and grimace which reflect the expressive miming of the *commedia dell'arte* and the extravagant gestures of French farce. It is not the plot then, as in Roman Comedy, that shapes the play, but the farcical structures of character and quarrelsome confrontation. The plot on its own is a collection of bits and pieces: Alceste's court case crops up in the first and fifth acts; his row with Oronte in the first act is followed by a forced offstage reconciliation reported in the fourth; we become aware of Arsinoé's threat to expose Célimène's double-dealing only in III, 5; the prospect of marriage between Philinte and Éliante, giving the comedy at least the appearance of a conventional happy ending, is touched on only in the fourth act and in the last few lines of the play; the links between these elements of plot and subplot are sometimes so shadowy as to pass unnoticed, especially by live audiences caught up in the explosive confrontations between characters. The complex structure of action and argument which shapes the play then rests upon a farcical underpinning.

It might seem paradoxical too that *Le Misanthrope*, though closer to farce than to Terentian comedy, has some of the structural features of tragedy. But of course the line between the comic and the tragic is a thin one. What, potentially at least, could be more farcical than the plot of *King Lear*, where a silly old man quarrels with his honest daughter and gives all he has to the two whose hypocrisy is transparent to everyone but the old man himself? Characters in farce and tragedy equally are victims of their own characters and temperaments; their inflexibility is a kind of fate. Characters in New Comedy, on the other hand, must show a degree of flexibility; they must, at least at the denouement, forget enough of their resentments, prejudices and fears to allow love to perform its work of reconciliation. Molière's characters in *Le Misanthrope* are so saddled with their particular temperaments and worldviews that no amount of affection or love can change them. Alcestes and Célimènes, spectators feel, will be at war until the end of time. Theirs are not the conventional lovers' quarrels which make reconciliation all the sweeter; they are not sparring wits like Shakespeare's Benedick and Beatrice in *Much Ado About Nothing*, or Congreve's Mirabell and Millamant in *The Way of the World*, where discord finally yields to love, providing typical New Comedy endings to both plays. When Benedick, a seasoned mocker of marriage and women, finally decides to marry, the reversal is complete: 'a college of wit-crackers,' he says, 'cannot flout me out of my humour' (V, 4); the teasing Millamant yields to Mirabell with a smiling 'Well, you ridiculous thing you, I'll have you. – I won't be kissed, nor I won't be thanked' (IV 1). At the end of *Le Misanthrope*, in contrast, all four of Célimène's lovers leave the stage cursing her for her fickleness. The play might be said to end happily only in the sense that at least the ill-matched lovers are to be spared a marriage likely to bring mutual torment. The contrast between the two kinds of comedy emerges with particular sharpness at the parallel moments in the denouements of *Much Ado About Nothing* and *Le Misanthrope*, where written evidence is produced to reveal the true state of the lovers' feelings: in the first, a sonnet by Benedick and a note in Beatrice's hand show that, beneath their surface conflicts, their love has remained unswerving throughout; in *Le Misanthrope*, the letters written by Célimène demonstrate on the contrary that her surface professions of love conceal contempt for her lovers. She does, of course, feel some attachment to Alceste (whom she is quite willing to marry), and Alceste is in his own peculiar way head-over-heels in love with Célimène, but theirs in both cases are self-obsessed loves which will never triumph over the obstacles that separate them. At the end of *Le Misanthrope*, the audience is left to question whether love's magical powers are sufficient to heal life's wounds, a frame of mind quite inimical to the carnival world of comedy. While there is no doubt that Alceste and Célimène are comic characters, they function like tragic characters to the extent that it is their flaws – or their defective humours – which structure the action of the play and not all-conquering love: Alceste is incurably bilious, while Célimène is compulsively coquettish; the comic perspective in the case of *Le Misanthrope* heightens our awareness of the lovers' limitations rather than allowing love to sweep these limitations to one side.[1]

This structural pessimism is in fact a hallmark of Molière's work: even in the lighter plays that bathe in an atmosphere of carnival and celebration it is the crooked perspectives of his protagonists, translated into gestures, words and encounters, which make them comic. Molière's œuvre belongs to the genre of *vanitas* literature according to which 'that which is crooked cannot be made straight' (Ecclesiastes 1. 15).[2] Truly happy endings would make aesthetic nonsense of his plays. *Le Misanthrope*, then, explores one of the commonest of themes, the vanity of a world filled with double-dealing, hypocrisy, ambition and self-love. For Renaissance and baroque writers (and painters), there were two principal angles from which such a world might be viewed: we might laugh at its foolish ways like Democritus, or weep at its tragic errors like Heraclitus.[3] Molière, like Erasmus, Rabelais and Montaigne, was a Democritus. In *Le Misanthrope*, he is mocking a world he knew well: the polite circles of Paris and the court. The extent to which it is his own world is emphasised by the many allusions to writing and theatre in the text: Oronte plagues the public with readings of his verse; there are hints that Alceste might be a writer too – he is treated as a poet by

courtiers who crave his approval of their verse, and his enemies would have
been unlikely to brand him as the author of a dangerous polemic if he were
not a writer already (1096 and 1500–4); we know from Philinte's allusion
to Molière's *L'École des maris* that he is a theatre-goer (99–100); and
Acaste, a lover of all literary novelties, is a theatre-goer too (791–6). To
evoke a concentrated picture of this comic and courtly world, Molière
focuses on a small number of stereotypical figures and on the conversations
and incidents of a single day in one Paris salon. He adds variety to his
picture by having characters express their views on the way of the world in
general, by having them draw portraits of one another and by adding –
mainly through the witty Célimène – a gallery of supplementary portraits of
figures who do not appear on stage (especially in II, 4). The principal
exemplars of a world ruled by vanity and self-interest in the play itself are
the four courtiers. We learn that Clitandre, an idle *marquis*, has no com-
mitments between the *levé du roi* and the *petit couché* (the ceremonies of
the King's rising and of his retirement to bed) (567 and 739–40). Acaste, the
second *marquis*, paints a self-portrait which covers the pair of them: on self-
examination, he tells Clitandre, he is pleased to find himself rich, young, of
noble lineage, fit for any position, courageous, clever, shrewd and an arbiter
of the best taste; from his seat on stage at plays, he cuts a fine figure as he
leads audience opinion with his loud interjections; he is stylish, good-
looking, has beautiful teeth and a lissom figure; none is better dressed than
he, his reputation is high, women adore him and he is well in with the King
(781–804). Such braying, foppish clowns, however, cannot be ignored: as
Célimène says, such figures, without anyone quite knowing why, are lis-
tened to at court, involved in every conversation, can do no one any good,
but have power to inflict great harm (542–8). The other two professional
courtiers are cleverer and still more menacing. Oronte, the obsequious
scribbler, another who boasts of his closeness to the King, seeks to buy
Alceste's approval of his verse by offering him undying friendship; then,
when the bargain is rejected, he becomes a dangerous enemy, lodging a
complaint with the court marshals – a procedure designed to do real harm
to Alceste's standing – and adding his voice to those naming Alceste as the
author of a treasonable anonymous tract.[4] The fourth courtier, Arsinoé, is
an ageing coquette, prude and gossip; jealous of Célimène and intent on
destroying her reputation, she can draw on a powerful court cabal to ensure
she succeeds. Other exemplars of court life, among Célimène's portraits, are
Cléonte, whose florid appearance and manners make him a laughing-stock;
Damon, the unstoppable talker with nothing to say; the busy, conspiring
Timante, who whispers everything, even 'good morning', into his listener's
ear; Géralde, whose tedious talk is all of dukes and princesses; Bélise, the

aphasic guest who, with all the commonplaces of conversation long exhausted, still refuses to budge from her chair; Adraste, the malcontent swollen with self-love; and the Vicomte, who has engaged Célimène for three long quarters of an hour while he spits into a well to make rings (II, 4 and V, 4). The most sinister of the absent figures alluded to in the play, however, is the unnamed villain with whom Alceste is locked in litigation: this man, we are told, is a hypocrite, whose crooked and grimacing climb to power has been observed by all; yet, though known to be an out-and-out scoundrel, he is welcomed everywhere (123–40). This figure serves to remind audiences of the truism that it is sufficient for good men to keep silent for evil to flourish. The corruption of court and society is further underlined by Alceste's and Philinte's judgements on them: for the misanthropist everyone is evil, some naturally so, the rest because they tolerate the others (118–22), while for Philinte, his phlegmatic friend, it is a truth hardly worth articulating that self-seeking cabals, greed and trickery abound everywhere (1,555–8); for him a man who is a money-loving rogue with no care for justice is no more shocking than a vulture hungry for carrion (173–8).

The world as a theatre of folly, however, is not the main focus of *Le Misanthrope*. As Philinte reflects, corruption and folly are too common to stir up much emotion in sensible people. The question the play explores much more interestingly is how individuals engage with such a world, and it is through Alceste and Célimène that we, as spectators and readers, are drawn into the debate. We like them and, on occasion, even identify with them because their very weaknesses are attractive: both cause social havoc, one by being a straight talker, the other a malicious wit. Both have an arresting stage presence: Alceste is admired by all three of the women in the play and Célimène by four of the five men. Both, like the playwright himself, are connoisseurs of the world's follies. Yet, even as we warm to them, we see them as exemplars of folly. We see that, for all their perspicuity, their social interactions are misjudged; we feel there is too much vanity and contempt in their attitudes to other people. As the morally well-informed Célimène reminds us, 'On doit se regarder soi-même un fort long temps / Avant que de songer à condamner les gens' ['We should spend a long time looking at ourselves before thinking of condemning others'] (951–2). But for all their knowledge of how people should behave, both Alceste and Célimène focus with lynx-eyed sharpness on others' faults while seeing their own with the eyes of a mole. Their perspectives reflect one of the commonest moral axioms of Renaissance Humanists: the much-quoted Aesop pointed out in the fable of the wallets that all carry a sack with two pockets; in the back pocket, where they are out of sight, they stow away their own faults, while other people's faults are kept in full view in the front one.[5] Alceste and Célimène, then, because we both laugh at them and like them, are both ridiculous and disturbing; they are comically wrong and yet uncannily like us.

Alceste fails spectacularly to measure up to Célimène's maxim. He will have no truck with self-examination. As militant and unquestioning a critic as any satirist could be, he believes there is a clear-cut line between right and wrong and that he alone knows where to draw that line. Yet one can easily agree with many of his views – on the gushing manners of modish courtiers for example:

> Quel avantage a-t-on qu'un homme vous caresse,
> Vous jure amitié, foi, zèle, estime, tendresse,
> Et vous fasse de vous un éloge éclatant,
> Lorsqu'au premier faquin il court en faire autant? (49–52)

[What use is it if a man makes a fuss of you, swears friendship, fidelity, esteem, affection, and praises you to the heavens, if he then runs off and does the same to the first rogue he meets?]

We applaud him when he tells the scheming Arsinoé not to bother using her influence to find him a place at court. A man of his temperament, he points out, has no place there:

> Être franc et sincère est mon plus grand talent;
> Je ne sais point jouer les hommes en parlant;
> Et qui n'a pas le don de cacher ce qu'il pense
> Doit faire en ce pays fort peu de résidence. (1,087–90)

[My greatest talent is for frankness and sincerity; I don't know how to flatter people in conversation; and a man who doesn't have the gift of concealing what's in his mind must keep his visits to that country brief.]

He acknowledges that shunning the court will block his worldly advancement, but is pleased at least to be freed from the pains of playing the fool there, of suffering repeated snubs, of praising the verse of scribblers, flattering Madame so-and-so and wilting under the babblings of aristocratic fops.

However, the self-knowledge revealed in this speech is fragile at best. In his encounters with others, Alceste's choleric black bile quickly usurps the role of judgement; he treats all around him, whether they deserve it or not, with anger and contempt. In the opening encounters of the play he curses his friend Philinte for sharing the affable embrace of a man whom he hardly knows, comes almost to blows with a scribbler whose sonnet he does not like and angrily scolds his mistress for her fickleness. Later, knowing that

Éliante loves him, he proposes marriage – as he frankly explains – to spite her cousin Célimène (1,246–58). His blind rage leads him to harm himself even more than others: he refuses to defend himself against the villain who is cheating him at law (182–202); most importantly, however, it renders him incapable of happiness; there is not a moment in the five acts when Alceste is to be observed enjoying the company of other people. His rages, like Heraclitus' tears, are symptoms of a radical problem of judgement: they leave no room for the irony which would make it possible for him to see himself and the world in proportion. In consequence, he views himself as a tragic hero, while for others he is the butt of comedy. His skewed perspective is revealed in the opening incident: without a hint of humour, Alceste says that, had he been guilty of Philinte's insincere show of civility, he would have hanged himself – the classic response to a tragic dilemma. Philinte, understandably, finds the sentence disproportionate, laughs and begs to be spared the full rigours of a hanging. The Heraclitean and the Democritean perspectives are tested out face to face and, clearly, audiences find Philinte's smiling response more fitting. His ironical quip offers Alceste a chance to forget his anger, smile at having sentenced his friend to the gibbet and return to enjoying his company. Instead, his brooding anger deepens as he complains bitterly that Philinte's flippancy is in bad taste. The misanthrope's flawed sense of humour is confirmed a few moments later when, scorning Philinte's comparison of the two of them with the two brothers in *L'École des maris*, he reveals that he has no time for Molière.[6] His doctrine of complete sincerity is turning him into a laughing-stock. When Philinte asks if Alceste would tell old Émilie to her face that she is too old to attempt to look pretty and should stop wearing make-up, his answer, 'Sans doute' ['Undoubtedly'], inspires smiling disbelief. As the action develops, Alceste will frequently be the butt of others' laughter: his reading of a street ballad as if it were high poetry amuses Philinte (401–16); all on stage enjoy Célimène's satirical (and accurate) portrait of him (669–82); the two *marquis* dissolve into giggles when Alceste asserts that only a command from the King in person could make him find merit in Oronte's sonnet (769–72); when Philinte tells Éliante of Alceste's appearance before the court marshals, both smile at the picture of an Alceste who, finally persuaded to concede that he wished with all his heart that he had liked Oronte's sonnet better, is bundled into a quick embrace with his resentful rival (1,133–62).

Alceste's ill-judged tragic spleen is most damaging, however, in the matter which most affects his happiness: his pursuit of love. He is at his most touching and at his most comic in the conduct of his courtship of Célimène. It is here that the discrepancy between his view of himself as a tragic figure and the audience's view of him as a comic one is greatest. The audience sees a bilious moralist who, having fallen out with the entire human race, is still hopelessly infatuated with a woman who collects proposals of marriage from all and sundry; it also sees a bad-tempered lover fending off rivals while persuading himself that his rages are prompted by the highest moral regard for integrity. 'Je veux qu'on me distingue,' he says, which might be paraphrased as 'I do not wish to be confused with other men' (63). For the audience, Alceste's misadventure is just another episode in the age-old war of the sexes.[7] His outburst when he discovers that Célimène has deceived him points up the contrast between his tragic perspective and our comic one:

> Ah! tout est ruiné;
> Je suis, je suis trahi, je suis assassiné:
> Célimène ... Eût-on pu croire cette nouvelle?
> Célimène me trompe et n'est qu'une infidèle. (1,227–30)

[All is ruined; I am ... I am betrayed, I am assassinated: Célimène ... who would credit it? Célimène has betrayed me and is no more than a faithless woman.]

The audience may be too fond of Alceste to laugh out loud, but it cannot suppress an ironical smile because, of course, the answer to his question is that everyone except him can believe quite easily that Célimène has betrayed him. Decidedly, his love for this glamorous flirt is not (as he claims) the greatest love which ever man experienced for woman; it is possessive, whingeing, ungenerous and displays the run-of-the-mill selfishness of the most banal of loves. Molière's portrait of Alceste reminds us of La Rochefoucauld's observation that there is no passion in which selfishness is more powerful than the passion of love.[8] The portrait of Alceste of course – like this maxim – has implications for all. It is an invitation to urbane spectators (and this play assumes urbanity in its audience) to reflect with irony on their own misanthropy and their own conduct as lovers; to smile at the promptness with which, on occasion, they have so liberally identified the faults of others; and to acknowledge cheerfully that they – like lovers from the beginning of time – have tended to take their own heart-rending loves and jealousies every bit as seriously as the comic Alceste takes his.

Célimène with 'son humeur satirique' ['her satirical humour'] (661) has no difficulty seeing the funny side of things. If Alceste incarnates the angry satirist's crusading spirit, Célimène captures that part of every good satirist's make-up which revels in the sheer absurdity of people. Though a gossip and coquette, she is shrewd, witty, resourceful and irresistible. Her portraits ring true on the whole: Philinte is quick to point out to Alceste when he scolds her as a gossip that he too would condemn the very same faults ridiculed by Célimène (667–8). We particularly enjoy her fluent assault on Arsinoé when the latter advises her glamorous young 'friend' that, in circles where virtue is prized, her flirtatious ways and the crowds of men who flock to her salon are attracting censure (III, 4). We admire Célimène's misuse of the conventions of politeness to outmanœuvre and humiliate her malicious opponent. We are amused, too, by the ease with which she dominates her whole circle and deceives her four lovers. Spectators have always applauded inventive schemers and manipulators, such figures as Terence's Phormio, Molière's Scapin or Beaumarchais's Figaro. Yet we are not quite free to make a romantic heroine of Célimène. Here again a parallel with Congreve's Millamant, a salon beauty and wit of a similar stamp, points up the particular character of Molière comedy. Millamant, though one of a circle (rather like Célimène's) which meets three times a week for 'cabal nights ... where they come together like the coroner's inquest, to sit upon the murdered reputations of the week', is a fully-fledged romantic heroine.[9] While Millamant's wit and charm generally display magnanimity, Célimène's more often conceal malice and dissimulation.

Célimène's strategy, for all its surface polish, in fact works no better than Alceste's. She too ends the play isolated from her circle and – still more dangerously – from herself: in the midst of her many liaisons, she cannot tell when love is real and when feigned (1,180–4). Her satirical wit has brought disorder to her outer and inner lives. While knowing the theory that good satirists begin by laughing at themselves, she keeps hers for others; she says it is a good friend's duty to alert us to our own faults (965–72), but prefers to hear no criticisms. While she has enough self-knowledge to know that she could not endure exile in the provinces with Alceste, she does not have enough to find happiness in the society of court and town. She uses her wit to flatter insiders, to ridicule absent friends and acquaintances and to attract admiration. With each succeeding sketch in the portrait scene (II, 4), her wit, fed by flattering applause, becomes more malicious so that by the time she reaches Damis, a man of reputation whom Philinte admires, his intelligence, discernment and refinement are amusingly turned into defects. Her brilliant gossip makes her giddy with power; her contempt for the world she mocks with such brio is perhaps greater than Alceste's. Her obsessive scheming mirrors Alceste's immoderate anger and, oddly, their opposing strategies drive both into excessive involvement with others and neglect of themselves; both give too little time to knowing themselves and their own needs so that they can live at ease with themselves and others. Célimène's social strategy leaves her at the denouement without allies and with a shattered reputation. Hers is every bit as disconcerting a comic portrait as Alceste's. Beauty, wit and intelligence, especially on stage, can hardly fail to captivate, yet spectators are left, even as they smile, with a sense of waste and loss.

Philinte and Éliante, though structurally essential as counterpoints to Alceste and Célimène, pose problems for directors, actors and, sometimes, for spectators too. Especially when set against the two central figures, their dramatic colouring is pale; also, they are too self-knowing to be really ridiculous. Their function in the structure of the play is to serve as pointers to social strategies that work. Philinte is closer to Célimène, a cool ironist, a self-confessed social animal adept at playing the games required by etiquette. He has almost no fixed character because he changes with changing contexts, closely observing himself and the world in order to respond appropriately. His awareness of the unending cruelty of man to man inspires not lonely misanthropy, but ironical watchfulness. His advice to Alceste is practical: to fight the villain who is suing him with all the means at his disposal; to drop his damaging policy of absolute frankness; to resist the passion which is making him miserable; and not to abandon the society of others, a policy likely to end in madness. Unlike Célimène, he uses humour sparingly and only with friends: to attempt to laugh Alceste out of his rages, or to share his ironic perspective on Alceste and their circle with Éliante. Frankness, too, he reserves for his friends; with others he is accommodating. His approach to society is conciliatory: he praises Oronte's sonnet to keep the peace, forgives Alceste's unmannerly snubs, bears with the salon gossip, attempting only occasionally to divert it along more kindly lines. He knows that there is no greater folly than seeking to put the world to rights (157–8). He sees his own modest place in the general scheme of things in a true perspective, keeping in check even the stronger emotions stirred by love: he twice acknowledges without apparent resentment Éliante's preference for Alceste (245 and 1,203–6). The only moment in the play when anyone truly enjoys another's company is the scene where Philinte and Éliante mull over the problems of Alceste and Célimène, reflect on the quirks of human nature and frankly confess their own feelings (IV, 1).

Éliante, though rather like Alceste, is the proof that a love of sincerity can work in a corrupt society. She is an unwilling player of social games, repelled by gossip (583–4), admires Alceste for his sincerity (1,163–8) and declines to support Célimène when she refuses to choose between Oronte and Alceste, replying that she prefers people who speak their mind (1,660–2). Her key contribution is in the portrait scene, where, echoing Lucretius and Horace, she gently and affectionately ridicules all lovers, noting that it is in the nature of love to transform the very faults of the beloved into strengths (711–30).

This speech has a broader application, implying that all relationships, not just those between lovers, become easier if one takes as generous a view as possible of the faults of others. Éliante echoes the generalised and gentle satire of Horace, which smiles at the world's ways while avoiding castigating named individuals.[10] Yet it is perverse to seek in this pale pair the voices of either Molière or the spectator.

Where, then, should we look for Molière? It is hardly surprising that in this lovingly composed play, in which there was no pressing or immediate need to please King or court, the playwright has chosen to explore the comedy of his own calling, to look at questions of balance between lucidity, sincerity and censure, and at the boundaries between appropriate and inappropriate uses of humour and satire. As usual with Molière, we cannot be sure what (if any) were his conclusions. There is a strong Montaignian vein running through the play. Philinte's philosophy is very close to Montaigne's in 'De Democritus et Heraclitus', where the essayist warns of the dangers of taking people too seriously. Perhaps Molière, like Montaigne, feels that human beings are too silly to deserve our tears, and that smiling indifference shows a proper and well-judged detachment from foolish humanity? A Montaignian emphasis on the mean can also be felt throughout the play; excesses of sincerity and sociability are shown to be equally damaging, while the middle ground occupied by Philinte and Éliante leads to understanding and love. One feels, however, that, both in this play and in his work as a whole, it is less the mean than the extremes that really interest Molière. Philinte and Éliante function effectively as moral pointers, but we find them almost too good to be credible: most will share Alceste's disbelief on hearing Philinte's assurance that he could accept calmly the treachery of a friend seeking to ruin his good name and fleece him through a crooked lawsuit (167–74); we wonder, too, at Éliante's patience when faced with Alceste's insulting proposal of marriage (1,252–68). Such phlegmatic calm and kindly forbearance certainly do not echo Molière's satirical practice. On the contrary, his comedies come closer to combining Alceste's rage and Célimène's merciless wit: in his satirical portraits of the *précieuses*, of his many *marquis*, of Tartuffe, Trissotin and all three learned women, there is no question of Molière's finding as much good in them as possible; rather, he exposes them to hyperbolic ridicule. In *Le Misanthrope*, too, the laughter can seem harsh: Alceste and Célimène, after all, are a likable pair whose crimes, measured on any kind of general scale, are minor. Molière's job, of course, was to fill theatres rather than to tiptoe through the minefield of salon life. We cannot be sure to what extent his use of hyperbolic ridicule is a reflection of his temperament and to what extent the technique of a master caricaturist. Nor perhaps do we need to know. It is enough that *Le Misanthrope* is a delightful, provoking and elegant entertainment and that in Alceste, whom he played himself, Molière gave the comic theatre one of its richest and most demanding roles.

NOTES

1 Molière drew attention to the importance of Alceste's bilious humour in an earlier title for the play, *L'Atrabilaire amoureux* (*Œuvres complètes*, ed. G. Couton, 2 vols. (Paris: Gallimard, 1971), II, p. 125). Explicit and implicit references to Alceste's bilious and melancholic humour can be found in lines 143–4, 166, 685, 688, 1,082, 1,521–4, 1,582–6, in Célimène's portrait of him in the letter read out by Acaste (after 1690) and 1,803–6.

2 The most important *vanitas* text, 'Vanity of vanities; all is vanity', occurs earlier in the same chapter (5. 2). For parallels between *vanitas* themes in literature and in painting see my 'From Epic and Tragic to Comic and Satiric: Reversed Perspectives in Painting and Writing from the Renaissance to the Seventeenth Century', *Seventeenth-Century French Studies*, 21 (1999), 261–75.

3 See especially Montaigne's chapter 'De Democritus et Heraclitus' (*Essais*, I, 50), in which he explains his preference for a smiling perspective. See also my *Molière: The Theory and Practice of Comedy* (London and Atlantic Highlands, NJ: Athlone Press, 1993), pp. 89–92.

4 This is probably a reference to attempts by Molière's enemies to pin the authorship of a dangerous polemical text on to him. For more details, see *Œuvres complètes*, ed. Couton, I, pp. 1,343–4.

5 This fable was a favourite text of Renaissance and seventeenth-century moralists, including Erasmus, Rabelais, Montaigne and of course La Fontaine ('La Besace', *Fables*, Book I, 7). For more details, see my *The Fables of La Fontaine: Wisdom Brought Down to Earth* (Geneva: Droz, 2001), pp. 75–8.

6 The reference is especially to the opening scenes of *L'École des maris* (1661), where an aggressive and misanthropic younger brother quarrels with his urbane and modest older brother. The judgement of Argan in *Le Malade imaginaire* is similarly undermined when he dismisses the therapeutic value of Molière's comedies (III, 3).

7 Other variations on this theme in Molière's opus include *La Jalousie du Barbouillé* (no date), *Sganarelle ou Le Cocu imaginaire* (1660), *L'École des maris* (1661), *L'École des femmes* (1662) and *George Dandin* (1668).

8 François de la Rochefoucauld, *Maximes*, ed. J. Truchet (Paris: Garnier-Flammarion, 1977), no. 262 (p. 68).

9 William Congreve, *The Way of the World* (1700), I, 1. See *The Comedies of William Congreve*, ed. by E. S. Rump (Harmondsworth: Penguin, 1985), p. 325. For a sustained parallel between these plays, see my 'On Humour and Wit in Molière's *Le Misanthrope* and Congreve's *The Way of the World*', in Sarah Alyn Stacey and Véronique Desnain (eds.), *Culture and Conflict in Seventeenth-Century France and Ireland* (Dublin: Four Courts Press, 2004), 151–62.

10 See Ruth Calder, 'Molière, Misanthropy and Forbearance: Éliante's "Lucretian" Diatribe', *French Studies*, 50, 2 (1996), 138–43.

8

CHARLES MAZOUER

Comédies-ballets

The resurgence of baroque music in the twentieth century, particularly the music of seventeenth-century France, has boosted interest in a traditionally neglected yet important part of Molière's work: his twelve *comédies-ballets*. It is high time to remind ourselves that 40 per cent of his output consists of works which combine the spoken word with the arts of music and dance.[1]

In truth this new composite genre created by Molière, a genre which encompasses such a diversity of productions, has an unlikely look about it. Not only is it impossible to classify it or codify its rules with any precision, but even its name is problematic. We call it *comédie-ballet*, but this term (a poor fit, as it downplays the role of music) was imposed only in the eighteenth century; Molière used the term only once – in his edition of *Le Bourgeois gentilhomme* (1671) – and then in quite special circumstances: not in order to draw attention to the presence of the three arts throughout the comedy, but precisely because the comedy was followed by a ballet, the *Ballet des nations*, inserted at the end of the spectacle. In the seventeenth century, gazetteers, chroniclers and publishers were puzzled by this strange genre and uncertain what to call it; they most often used an expression which listed the three arts while giving precedence to comedy; thus *Le Malade imaginaire*, published after the death of Molière (who, with the exception of *Le Bourgeois gentilhomme*, always sent his *comédies-ballets* to the publishers as *comédies*), was entitled 'comédie mêlée de musique et de danse' ['comedy mingled with music and dance'].

This improbable genre was born quite by chance; Molière himself tells us how in the Preface to *Les Fâcheux* (1662). Under the pressure of circumstances, when Fouquet was putting on a series of spectacles at Vaux-le-Vicomte in the summer of 1661, the performers had to find an emergency solution to a practical problem: there were too few ballet-dancers and they had too little time to change between their entrées, so they divided up the ballet entrées and slipped them in between the acts of the comedy of *Les Fâcheux*, where they served as ornamental enrichments to the comic action.

Comédie-ballet was born from the dismembering of a ballet! Note that at that stage the mixture was only of comedy and ballet, supported by music; not until *Le Mariage forcé* in January 1664 was instrumental and vocal music to play a full autonomous role, alongside ballet, in the spectacle. From that date all the *comédies-ballets* were to involve the three arts, with their three distinctive languages.

'C'est un mélange qui est nouveau pour nos théâtres' ['It is a combination which is new to our theatres'], Molière proclaims in the same Preface to *Les Fâcheux*. Of course Molière could have found in the traditions of France and Europe examples of theatrical forms and experiments which combined the arts; to look no further than his own immediate context, the *commedia dell'arte*, Italian opera, French machine-plays and court ballets offered varied examples of such mixtures. But Molière was responsible for a wholly original and creative bringing-together of the three arts in new forms. We can endorse Donneau de Visé's affirmation in the *Mercure galant* of 1673 that it was Molière who 'first invented a manner of combining musical scenes and ballets in his comedies'.

Court Spectacle

When *Les Fâcheux* was performed, Louis XIV was Fouquet's guest; the young King was from the first delighted by this kind of spectacle and encouraged Molière to work for him and contribute to his entertainments. From 1664, all Molière's *comédies-ballets* were written to be performed at royal festivals or entertainments. We should take literally the words of the musical prologue to *L'Amour médecin* (Versailles, September 1665), sung by Comedy, Music and Ballet – three allegorical figures symbolising the arts of *comédie-ballet*:

> Quittons, quittons notre vaine querelle,
> Ne nous disputons point nos talents tour à tour,
> Et d'une gloire plus belle
> Piquons-nous en ce jour:
> Unissons-nous tous trois d'une ardeur sans seconde,
> Pour donner du plaisir au plus grand roi du monde.

[Let us abandon our fruitless quarrel, and argue no more, turn and turn about, as to which of our talents is best; let us boast of a greater glory this day: let us all three combine with a new ardour to give pleasure to the world's greatest monarch.]

Yes, Molière was a courtier! Providing royal entertainments together with his company, proclaiming the King's glory and supporting the monarchy, Molière gave unstinting service to the King, though often rushed and harried by the pressure from royal demands. Almost every year, right up to *Le Malade imaginaire*, saw one or sometimes two new *comédies-ballets* commanded by the King who, along with the peers of the realm, loved to dance before court circles and did so in the *comédies-ballets* – at least until *Les Amants magnifiques* (1670). The truth, however, was that the relationship between Molière and the King was a good deal more interesting and profound than that between a common courtier and his King, as the quarrel of *Le Tartuffe* demonstrated. A real complicity – on, for example, the philosophy of pleasure and love shared by a young King and a libertine playwright – bound them together; this complicity, however, did not prevent Molière from retaining his freedom of judgement, as the *comédies-ballets* themselves often showed. In a word, while pleased to serve the King at royal festivals, Molière was thoroughly at home with the genre which gave the King so much pleasure.

We must keep in mind that royal festivals were at the behest – and under the orders – of the King, and that their purpose was to add to his glory: they were an expression of royal power and part of his political strategy. The royal provider, the magnificent ordainer of court spectacles, their principal spectator and often their hero, made use of them to display to the aristocracy, to his peoples and to Europe his greatness and his glory, the very concepts on which the order of his realm was founded. The occasions for such entertainments were diverse. Each year brought its carnival season, a time for every kind of pleasure, and, in the opposite season, the royal hunts of autumn. To mark a victory, to offer a present to Queen Marie-Thérèse (officially), to the current mistress (unofficially) or, later, when he had put gallantry behind him, to the Princess Palatine, the King would order a celebration and set Molière to work on it.

The *comédies-ballets*, then, had their origins in festivals of which they were often only one constituent element; they followed the King's sojourns in his various residences. A number of them would have been performed in royal palaces as part of loosely programmed entertainments on which our information remains sketchy. This was the case with *Le Mariage forcé* (at the Louvre), *L'Amour médecin* (Versailles), the three Molière spectacles contained in *Le Ballet des Muses* (Saint-Germain-en-Laye, December 1666 to February 1667), *La Comtesse d'Escarbagnas*, which brought together the anthology from the *Ballet des ballets* (Saint-Germain-en-Laye, December 1670), *Monsieur de Pourceaugnac* and *Le Bourgeois gentilhomme* (Chambord, respectively October 1669 and October 1670). Other *comédies-ballets* were integrated into open-air festivals given in the summer season with much greater splendour, and on these we have much fuller information. *Les Fâcheux*, Fouquet's entertainment at Vaux-le-Vicomte (of which La Fontaine has left us a brief but evocative account), was of this kind. So too were *La Princesse d'Élide* and *George Dandin* at Versailles – the early Versailles, that is, consisting principally of gardens. *La Princesse d'Élide* was performed on 8 May 1664, on the second day of *Les Plaisirs de l'Île enchantée*, a festival on a theme based upon the figure of the enchantress, Alcine, from the *Orlando furioso*, and whose *plaisirs* [pleasures] were staged over several days. *George Dandin*, encased within a pastoral musical entertainment, took place amid the set ritual of a great royal feast: collation, dinner, ball, illuminations and fireworks. A glimpse at Félibien's account of this *Divertissement royal de Versailles* of July 1668 gives some sense of its miraculous inventions and the wonder they inspired: architectural effects, abundant ornament, plays of light, displays of fountains and the magnificence of the banquet itself, were all designed to amaze. It was precisely in this enchanting framework, amid this riot of display and profusion of sensations, that Molière's artistic project found its proper place; an echo of such profusion is to be found in the *comédies-ballets* themselves.

Thus the King, not content merely with giving the initial impulsion but determined to enter into the detail of execution, requiring accounts of everything, employed painters, sculptors, decorators, engineers, machinists, gardeners, pyrotechnists, hydraulic engineers and, of course, musicians, dancers, poets and playwrights, who pooled their efforts to create events which were to become veritable meeting-places for all the arts. Certainly these celebrations were quintessentially baroque, staged as they were to the accompaniment of Lully's music and Vigarani's sumptuous scenery. While revelling in the sheer profusion, brilliance and capacity to surprise with which they aimed to satisfy all of the senses, Molière saw no objection to slipping into these baroque festivals comedies whose realism was at times violently at odds with their celebratory tone.

How, then, were Molière's *comédies-ballets* incorporated into the royal entertainment? Most occurred as spectacles in their own right, which took their place among other pleasures – hunting, walking, dancing, ballet, concerts, collations, fireworks and other theatrical performances. There was no necessary link binding *Les Fâcheux*, *Le Mariage forcé*, *L'Amour médecin*, *George Dandin* and its pastorale, *Monsieur de Pourceaugnac*, *Les Amants magnifiques* or *Le Bourgeois gentilhomme* to particular programmes of entertainments.

However, in a court context, certain entertainments were organised around a central theme so that each of them took its place in an ordered sequence. The programme of events for *Les Plaisirs de l'Île enchantée* took care to link Molière's *comédie-ballet* to the theme for the second day: pressed by the sorceress Alcine, who is holding them on an island, Roger and the other warriors first entertain Queen Marie-Thérèse with races and then with a comedy – more or less the situation in *La Princesse d'Élide*. With *La Pastorale comique* and *Le Sicilien*, which constitute respectively the third and fourteenth entrées of the substantial *Ballet des Muses*, the unifying structure is a little tighter. The very supple overall shape of the ballet made it possible to add to it danced entrées together with a *comédie-ballet*; this is precisely what happened with *Le Sicilien*, a last-minute addition with two new entrées for Turks and Moors. Even then, care was taken to link these elements, too, to the overall theme: the visit of the Muses to the court of the Great King. *La Pastorale comique* was intended to honour the Muse of comedy, Thalia. The Muses rounded off the King's entertainment with the entrées of the Turks and the Moors combined with the little comedy of *Le Sicilien*.

The other way round, as one might say, a Molière comedy could serve as a frame, providing the linking context for several entertainments. This is the pattern in *Les Amants magnifiques*; it is very clear in *La Comtesse d'Escarbagnas* and the lost pastorale which Molière composed for the *Ballet des ballets*. Wishing to offer an anthology of the best ballet scenes from earlier years, all taken from the *tragédie-ballet* of *Psyché* and the *comédies-ballets* of Molière and Lully, the King naturally turned to Molière, who wrote *La Comtesse d'Escarbagnas* – a framework for a sort of giant *comédie-ballet*, as the comedy contained a pastorale which in turn served as a frame for balletic interludes.

The most surprising thing to modern eyes is that Molière integrated into these entertainments or these great baroque celebrations *comédies-ballets* whose tone and subject were very different from what one might have expected in such a setting – need one recall that the staging of the first *Tartuffe* occurred precisely during one of the days of *Les Plaisirs de l'Île enchantée*? For Molière, all kinds of subjects and all forms of comedy could be adapted to this new genre, which makes it impossible, moreover, to draw a clear dividing line between *comédies-ballets* and the rest of Molière's œuvre; the ornaments of music and dance are integrated into the comedy which, whatever its theme, remains the base on which the genre of *comédie-ballet* rests.

Les Fâcheux introduces us into a noble world; still nobler are the worlds of *La Princesse d'Élide* and *Les Amants magnifiques*, whose heroes are princes and aristocrats, and which often aspire to a heroic tone. This gallant side of the *comédie-ballet* blends easily with the world of pastoral entertainments, whether taken seriously or perpetually parodied as in *La Pastorale comique*.

On the other hand, *comédie-ballet* can be frankly comic, lending its fantasy to plays which portray bourgeois reality, such as *Le Mariage forcé*, *L'Amour médecin*, *Monsieur de Pourceaugnac*, *Le Bourgeois gentilhomme* and *Le Malade imaginaire*; or to plays which portray the reality of the provinces and the country, such as *George Dandin* and *La Comtesse d'Escarbagnas*. We would be hard put to it to classify *Le Sicilien*, whose Sicilian reality gives off a slight whiff of fantasy!

Farce, poetic fantasy, gallant or heroic comedies, caricatural sketches, comedies of character or manners, all forms, whether in five acts or not, in verse or in prose, call upon the collaboration of musician and choreographer for court festivals.

Court celebrations are ephemeral; their glamour has gone by the next day, after the fading of their profusion and magnificence. But Molière did not believe that his personal contributions to them could not live on. Having served the King in his residences, he offered his *comédies-ballets* to his Parisian public in the Palais-Royal – which was not exactly a courtly public. With few exceptions, the *comédies-ballets* created for the court were performed again before the town, and almost always with the ornaments of music and dance – and the expense that went with them! Molière then succeeded in pleasing two publics, and took care to focus on each of them in turn with clear eyes and unclouded judgement.

A Composite Genre

The originality of the *comédie-ballet* came from combining three arts and their three distinct languages: the word in the dialogue of the spoken comedy, and the music and dance which are present in what Molière and his contemporaries called the *ornements* or *agréments* (embellishments), which might be spread throughout the comedy or appear as interludes between acts. A *comédie-ballet*, then, should be considered as a common undertaking: involving Molière, of course, who wished to retain overall control in order to assure the unity of the spectacle – which he achieved with varying degrees of success – and also the composer and choreographer.

The goal in *Les Fâcheux* was to harmonise the ballet entrées with the comedy; dance played a crucial role in the birth of the genre of *comédie-ballet*. Its central place in the civilisation of the seventeenth century and the importance accorded to it by Louis XIV are well known; in 1662 the King founded an Academy of Dance. One of the most celebrated masters of the Academy, Pierre Beauchamp, who was to become its director, was equally skilled in composition (he wrote and directed the music for *Les Fâcheux*). Beauchamp, who with Lully had created the great court ballet and who was later to choreograph Lully's operas, choreographed all of Molière's *comédies-ballets*.

Molière, who had perhaps been taught to dance by the Jesuits at the Collège de Clermont, had a thorough acquaintance with all the aesthetic ideas of his time on dance. According to the doctrine of *imitatio*, everything in the spectacle of dance had to imitate: décors, costume, stage props, but above all the gestures and movements of dancers' bodies. Dancers had to be able to imitate everything: first and foremost the feelings and passions, but also social stereotypes, mythological figures, even the phenomena of nature. Dance, say the theorists of the time, expresses the nature of things and the habits of the soul; it expresses, depicts and recreates through action. Molière had an acute awareness of the beauty and charm of dance, of its expressive and emotive power, of the sense of harmony it can inspire in an individual or in a larger public when it is allied with music. He would place before his choreographer – and at the same time before his composer – a crowd of characters who were to people his interludes or provide ornamental musical moments in the action: allegorical figures, gods, pastoral figures or types from the *commedia dell'arte*, and various characters borrowed from everyday life, familiar or exotic. Costumed, bringing into play all the resources of their bodies, dancers – King and nobles mingling with professionals – would, to the accompaniment of a variety of airs for dancing, perform set steps and figures, the detail of which, and even the general style, are now difficult to recapture.

Molière, by family (he was related to the old and musical family of the Mazuels), taste and upbringing, must have been still more sensitive to the power of music. As with dance, music had its special place at court and in society as a whole; like dance, it imitates nature, and in particular the passions and moods of the soul for which the imitative language of music could find all the appropriate accents. It moves powerfully all who listen to it. Molière integrated the charm of music into the creative synthsesis of the *comédie-ballet*.

He worked with a number of composers. He and Lully – the other Baptiste – who, thanks to Louis XIV, who was charmed by him, had recently shot into prominence, rapidly found themselves aesthetically and personally on good terms; Lully was ready to place his talent and verve, his sense of drama and stage and all the musical experience he had acquired through court ballet at the service of *comédie-ballet*. The successful collaboration between the two Baptistes, as they were known, lasted from 1664 to 1672, the date at which Lully turned to opera, or *lyrical theatre*, and did his best to make the performance of *musical theatre*, to which Molière's *comédies-ballets* belonged, impossible. Following this aesthetic parting of their ways – opera gave precedence to the composer while *comédie-ballet* gave overall control and precedence to the playwright and to the spoken word – Molière turned to a young composer of genius, Marc-Antoine Charpentier, whom the ubiquitous Lully had kept in the shade. Though the collaboration was brief, it resulted in the score for *Le Malade imaginaire*, which reached a peak comparable to that attained by Lully in *Le Bourgeois gentilhomme*.

Musicologists have long analysed the musical forms used by the two composers whose airs sustained the dancers. Together with its airs for dancing, and more important than its orchestral pieces (overtures and ritornelles), *comédie-ballet* gave special prominence to vocal music; characters performing musical passages or interludes, sometimes taking the form of a brief drama-in-itself (for Lully and Charpentier composed truly dramatic music), sang solos, combined in duets or trios (which made possible a rich diversity of registers and emotive colourings) or else merged into a combined chorus or double chorus. The lyricist Molière wrote with music in mind and the composers adjusted their music to the words so as to bring out more strongly their expressive and emotive power.

It is essential therefore to return to the scores and seek to imagine the dancers in action if we are to appreciate the richness, variety and beauty of the ornaments of music and dance whose omission literally disfigures *comédies-ballets*. After the French-style overture, the purpose of which was to transport audiences into a world of fantasy, the ornaments of dance and music stirred the emotions and evoked a particular mood as the spectacle unfolded. Two principal moods dominated: one brought together the range of emotions peculiar to the pastorale, with its cold-hearted shepherdesses and suffering shepherds finally united in happiness – though Molière and Lully sometimes mocked pastoral conventions too; the other was a mood of laughter, inspired by the various musical and verbal languages working closely together, bringing joy to daily routines, making fun of ponderous characters (such as lawyers or doctors) and leading into the grand burlesque ceremonies which formed the climaxes to *Le Bourgeois gentilhomme* and *Le Malade imaginaire*, veritable masterpieces of musical comedy.

While it was the combining of the arts that made the *comédie-ballet* original, it was also this that gave rise to the aesthetic problems of the genre, emphasised by Molière as early as *Les Fâcheux*, where he tried as best he could to graft the ballet entrées on to the plot of the play 'so as to make a single work out of the ballet and the comedy' ('Avertissement au lecteur'). Musical ornaments inspire laughter, charm us, move us in a word by the combined grace of poetry, melody and dance. But how are such musical pleasures to be successfully integrated with the pleasures of the comedy? How is one to 'enchaîner ensemble tant de choses diverses' ['bring coherence to such different things'] ('Avant-propos' to *Les Amants magnifiques*)? How is their union to be made aesthetically plausible?

Before even addressing the question of the coherence of music and dance and their integration into the comedy, we must first appreciate what is the place and relative importance, within each *comédie-ballet*, of musical and choreographic elements as compared to the comedy itself; we must ask in short what is the aesthetic balance in this hybrid genre which was so new to the theatre. Two patterns can be distinguished.

In one, the more successful one to our taste, the comedy remains pre-eminent while those parts which are sung or danced have a relatively modest role and slip easily into the development of the play's action. This pattern is clear in *Le Mariage forcé* and *L'Amour médecin*, in *Le Sicilien* especially, perhaps the most exquisite of Molière's *comédies-ballets*, and in *Monsieur de Pourceaugnac*. The second pattern makes its appearance in *La Princesse d'Élide* and, no doubt under pressure from Lully and in any case following the tastes of King and court, was to become the dominant one: here, the musical interludes grow in importance to become dramatic episodes in themselves. *La Princesse d'Élide* includes six interludes, all interconnected. In *George Dandin* the interludes were developed to the point where they turned into a huge musical pastorale in four acts, which enclosed within them the three acts of the brief peasant farce; in other words, in a strange reversal, Molière's comedy provided interludes for Lully's pastorale! *Les Amants magnifiques* returned to a less paradoxical hierarchy, but one has the impression at times that the intrigue of this *comédie galante* imagined by Molière (too little known, rather like *La Princesse d'Élide* where the classical playwright gives us a foretaste of Marivaux) served rather as a pretext for displaying a series of six internal spectacles.

Le Bourgeois gentilhomme is the apotheosis of the genre, encapsulating all the various delights of music and dance within the comedy itself, which remains the focus of a spectacle enriched by composer and choreographer, integrating all its various elements naturally into its comic progress. When one adds, after the comedy, the *Ballet des nations*, which lasts more than forty minutes, one sees the culmination of the tendency to let the musical elements run to excess. Molière doubtless sought to achieve a better balance with his new composer for *Le Malade imaginaire*, where he returned essentially to a pattern of separate interludes; but more than half of Charpentier's score is devoted to the Prologue, a long eclogue with music and dance which Molière was unable to perform for the King before his own death.

Chronology signifies nothing in this context; there is no linear development of the genre of *comédie-ballet*, no organic progress. Responding to a
variety of impromptu demands, from both taste and necessity, Molière tried
different formulas, experimenting with elements of continuity and rupture,
advancing in one area and retreating in another. We shall find no linearity
either when we come to examine the major aesthetic problem posed by this
hybrid genre: the structuring of musical elements in relation to the comedy.
I am persuaded that Molière did have before his eyes an ideal in which
musical ornament and comedy would form a natural unity, and that he did
seek natural links, rational connections, and a necessary fusion of disparate
elements; but there was no steady evolution towards the attainment of such
an ideal; we see him experimenting, feeling his way, sometimes succeeding
and at others turning back to earlier solutions. The best we can do, then, is
present a sort of rising logical – but not chronological – table of solutions to
the problem, ranging from the loosest of structures to others displaying the
tightest unity.

In certain spectacles, the prologue, or a particular musical ornament, is
detachable: such as the prologues to *Les Fâcheux*, *L'Amour médecin* and
Le Malade imaginaire, and the first interlude of *Le Malade imaginaire*. The
entire musical pastorale which enfolds *George Dandin* – which is complete
and self-sufficient – can be performed separately from the comedy; contemporaries were aware of this and Molière was to perform *George Dandin*
on its own in his Paris theatre, though not, of course, without changing the
meaning of the spectacle.

The next step shows the playwright seeking to make the musical
ornaments integral, increasing their *vraisemblance* to fit them more aptly
into the *comédie-ballet* as a unified whole. He sometimes achieved this by
turning them into little musical scenes which the characters in the play
perform for one another as entertainments. Of this kind are the interludes
in *Les Amants magnifiques* and the *Ballet des nations*; entertainments
which a lover offers to his mistress or which celebrate a joyous marriage in
the denouement; diversions laid on to dissipate the melancholy of the comic
protagonists in *Monsieur de Pourceaugnac* and *Le Malade imaginaire*; and
the many music and dance routines in the first act of *Le Bourgeois gentilhomme*, where the masters' demonstrations of their arts before Monsieur
Jourdain are essential to the action of the play.

The final step was to harmonise the action in the balletic and operatic
interludes with the action of the comedy so that musical elements, assimilated into the story of the play, unfolded seamlessly as part of the intrigue.
This occurred as early as *Les Fâcheux* and *Le Mariage forcé*, using a
formula which was to be repeated in those *comédies-ballets* where the

proportion of musical entertainment in the play remained moderate. It was achieved in *La Princesse d'Élide*, where interludes between acts develop a sub-plot in which scenes of burlesque comic relief are performed by Moron (played by Molière), who appears as a character both in the play itself and in the musical interludes. It was achieved finally and most successfully in the two major burlesque ceremonies of *Le Bourgeois gentilhomme* and *Le Malade imaginaire*; these two great set-pieces of verbal, musical and balletic high comedy are essential to the action but still more essential to the characterisation of the comic heroes. By turning Monsieur Jourdain into a *mamamouchi* and Argan into a doctor – a veritable metamorphosis for each of them and a feast of carnival disguise for everyone else – Molière could stage the flowering of their illusions into folly and give the last touches to his portraits. The ornament of music could not be more necessary or integral to the comedy.

Meanings

The search for believable dramatic unity leaves unresolved the question of the *comédie-ballet* as a hybrid creation which combines aesthetic values from fundamentally different domains: word, sound and dance. Should we be happy simply to label this heteroclite mixture *baroque* and be content with this historical designation? I think not. I am persuaded that Molière adopted this new combination not only to harness the pleasures intrinsic to the three arts and explore the effects of surprise and charm inspired by the three of them working in harmony, but also because he counted on finding new effects of meaning through the use of mixed-genre spectacles. It is a fact that the *comédie-ballet*, through both content and composition, implies a particular vision of the world.

To begin with, Molière, so careful to give dramaturgical unity to the *comédie-ballet*, was keen, along with his co-artists, to underline the gap between the realism of comedy and the fantasy of music and dance, to exploit the contrapuntal effects to be gained from contrasting the imaginary and the real. Thanks to music and dance and to the contrapuntal play between these and the comedy, the playwright could reject a unilateral vision of things, providing instead – in a kind of polyphony – multiple perspectives and judgements upon his characters. The role played by Moron in the interludes of *La Princesse d'Élide* creates an ironic distance between the audience and the pastorale and the values of the nobility portrayed there. Two visions of love enter in turn into conflict and resolution in *George Dandin* and its accompanying pastorale in the Versailles performance. The musical ornaments of *Le Bourgeois gentilhomme* allow us to judge the naive Monsieur Jourdain but also the rogue Dorante.

We could go a little further and look at Molière's work in its entirety. His critical eye on the world inspires laughter and the writer has chosen to see the world through a smiling perspective. The introduction of the musical ornaments does not in the least destroy such an artistic perspective, but – as it were – adds to the means at Molière's disposal for leading us from the real to the euphoric, enriching his thought with a new harmonic. The sometimes caricatural distortion which results from his comic strategy, and the distance which laughter creates, already tend to make the world unreal, to exorcise violence and stupidity and to soften the hard edges of the real. With its own intrinsic fantasy, musical ornament serves this end perfectly; it attains the very goal pursued by the comic, tipping the familiar prose of reality into a world of the imagination. The poetry of music, charming scenes of pastoral gallantry, the grace of dance which makes everything agreeable, the unbridled clowning in which both arts join, everything that such ornaments bring to the performance lightens the gravity of the spoken play, laughs alongside it and draws it into a light and playful dance. Yes, *comédies-ballets*, though born of chance, might be seen as the fulfilment of Molière's genius, the completion of his journey, as Romain Rolland proposed.

As *Les Fâcheux* showed from the start, the hard edge of comedy is softened by the fantasy of music. The presence of singing and dancing helps us forget the bitterness of ambition and the social violence and double-dealing which go with it. The satire of medicine and doctors is pitiless and fierce; their menace and the anguish they inspire, however, exorcised initially by the stylisation and the sense of unreality which the comic imparts to things, are finally calmed by the musical ornaments which embrace and expand the comic vision, transforming medicine into masquerade.

Comédie-ballet glorifies love. In the spoken comedy, love which is mutual and unconstrained overcomes all obstacles. In the pastoral interludes, shepherdesses finally allow themselves to be won over by the love and pleasure whose praises are constantly sung. Musical ornaments and comedy join together to ensure and proclaim the triumph of love; song and dance diminish the obstacles to love and conquer those who oppose it; singing love's praises, they bathe the comedy in their own optimism and sustain the will of the young lovers until they can celebrate its final victory.

Above all, *comédies-ballets* are an affirmation of joy. The part played by the comic musical ornaments is crucial: from the humorous to the burlesque they inspire gaiety without bounds; interlaced with the spoken comedy, they collaborate in the creating and perfecting of laughter. Molière counted on the alliance of laughter, vocal harmony and dance to create serenity as well as joy. The point has been made that *comédies-ballets* were often either composed for the carnival season or else their actions were set in a period of carnival. The spirit of carnival – the satirical questioning of order and hierarchy, the taste for games of mask and disguise which inspire riotous farce and allow Molière to deepen his analysis of certain human illusions – is conducive to the expression of joy. In sum, the *comédies-ballets* allowed Molière to add a final touch to his comic wisdom. Through ambivalent laughter, which both punishes and brings peace, he wishes to deliver us from the cold and violent world which his penetrating analysis of humankind and its relationships has laid bare; the ornaments of *comédie-ballet*, with the fantasy which is proper to them, complete the work of laughter and lead to a sense of complete well-being. He would concur with the view that stage happiness has its limits; but his affirmation of joy carries with it a conviction, or at least a longing: that the world could be a better place and that humankind could be happy.

In rehabilitating the *comédies-ballets*, which were produced as much for the Parisian public as for the court where they were first created, inviting appreciation of their beauty and of the charm of their musical ornaments, and demonstrating the originality of their subject matter and of the meaning attained by the combination of the three arts, we should not seek to separate them off from the rest of Molière's œuvre. If the *comédies-ballets* emphasise the extent to which Molière was a baroque playwright, they also have many strands linking them to other comedies where the element of fantasy is absent.

For the rest, remarkably, this genre, created by Molière with the help of his composers and choreographer, died with him. True, one finds comedies enlivened by music and dance written by various of his contemporaries and successors. But Molière's secret is lost: other playwrights have not found the inner necessity born of the union of the arts, nor the unity with which Molière embraced opposites to create new meanings. All the more reason then for urging that his *comédies-ballets* be staged and recorded more frequently, both in their integrity and in their integrality!

NOTE

1 For further reading on *comédies-ballets* please see the section at the end of this book devoted to the bibliography and discography of *comédies-ballets*.

9

JOHN S. POWELL

Le Bourgeois gentilhomme: Molière and music

With *Le Bourgeois gentilhomme* (1670), Jean-Baptiste Molière and Jean-Baptiste Lully created a masterwork of musical comedy. This was the ninth collaboration of their seven-year association, and *Le Bourgeois gentilhomme* became by far their most popular work – one that remained among Louis XIV's favourite entertainments throughout his life. This *comédie-ballet*, glowing with comic inspiration, proved 'les deux grands Baptistes' (as Mme de Sévigné called them) to be simply the best team of comic collaborators before Mozart and da Ponte. In fact, it was for *Le Bourgeois gentilhomme* that Molière coined the term *comédie-ballet*.

Le Bourgeois gentilhomme also marked a new direction in the genre of *comédie-ballet*. The early *comédies-ballets* were intended for court *fêtes* in which the King and his courtiers would participate as dancers in the *intermèdes* [musical interludes]. Louis XIV had performed a variety of colourful and exotic roles in these early works – including those of gypsy (*Le Mariage forcé*), peasant (*La Pastorale comique*) and Moor (*Le Sicilien*). But after the King's retirement from the stage with *Les Amants magnifiques* (where he was to portray Neptune in the first *intermède*, and Apollo in the last) the genre broke with tradition.[1] *Le Bourgeois gentilhomme* was the first wholly professional *comédie-ballet* in which noble amateurs did not participate.

As with many of the earlier *comédies-ballets*, Louis XIV had a hand in selecting the subject matter. The visit of an envoy, Suleïman Aga, from November 1669 until May 1670 provided the comic inspiration for the central musical episode. This diplomat, charged with repairing diplomatic relations between France and the Ottoman Empire, proved a difficult personality. Unimpressed by the splendour of Louis XIV's court and scornful of the Turkish-style reception given in his honour, Ambassador Aga was overheard to remark that the sultan's horse was more richly adorned than the French King. Following the ambassador's departure, Louis commanded the Chevalier Laurent d'Arvieux, recently returned from the Middle East, and an expert in Turkish customs, to join with Molière and Lully in preparing a Turkish masquerade.

Later that summer, the three retired to the village of Auteuil, where the Parisians went to escape the stifling heat of the city, to continue preparations. D'Arvieux recounts that, once the play was finished and approved by the King, he 'spent eight days at the home of the master tailor Baraillon, to have the Turkish clothes and turbans made'.[2] Evidence suggests, however, that the play was far from finished. Most probably D'Arvieux was referring only to the central 'Cérémonie Turque', and Molière and Lully had yet to set their musical and comic imaginations to work building up plot and action and fleshing out the entertainment around the Turkish centrepiece. Much of the elaboration and many details of the *comédie-ballet* were left to the eleventh hour. On 3 October, only six weeks into their busy autumn season at the Théâtre du Palais-Royal, Molière and his actors left for Louis XIV's fairy-tale château at Chambord, where the King and court had retired for a season of hunting and relaxation. Molière and Lully therefore had a scant ten days to set up, rehearse and coordinate the music, dance and spoken episodes of the play. The printed booklet (*livret*), distributed to the audience at the court performances (an action depicted in the opening scene of the concluding 'Ballet des Nations'), offers a rare glimpse into this comic masterwork-in-progress. One undated *livret* that survives in a single copy evidently served as a first proof.[3] In it, the *dialogue en musique* and the second drinking song do not appear, and the sung minuet 'Ah, qu'il fait beau dans ces bocages' ['How fair the day in these woodlands'] is placed in the fourth (not the fifth) entrée of the 'Ballet des Nations'. These and other minor discrepancies between the two *livrets* suggest that Molière and Lully were still working out the sequence of events during this ten-day period.

The Chambord premiere was given at a staggering cost to the royal treasury – a total of 49,405 *livres* according to the royal accounts.[4] These accounts reveal many details relating to the premiere performances. Jean Baraillon, royal tailor, and the tailor Forestier received 5,108 *livres* and 3,571 *livres* respectively for furnishing 81 costumes. This did not include those worn by the actors (for which Molière's company received 4,400 *livres*); nor did it include the costumes worn by Lully (who played the Mufti) and the court singer Mlle Hilaire (who appeared onstage once, to sing the air 'Je languis') – for which they received 900 *livres*. Further payments made for silk hose (ninety-three pairs), ribbons, masks, garters, wigs, beards, feathers, gloves (eleven dozen), and precious stones reflect the magnificence of the production. The ninety pairs of stage shoes (*escarpins*) supplied to the performers give an idea of the great host of participating singers, instrumentalists and dancers.

14. Drawing by Henry Gissey (1621–73), Stockholm, Nationalmuseum, Collection Tessin, K. 8, fol. 27.

The quality and cost of costumes can be gauged from those worn by Lully and Molière, of which there are surviving illustrations. The first, a drawing by Henry Gissey (1621–73), depicts that of the Mufti – played by Lully (listed in the *livret* under the stage-name 'le Seigneur Chiacheron'). On his head is a 'turban de cérémonie', and under his arm he carries the Koran. This costume cost the royal treasury 200 *livres*, plus an additional 100 *livres* for ribbons and garnishes. The second illustration, by Pierre Brissart, depicts the initiation of Monsieur Jourdain into the Turkish aristocracy. While this engraving lacks the detail of Gissey's drawing, an inventory of

15. Engraving by Pierre Brissart, *Les Œuvres de Monsieur de Molière. Revues, corrigées, & augmentées. Enrichies de Figures en Taille douce* (Paris: Denys Thierry, Claude Barbin and Pierre Trabouillet, 1682).

Molière's wardrobe made after the playwright's death in 1673 describes

> a costume for the performance of *Le Bourgeois gentilhomme*, consisting of a dressing gown, double striped with rosy-gold and green taffeta, breeches of red velvet, a camisole of blue velvet, a nightcap with lining, some shoes and a cotton Indian-painted scarf, a Turkish jacket and a turban, a sabre, shoes of musk-deer trimmed with green and rosy-gold ribbons and two Sedan points, a taffeta doublet trimmed with lace of faux silver, the belt, green silk stockings and gloves, with a hat trimmed with rosy-gold and green feathers.[5]

Royal accounts list payments for food and lodging, for carriages to transport the singers, dancers, and actors from Paris to Chambord, for carpenters and painters, for lumber, nails, rope and canvas to construct a temporary theatre, designed by Carlo Vigarani, in the *salle des gardes* (where the marks of the rings to which curtains were attached are still visible), for face powder, pomade and make-up assistants, and much else besides. Then, after Chambord, the court and the performers picked up and moved the entire production to Saint-Germain-en-Laye, where performances continued on 9, 11, and 13 November. The cost of transportation by carriage and waggon to Saint-Germain added some 10,000 *livres* to the mounting costs.

According to D'Arvieux, early performances were an outstanding success.[6] According to Grimarest, however, the King remained silent after the first performance, prompting courtiers to round on Molière, accusing him of attempting to entertain them with childish inanities, and leaving him in great distress. Then, after the second performance, the King said to his playwright: 'I did not speak to you of your play at the first performance, because I feared being influenced by the manner in which it had been performed: but in truth, Molière, you have never written anything that has entertained me more, and your play is excellent.'[7] Mortified courtiers, Grimarest recounts, then joined in the applause. Such a prank at the expense of his sycophantic courtiers has the ring of truth, for Louis XIV on occasion revealed a theatrical flair for keeping his courtiers off balance.

Music and ballet inform *Le Bourgeois gentilhomme* on multiple levels. The entertainment begins ceremoniously with an instrumental overture, and concludes with a *ballet à entrées* – for the entertainment of Monsieur Jourdain and his family. Moreover, each act (of the recast five-act version[8]) concludes with an *intermède* that grows out thematically from the preceding spoken scene. The first is a kind of dance-demonstration, in which 'the four dancers execute all the different movements and all the kinds of dance steps that the Dancing Master orders'. For the second, choreography informs stage action as four apprentice tailors dress Monsieur Jourdain to musical accompaniment, and then dance their delight with the tips they have received from him. Then, at the end of Act III, the six cooks enter dancing to present their succulent dishes for the banquet.[9] Collectively, these balletic episodes form a dramatic arc to the apotheosis of Monsieur Jourdain in the fourth *intermède*, the Turkish Ceremony – an irruption of music, dance and *fantaisie* (a term which includes notions of both an outer fantasy world and an inner creative imagination).

From the very start of the plot, when the curtain opens to reveal the pupil composing a vocal *air*, we are made aware that artistic inspiration, comic and musical *fantaisie* lie at the heart of this work. According to a stage direction in the *livret*, 'a pupil of the Music Master is seated at a table composing an air which the Bourgeois has ordered for a serenade'. This laconic rubric gives little insight into the *mise en scène* that would bring this comic action to life in performance. Fortunately, André Danican Philidor, Louis XIV's music librarian, preserved the musical score for this scene in his manuscript copy of *Le Bourgeois gentilhomme* made for the king's library.[10] By means of this silent score – these mute notes attached to a musical staff, with the syllables to be sung placed below – we are given insight into the inner workings of the creative process. Here the composer 'invents' a melody phrase by phrase, while striving to duplicate in musical rhythms and pitches the speech inflections of a skilled orator. As he fashions the melodic shape of each phrase (without the aid of a harpsichord, judging by the stage direction), he writes it down on manuscript paper to his own sung dictation. Musical example 1 shows his setting of the first three lines of text; above the vocal staff, placed in italics, is my analysis of the implied stage action that accompanies each measure of music.

Yet the question remains: if no harpsichord is present on stage, just what does the bass line represent? Clearly, this bass does not correspond to that of the finished air, which has decidedly more melodic contour and harmonic direction. Rather, this bass is a stream-of-consciousness succession of germinal phrases, a series of partially formed musical ideas with the forward impetus of a 'walking bass'. Indeed, this bass could be viewed as a musical representation of the composer's thought-processes while in the throes of creative inspiration. As the harpsichord is not present onstage, its music must therefore exist only in the mind of the composer-student as a product (or perhaps by-product) of his musical *fantaisie*. It is precisely this artistic fantasy-world that lies just beneath the surface of *Le Bourgeois gentilhomme* – which irrupts periodically in the form of the twisted logic of the Maître à danser (for whom 'Tous les malheurs des hommes, tous les revers funestes dont les histoires sont remplies, les bévues des politiques, et les manquements des grands capitaines, tout cela n'est venu que faute de

Musical example 1: *Élève de musique* scene, transcribed from BnF, Rés. F. 578, p. 4.

savoir danser' ['All the misfortunes of mankind, all the dreadful disasters that fill the history books, the blunders of politicians and the lapses of great commanders proceed from not knowing how to dance'], I, 2) and in the increasingly hyper-real *intermèdes*. Artistic *fantaisie* comes to the foreground in the carnivalesque Turkish Ceremony and is compounded meta-theatrically in the 'Ballet des Nations' – where the new Mamamouchi and his family become onstage spectators at a second theatrical entertainment as exotic as the first.

At any rate, we learn that the Maître de Musique has assigned the task of composing this air to one of his pupils 'who has an admirable talent for these kinds of things'. This elicits the peevish and ignorant response from the bourgeois that the master should have done it himself. The master replies: 'Il ne faut pas, Monsieur, que le nom d'écolier vous abuse. Ces sortes d'écoliers en savent autant que les plus grands maîtres; et l'air est aussi beau qu'il s'en puisse faire' ['You must not let the name of pupil fool you, sir. Pupils of this sort know as much as the greatest masters, and the song is as fine as could be made']. We may appreciate the delicious irony (as did the audience) that the actual composer of the air was *not* the Music Master's student, but none other than Lully, Louis XIV's Superintendent of Music. Lully was a gifted musician who had sprouted from humble roots. Brought from Florence by the duc de Guise to teach Italian to his wife, he rose through the ranks to become not only the most influential musician in France but also a lifelong friend of the King. Lecerf de la Viéville tells us that the intuitively gifted Lully composed music in a manner similar to that depicted here. Once he had the text of an operatic scene:

> Lully read it until he knew it nearly by heart; then he sat down to his harpsichord, sang and re-sang the words, playing his harpsichord and fashioning a basso continuo. When he had finished his melody, he would commit it to memory in such a way that he would not forget a single note. Lalouëtte or Colasse [Lully's secretaries] would then come, and he would dictate it to them. The next day he would hardly remember anything of it.[11]

This scene was played for laughs at the premiere of *Le Bourgeois gentilhomme*, when the versatile court singer Jean Gaye (who played the music student) sang in falsetto and notated the melodies onto manuscript paper with a flourish. Contrary to our expectations, what follows is a masterwork: an *air tendre* [love song] of ravishing beauty which, when sung by the delectable court singer Hilaire Dupuis,[12] must have left the audience transfixed.

Musical example 2: Finished *air tendre*, transcribed from BnF, Rés. F. 578, p. 10.

Je croy-ais Jean-ne - ton aus-sy dou-ce que bel - le, Je croy-ais

Jean-ne - ton plus dou-ce qu'un mou - ton: hé - las! hé - las!

elle est cent fois, mil-le fois plus cru - el - le que n'est le tigre en bois.

Musical example 3: *Chanson*, transcribed from BnF, Rés. F. 578, p. 11.

Monsieur Jourdain's musical tastes, however, run in quite a different direction, and he finds the student's composition a bit lugubrious. Expressing his preference for a rustic chanson ('There's sheep in it', he recalls), Monsieur Jourdain sings the ditty in falsetto, taking pride in being able to do so without ever having studied music.[13]

The drinking songs found in Act II of the *livret* (or Act IV of the printed play) provide a lively counterpoint to the earlier *air sérieux* of Act I. These performances, like the banquet they accompany, have been laid on, not by Monsieur Jourdain (who merely foots the bill), but by his aristocratic fair-weather friend Dorante. An easily recognisable type of parasite, Dorante is a penniless courtier driven to trading on his nobility to raise money in a sham alliance with someone below his station. He uses Monsieur Jourdain's food and music to whet the sensual appetites of Dorimène – an aristocratic lady he intends to court – and right under the bourgeois's nose. Yet, even this farcical scene is ennobled by Lully's music. The first song ('Un petit doigt [a little drop] Philis') tells of how wine inflames love, while the second ('Buvons, chers amis, buvons' ['Drink, friends, drink']) expands on the familiar *carpe diem* theme (wine being a metaphor for love). Indeed, Lecerf de la Viéville tells that of all his airs 'Buvons, chers amis, buvons' was the one that Lully loved most throughout his life. Thus, the diverse vocal music so far presents a cross-section of the different secular song traditions popular in mid-seventeenth-century France: the *air sérieux*, the *air bachique* or drinking song and, as will be discussed presently, the pastoral *dialogue en musique*.

In his performance of 'Je croyais Janneton', Monsieur Jourdain is evidently unaware that these sheepish lyrics were by Pierre Perrin – who the previous year had acquired the royal *privilège* to establish French opera. Molière and Lully took every opportunity to ridicule this rival poetaster and his eccentric theories on opera. Two years later Lully would break with Molière, take over Perrin's opera monopoly and establish his own

Académie Royale de Musique. Thus, the vocal concert that follows in I, 2, might well spoof the kind of pastoral operas performed in Perrin's short-lived 'académies d'opéra'. The Maître de Musique explains that 'c'est un petit essai que j'ai fait autrefois des diverses passions que peut exprimer la musique' ['this is a little essay that I once wrote of the various and sundry passions that music may express'], and he directs Monsieur Jourdain to imagine the singers dressed as shepherds. 'Pourquoi toujours des bergers?' asks the mystified bourgeois. 'On ne voit que cela partout' ['Why always Shepherds? You see nothing but that everywhere']. With tongue in cheek, the Dancing Master appeals to Monsieur Jourdain's rationalist sensibilities – explaining that 'Lorsqu'on a des personnes à faire parler en musique, il faut bien que, pour la vraisemblance, on donne dans la bergerie. Le chant a été de tout temps affecté aux bergers, et il n'est guère naturel en dialogue que des princes ou des bourgeois chantent leurs passions' ['When we have characters that are to speak in music, it has for the sake of plausibility to be a pastoral; singing has always been assigned to shepherds, and it is not natural in dialogue for princes or shopkeepers to sing their passions']. Yet there is more to this than the obvious burlesque of pastoral convention, for here Molière and Lully ridicule the very aesthetic premise of Perrin's operas. Perrin had sought to avoid the *invraisemblance* [lack of verisimilitude] of 'operatic' singing by replacing all serious discourse with the lyric sentiments most suitable for pure musical expression (love, joy, despair, etc.). Indeed, Molière modelled his three nameless characters after the pastoral archetypes found in Perrin's first opera, the so-called *Pastorale d'Issy*. Here we easily recognise Perrin's inconstant shepherdess, the faithful shepherd and the rejected satyr. In Molière's and Lully's version, 'La musicienne' prizes her freedom from love; the 'premier musicien' embraces the philosophy of the faithful shepherd; while the 'second musicien' is a worldly-wise satyr who vehemently and operatically denounces 'ce sexe inconstant'. Each of Molière's characters receives music that befits his/her character: lightheartedly mocking music for the fickle shepherdess, passionate lyricism for the lovesick shepherd, dramatic recitative for the misogynistic satyr. The three singers resign their positions in the concluding trio and join in singing the platitude 'Oh, how sweet it is to love when two hearts are faithful'. From chaos emerges order in Lully's music, and the three richly divergent musical personalities eventually coalesce in sweet harmony.

Music and the arts also serve a greater philosophical purpose in *Le Bourgeois gentilhomme*, as an idealised metaphor for social harmony and stability. Monsieur Jourdain shows little taste in music and poetry – or, for that matter, little appreciation for the arts – and this failing becomes symbolic of the disharmony that he has brought about in his family life. Just as surely as his determined social climbing draws attention to, and indeed exacerbates, his poor taste in the realm of the arts, it also ruins such judgement as he has in family matters. While he wishes (harmlessly enough) to learn music to ape 'people of quality', he (rather more seriously) disregards his daughter's wishes and insists upon marrying her to a gentleman. Trapped in his narrow world of a vulgar, social-climbing bourgeois, Monsieur Jourdain is hell-bent on underlining his bleak philistinism by decking himself, his house and his family in the trappings of nobility. Yet increasingly, as the action unfolds, his vulgarity is little more than an artistic motif: Monsieur Jourdain becomes no more than a bourgeois clown, around whom playwright, composer, choreographer and costumier create a swirl of richly inventive comic dialogue, music, dance and image.

The arts, always kind to young lovers, will set this situation aright by means of a musical ruse – the Turkish Ceremony. We have seen the *comédie-ballet* setting up a delightful counterpoint of comic scenes and musical episodes drawn from the tradition of court ballet. As the plot unfolds, however, these musical interludes, first presented to Monsieur Jourdain and his household as mere entertainment, become increasingly fantastic and meta-theatrical. They will serve as stepping-stones away from his comfortable life of middle-class reality and toward an exotic, musical fantasy-world.

Not surprisingly, patterns and rhythms of music and choreography inform many of the spoken episodes of the play: we see this formal patterning in the articulation of comic set pieces, in dialogues and in verbal games. In the first scenes we meet the five masters, of music, dance, fencing, philosophy and tailoring. The first two, obsessed with earning money, full of themselves and their professions, are taken to their hyperbolic limits: for them, everything in the world is explicable only in the narrowest terms of music and dancing. Molière adds to the squabbling pair the still more lunatic self-admiring figures of the Fencing Master and the fist-waving Master of Philosophy. It is no accident that none of these cultural parasites has a proper name, for they are depersonalised archetypes drawn from the realms of farce and *ballet de cour*. Moreover, in true ballet tradition, each appears with his entourage of followers: the first with three musicians, the second with four dancers, and the tailor with four apprentices.

The linguistic symmetries of these scenes in particular mirror balletic choreography. The opening dialogue is a verbal *pas de deux* in which the Music and Dancing Masters have a professional quarrel which, like so many professional quarrels, begins with a tiny difference of opinion. The one, preferring to display the indifference to money of a man devoted to his art, feels that fulfilment can be attained only if he is paid to the accompaniment of lavish and discriminating praise, while the other is content to take his wages from a rich fool while gathering approval from less well-off connoisseurs. In the second scene, their rivalry grows as one evokes a world which could only attain perfect harmony if all studied music, while the other believes that universal peace can be attained only through the study of dancing, which would eliminate all *faux pas* from human affairs. When the Fencing Master arrives in the second act, the heated verbal interplay between the three gathers pace, threatening to break out in song and dance:

MAÎTRE D ARMES: Et c'est en quoi l'on voit de quelle considération nous autres nous devons être dans un État, et combien la science des armes l'emporte hautement sur toutes les autres sciences inutiles, comme la danse, la musique, la ...

MAÎTRE À DANSER: Tout beau, Monsieur le tireur d'armes. Ne parlez de la danse qu'avec respect.

MAÎTRE DE MUSIQUE: Apprenez, je vous prie, à mieux traiter l'excellence de la musique.

MAÎTRE D ARMES: Vous êtes de plaisantes gens, de vouloir comparer vos sciences à la mienne!

MAÎTRE DE MUSIQUE: Voyez un peu l'homme d'importance!

MAÎTRE À DANSER: Voilà un plaisant animal, avec son plastron!

MAÎTRE D ARMES: Mon petit maître à danser, je vous ferais danser comme il faut. Et vous, mon petit musicien, je vous ferais chanter de la belle manière.

[FENCING MASTER: And by that you see in what consideration men like me should be held in the State, and how the science of arms excels greatly all other useless sciences, such as dancing, music, and ...

DANCING MASTER: Easy, easy, sir wielder of arms. Don't speak of dancing except with respect.

MUSIC MASTER: I pray you, learn to treat better the excellence of music.

FENCING MASTER: Amusing folk, to want to compare your sciences with mine!

MUSIC MASTER: Do but see the importance of the man!

FENCING MASTER: My little dancing master, I'll make you dance as you should! And you, my little musician, I'll make you sing in the prettiest way.]

The rhythm and patterning of these exchanges lead up to the arrival of the Maître de Philosophie, who, having commended Seneca's treatise on anger to the warring masters, rapidly takes the quarrel to a new intensity, dismissing the other three as mere practitioners of the 'pitiful trades of gladiator, songster, and mountebank'. The exchange concludes with insults and fisticuffs:

MAÎTRE D'ARMES: Allez, philosophe de chien.

MAÎTRE DE MUSIQUE: Allez, bélître de pédant.

MAÎTRE À DANSER: Allez, cuistre fieffé.

MAÎTRE DE PHILOSOPHIE: Comment ? Marauds que vous êtes ...
(*Le Philosophe se jette sur eux, et tous trois le chargent de coups, et sortent en se battant*).

[FENCING MASTER: Get out, you dog of a philosopher!

MUSIC MASTER: Get out, you scoundrel of a pedant!

DANCING MASTER: Get out, you cad of a pedagogue!

PHILOSOPHY MASTER: What! Villains that you are ...
(*The philosopher flings himself at them, and all three go out, fighting*).]

The masters of music and dance, together with their players, singers and dancers (for all their human limitations), are the very instruments of fantasy which lift audiences and performers out of their trivial and self-obsessed private worlds into a magical world of comedy and harmony, order and beauty.

For his part, Monsieur Jourdain is repeatedly drawn into the swirl of ballet surrounding him: with each master in turn, he sings his tasteless ditty, dances a clumsy minuet, fences ineptly, rehearses elocution and serves as a tailor's mannequin. As the musical episodes become increasingly fantastic and surreal, they lead inexorably to the apotheosis of Monsieur Jourdain in the carnivalesque 'Cérémonie Turque'. In the spoken dialogue preserved in the printed edition of the play, Molière linguistically prepares for this transformation from prosaic reality to musical *fantaisie* in three distinct stages. First, Covielle (Cléonte's valet) arrives in disguise to persuade the gullible Monsieur Jourdain that the son of the Grand Turk wishes to marry his daughter (IV, 3). As he prepares the ground, the bourgeois mechanically picks up and repeats Covielle's ends of sentences: as a baby, ladies took him in their arms, says Covielle, 'pour vous baiser' ['to kiss you']; 'pour me baiser' echoes Jourdain. Covielle proclaims himself a great friend 'de feu Monsieur votre père' ['of your late father']: 'De feu Monsieur mon père', he retorts. This flight of fancy continues with Covielle's delightful proof that Monsieur Jourdain was born of a noble father who was far from being a merchant but, 'comme il se connaissait fort bien en étoffes, il en allait choisir de tous les côtés, les faisait apporter chez lui, et en donnait à ses amis pour de l'argent' ['as he was a connoisseur of fabrics he went everywhere to choose them, had them brought to his house, and gave them to his friends for money']. The newly gentrified bourgeois instantly raises the register of his speech so that it corresponds to his new status: 'Je suis ravi de vous connaître, afin que vous rendiez ce témoignage-là, que mon père était gentilhomme' ['I'm delighted to make your acquaintance, so that you may testify to it that my father was a gentleman'].

In the second stage of this transformation, as Covielle announces the intention of 'le fils du Grand Turc' ['the son of the Great Turk'] to become Monsieur Jourdain's 'gendre' ['son-in-law'], these two terms – highlighting the preposterous imaginary relationship to which they allude – echo backward and forward between the two speakers. Then Covielle, having prepared the bourgeois to swallow anything, launches into *lingua franca*, taking audience and bourgeois into a world of the purest linguistic fantasy: 'Acciam croc soler ouch alla moustaph gidelum amanahem varahini oussere carbulath. C'est-à-dire; n'as-tu point vu une jeune belle personne, qui est la Fille de Monsieur Jourdain, gentilhomme parisien?' ['That is to say, "Have you not seen a beautiful young person who is the daughter of Monsieur Jourdain, a Parisian gentleman?"']. Bewitched by this exotic language, which tells him all he wants to hear, the bourgeois marvels at the discovery that '*Marababa sahem*' could mean 'Oh, how enamored I am of her!': 'Voilà une langue admirable, que ce Turc!' ['What an admirable language is this Turkish!'].

In the third and final stage of Monsieur Jourdain's linguistic journey to the land of music and make-believe, rituals of verbal repetition give way to pseudo-Turkish rituals. Now masquerade has become for the bourgeois the new reality, and he proudly assumes his role as the Mamamouchi in the 'Cérémonie Turque'. Hearing the heir to the Grand Turk personally declare 'Ambousahim oqui boraf, Iordina, salamalequi', translated by Covielle as 'Monsieur Jourdain, may your heart be all year long like a flowering rose-tree', the bourgeois responds with a formula at once florid and grovelling: 'Je suis très-humble serviteur de son Altesse Turque' ['I am His Turkish Highness's most humble servant']. Monsieur Jourdain's attempt to match Cléonte's metaphoric compliments is a measure of his psychic estrangement from his bourgeois past. The high watermark of absurdity is achieved when Covielle, suddenly tiring of this linguistic charade, translates Cléonte's 'Bel-men' as 'Il dit que vous alliez vite avec lui vous préparer pour la cérémonie, afin de voir ensuite votre fille, et de conclure le mariage' ['He says that you must quickly go with him to prepare yourself for the ceremony, in order to see your daughter afterwards and conclude the marriage']. 'Tant de choses en deux mots?' ['So many things in two words?'], marvels the bourgeois. 'Oui, la langue turque est comme cela' ['Yes, the Turkish language is like that'], says Covielle.

These symmetries, repetitions and *lingua franca* prefigure the patterns of the 'Cérémonie Turque', providing a seamless transition to its farcical musical ceremony and choreographed initiation rite. Monsieur Jourdain

Musical example 4: Excerpt from the 'Cérémonie Turque'.

expresses no surprise at the outlandish costumes, the pseudo-Turkish jargon, or the elaborate ceremonies performed in song and dance. In a brief scene missing from the first edition (but happily preserved in Philidor's music manuscript), the Mufti demands to know Monsieur Jourdain's religion – and the Turks assure him that he is Mohammedan. This vocal music illustrates the patterned and rhythmic *lingua franca* that is characteristic of the 'Cérémonie Turque' (see musical example 4).

Despite the broad farce of the 'Cérémonie Turque', Molière, Lully and d'Arvieux devoted a surprising amount of attention to authenticity. Not only do its lyrics contain several genuine Turkish words and phrases, but the ceremony itself draws upon the ritual for reception of novices into the order of Mevlevi Dervishes. In addition to the Mufti and Monsieur Jourdain, the participants include twelve Turkish singers, four Dervishes, and six Turkish dancers. While in Tripoli d'Arvieux had attended a Mevlevi Dervish ceremony, where he had heard authentic Dervish ceremonial music. However, in view of the fact that the 'Cérémonie Turque' is *not* a real Turkish ceremony, but a masquerade devised by Cléonte to dupe Monsieur Jourdain, one should not look too closely for authenticity, particularly in musical matters.[14] The Dervish songs attempt to achieve an 'exotic' effect through monotonous repetition, extended sequential progressions, hemiola rhythms, patter singing and disjunctive vocal leaps (see musical example 4). The *livret* indicates that singing and dancing were to be accompanied 'avec plusieurs instrumens à la Turquesque' ('with several instruments in the Turkish manner'), and therefore it seems unlikely that any authentic Turkish instruments were used.[15] Whatever the case, when on 13 June 1704 Hajji Mastapha, an envoy from Tripoli, saw the 'Cérémonie Turque' performed at court, he reportedly 'took great pleasure in seeing portrayed the customs of his country'. His main criticism was that 'the character of the Mufti ought never to have departed from the seriousness that he had affected when coming onstage, because gambols and prances are not at all appropriate for a Mufti'.[16]

The concluding 'Ballet des Nations' builds upon this linguistic and musical exoticism, while scaling new meta-theatrical heights. Before, we witnessed Monsieur Jourdain as the unwitting participant in a masquerade put on by his family; now, the masqueraders settle back to watch a *ballet à entrées* – which has its own onstage audience. In the first entrée a dancer arrives to hand out the livrets to the awaiting spectators and is immediately accosted by provincials who ask for them in chorus, and then by three troublemakers who harass him in dance. After the audience settles down, the ballet proper begins. In the third (Spanish) entrée, a lovesick Spaniard (counter-tenor) sings of the pains and pleasures of love, while another (bass) points out the folly of complaining so harshly of love; then a third Spaniard (bass) claims that no one who knows how to love dies of love, and the three agree that love is indeed a sweet death. In their concluding trio they call for feasting and dancing. The fourth entrée shifts focus to Italy and features the acclaimed *commedia dell'arte* actors who shared Molière's theatre. An Italian singer (soprano) proclaims that the more violent the love, the more it causes pleasure.[17] Then 'two Scaramouches, two Trivelins and an Arlequin represent night in the manner of Italian actors in time to the music', while another Italian (tenor) joins the soprano to urge everyone to enjoy youth while they can. In the end, 'the Scaramouches and Trivelins perform a dance of celebration' to the music of a chaconne. The fifth entrée returns us to the bucolic pleasures of the French countryside. Two Poitevins sing and dance minuets in praise of the sylvan landscape and invite the shepherdess Climène to follow the example of the love-birds. The sixth and final entrée joins together representatives from the three nations, and the entire onstage audience offers its choral applause for these 'spectacles charmants'. A tale of social-climbing ends in universal rejoicing.

NOTES

1 According to Boileau, Louis XIV quit dancing onstage after having taken to heart some lines in Act IV of Racine's *Brittannicus*, in which Nero is mocked for performing before the Roman people. However, Jérôme de La Gorce recently discovered in the dispatches of the Venetian ambassador that Louis XIV had abruptly stopped dancing because of occasional swooning sensations ('vapeurs à la tête'). The *Gazette ordinaire d'Amsterdam* (21 February 1670) confirmed that the king had been 'a little indisposed for some time'. See Jérome de La Gorce, *Jean-Baptiste Lully* (Paris: Fayard, 2002), pp. 156–7.

2 This account is to be found in the *Mémoires du Chevalier d'Arvieux* (Paris, 1735), IV. The quotation is on pp. 252–3.

3 See Albert-Jean Guibert, *Bibliographie des œuvres de Molière publiés au XVIIe siècle*, 2 vols. (Paris: Centre National de la Recherche Scientifique, Supplement 1977), II, pp. 468–9.

4 These costs are detailed in Madeleine Jurgens and Elizabeth Maxfield-Miller, *Cent ans de recherches sur Molière, sur sa famille et sur les comédiens de sa troupe* (Paris: Imprimerie Nationale, 1963), pp. 483–91.

5 See Jurgens and Maxfield-Miller, *Cent ans de recherches*, pp. 554–84 (at pp. 566–7).

6 D'Arvieux, *Mémoires*, IV, pp. 253–4.

7 Jean Grimarest, *La Vie de Mr de Molière* (Paris: Liseux, 1877), pp. 141–3.

8 The printed *livret* demonstrates that the *comédie-ballet* premiered at Chambord consisted of three acts. By the time Molière published the play in 1671, however, he had recast it in five acts, making a number of revisions to the spoken scenes in the course of the twenty-four public performances at the Théâtre du Palais-Royal.

9 The music for this dance, missing from Philidor's MS and long thought lost, was recently discovered in the Bibliothèque Municipale de Bordeaux; see Herbert Schneider, 'Zu den Fassungen und musikalischen Quellen des *Bourgeois gentilhomme* von J.-B. Lully', *Quellenstudien zu Jean-Baptiste Lully / L'Œuvre de Lully: Études des sources*, actes publiés par J. de La Gorce et H. Schneider (Hildesheim: Georg Olms Verlag, 1999), 175–99.

10 Philidor's manuscript score may be consulted online at <gallica.bnf.fr>.

11 Lecerf de la Viéville, *Comparaison de la musique italienne et de la musique françoise* (Brussels: François Foppens, 1705; repr. Geneva, 1972), Part 2, p. 215.

12 Hilaire Dupuis (known as 'Mademoiselle Hilaire', 1625–1709) was the sister-in-law of the court singer and composer Michel Lambert, whose daughter married Lully.

13 Henry Prunières points out that this text is found in Perrin's manuscript *Paroles de musique de Mr Perrin* (F-Pn, f. fr. 2208, fol. 29), where Sablières is listed as the composer; see 'Une chanson de Molière', *La Revue musicale*, 2, 4 (1921), 151–4. See also Louis E. Auld, 'Une rivalité sournoise: Molière contre Pierre Perrin', in Volker Kapp (ed.), *Le Bourgeois gentilhomme: Problèmes de la comédie-ballet* (Paris, Seattle, Tübingen : Biblio 17, 1995), 123–37.

14 Miriam Karpilow Whaples, in 'Exoticism in Dramatic Music, 1600–1800' (Ph.D. dissertation, Indiana University, 1958), p. 98, dismisses Despois and Mesnard's suggestion of bass drum, cymbals and triangle as an 'uninformed presumption based on the "Turkish music" of a later time'. She believes that the *instruments à la turquesque* may have included tambourines, nacaires (small kettledrums, similar to the Turkish *naqqara*), but doubts whether flutes and/or oboes were played with these 'Turkish' instruments, since none of the woodwind players of the Écurie are listed in the *livret* (pp. 99–100).

15 Couvreur, however, takes a different view, stating that 'pour renforcer la note exotique, Lully joignit "plusieurs instruments à la turquesque" appartenant aux collections royales'; see Manuel Couvreur, *Jean-Baptiste Lully: Musique et dramaturgie au service du Prince* (Brussels: M. Vokar, 1992), p. 204.

16 See Pierre Martino, 'La Cérémonie turque du "Bourgeois gentilhomme"', *Revue d'histoire littéraire de la France*, 18 (1911), 37–60, at p. 49; and Miriam K. Whaples, 'Early Exoticism Revisited', in Jonathan Bellman (ed.), *The Exotic in Western Music* (Boston: Northeastern University Press, 1998), 3–25, at p. 14.

17 Richard Strauss sets this text (*Di rigori armata il seno*) for the Italian singer in *Der Rosenkavalier* – for which *Le Bourgeois gentilhomme* serves as a prologue.

10

JULIA PREST

Medicine and entertainment in
Le Malade imaginaire

Critical consideration of *Le Malade imaginaire* is often shaped by the fact that Molière, playing the hypochondriac of the title, Argan, fell ill during the fourth performance of the work and died later that evening, on 17 February 1673. With this in mind, it is impossible not to be aware of the striking irony of the play's cheerful discussion of death, of the scenes in which Argan pretends to be dead (III, 12–14) and of his invective against Molière's stage depictions of the medical profession. In III, 3, for example, Argan declares that 'si j'étais que des médecins, je me vengerais de son impertinence; et, quand il sera malade, je le laisserais mourir sans secours' ['if I were a doctor, I would avenge his impertinence and, when he falls ill, I would leave him to die without any assistance']. With hindsight, his words seem almost prophetic, but there is no reason to believe that, in writing *Le Malade imaginaire*, Molière was somehow anticipating his own death. Rather, he was entering a new and challenging period of his theatrical career at the pinnacle of his creative inspiration, having just had his theatre renovated at great expense and having recently taken on a new musical collaborator.

While Molière was a genuine 'malade', Argan is only a 'malade imaginaire'. When Toinette and later Béralde (the two most sensible characters of the play) ask Argan what exactly is wrong with him, he is unable to provide a specific answer and responds instead with righteous indignation. Toinette informs the audience that Argan walks, sleeps, eats and drinks like everybody else (II, 2) and Béralde confirms Argan's physical health, saying, 'je ne vois point d'homme qui soit moins malade que vous, et … je ne demanderais point une meilleure constitution que la vôtre' ['I don't know a man who is less ill than you, and … I couldn't ask for a better constitution than yours'] (III, 3). He cites as evidence of Argan's good health the fact that his body has survived all the medical treatments it has endured. In several of his interactions with Toinette, Argan chases her around the stage, temporarily forgetting that he can supposedly only do so with the aid of a cane. In I, 5

Toinette obliquely suggests that Argan is mentally, and not physically, ill when she comments 'vous êtes fort malade ... et plus malade que vous ne pensez' ['you are very sick ... and much sicker than you think'] and in III, 5 Béralde articulates the true nature of Argan's illness, saying that he is suffering from 'la maladie des médecins' ['an obsession with doctors']. Argan is the latest in Molière's series of monomaniacs, whose fixation in this case is with his own health and with the medical profession. As Béralde suggests, Argan is 'embéguiné de [ses] apothicaires et de [ses] médecins' ['infatuated with his apothecaries and his doctors'] and wants to be ill 'en dépit des gens et de la nature' ['in spite of everybody and of nature'] (III, 3).

Le Malade imaginaire is, among other things, a compelling satire on the medical profession. Molière was an accomplished satirist who, in the course of his career, painted many types, including the philosopher, the lawyer, the marquis ridicule and the scheming servant. His most controversial types were the religious hypocrite (Tartuffe) and the libertine (Dom Juan). His most successful type, if we are to judge from the number of times he features in Molière's œuvre, was the medical doctor. Molière's most important medical plays are the two farces, Le Médecin volant (c.1647) and Le Médecin malgré lui (1666) and the two comédies-ballets, L'Amour médecin (1665) and Le Malade imaginaire (1673). In addition, the machine-play Dom Juan (1665) and the comédie-ballet Monsieur de Pourceaugnac (1669) feature important medical scenes. The fact that Molière returned to the theme of medicine and to the satire of the medical profession time and again throughout his career tells us less about any obsession or vendetta he might have had than about what a successful comic strategy he had found. Moreover, there are moments in Molière's non-medical plays where medicine is treated with a degree of respect: these include a medical (humoral) explanation of Alceste's condition in Le Misanthrope and the reference to Elmire's successful saignée in Le Tartuffe.[1] With this in mind, I would like to examine Le Malade imaginaire's relationship to Molière's earlier medical comedies, as well as its status as a form of theatrical entertainment (specifically a comédie-ballet) and its curious position in French theatre history.

Molière was not, of course, the first (or last) playwright to exploit the comic potential of the doctor figure. In both the French farce tradition and the Italian commedia dell'arte, the medical doctor and the pedantic lawyer or philosopher feature as recognised comic types. Indebted to their theatrical origins, even Molière's most sophisticated doctors remain rooted in farce and never feature as the more rounded, more plausible figures of higher forms of comedy (for that reason, it is significant that they appear only in the other-worldly genre of comédie-ballet and in farce). In addition to his many theatrical forerunners, Molière also drew on a long tradition of satirical comment on the medical profession and particularly on some of the remarks of the famous French essayist Michel de Montaigne (1533–92), whose influence is felt particularly in *L'Amour médecin* and *Le Malade imaginaire* itself. The popularity of the doctor figure is demonstrated in Molière's œuvre not simply by the number of doctors who are featured, but also by the number of times his characters choose to disguise themselves as doctors. Just as some of Shakespeare's heroines, for example, disguise themselves as men in order to escape unnoticed from an unhappy situation or to gain access to their beloved, so do some of Molière's protagonists find enabling the credibility which a medical appearance brings them. Clitandre in *L'Amour médecin*, for example, disguises himself as a doctor in order to meet with his beloved Lucinde, while Sganarelle in *Dom Juan* adopts the same strategy in order to escape from the scene of his master's crime. The Sganarelles of *Le Médecin volant* and *Le Médecin malgré lui*, on the other hand, find themselves posing as doctors for the benefit of others. It is significant that, in order to pass successfully as a doctor, they have only to don the appropriate clothing and to speak in a sufficiently impressive and obfuscatory manner. In *Le Médecin malgré lui*, for example, Sganarelle revels in tautologous arguments (Lucinde is mute because she has lost the power of speech) and deftly sprinkles his speeches with snippets of pseudo-Latin. Even a blatant error, as when Géronte notices that Sganarelle has located the heart and liver on the wrong sides of the body, can be defended by quick wit and convincing authority, as Sganarelle replies 'oui, cela était autrefois ainsi; mais nous avons changé tout cela, et nous faisons maintenant la médecine d'une méthode toute nouvelle' ['yes, that was the case in the past, but we've changed all that and we now practise medicine in a totally different way'] (II, 4). Of course Molière's use of doctoral disguise also serves to satirise the gullibility of his protagonists, of whom Argan was to be the most strikingly credulous.

If the success of Molière's phoney doctors suggests that the profession is easy to imitate and therefore somehow superficial and sketchy, his 'real' doctors present the profession in a still darker light. One of the most common characteristics of a doctor, from *Le Médecin volant* onwards, is that he is more likely to kill his patients than to cure them. When Lisette in *L'Amour médecin* asks why her master is consulting as many as four doctors about his daughter's mysterious illness, for example, she wryly comments 'n'est-ce pas assez d'un pour tuer une personne?' ['isn't *one* doctor enough to kill somebody?'] (II, 1). One might have expected the 'real' doctors to dispute their reputation for killing, but this is very far from being the case. For them, the death of a patient is of far less importance than the imperative that they should follow formal procedure as set down by their Faculty. As M. Tomès states quite categorically, 'Un homme mort n'est qu'un homme mort, et ne fait point de conséquence; mais une formalité negligée porte un notable préjudice à tout le corps des médecins' ['a dead man is only a dead man and is of no consequence; but an overlooked formal procedure casts a shadow over the whole medical profession'] (II, 3).

For all their insouciance with regard to their patients' lives, Molière's doctors are very keen to diagnose them and to propose suitable forms of treatment (which is particularly ironic since none of their patients is genuinely ill). Not only is the diagnostic procedure an opportunity for them to display their linguistic prowess and their erudition, it also provides Molière with additional satirical material. Perhaps the most striking thing about the doctors of *L'Amour médecin* is their conspicuous failure to reach an agreement regarding the patient's condition or treatment.[2] Where in II, 4, Tomès prescribes an immediate curative bleeding, for example, Des Fonandrès insists with equal resolve that what Lucinde needs is an emetic. Worse than that, both doctors believe that the other's proposed cure will prove fatal to the patient. In the scene that follows, the laborious Macroton and the babbling Bahys are at least of the same opinion, but their point of agreement is hardly comforting: 'il vaut mieux mourir selon les règles que de réchapper contre les règles' ['it is better to die according to the rules than to survive despite them'] (II, 5). A fifth doctor, M. Filerin, is brought in to mediate between his colleagues. His speech in III, 1 (much of it inspired by snippets from Montaigne's essay 'De la ressemblance des enfants aux pères') reveals a deep cynicism with regard to the medical profession and the relationship between doctor and patient. Filerin comments that 'le plus grand faible des hommes, c'est l'amour qu'ils ont pour la vie; et nous en profitons, nous autres, par notre pompeux galimatias, et savons prendre nos avantages de cette vénération que la peur de mourir leur donne pour notre métier' ['man's greatest weakness is his love of life; and we take advantage of this with our pompous prattle and we know how to make the most of the veneration that the fear of dying gives people for our profession'] (III, 1). Filerin spells out the doctor's best strategy by exhorting his colleagues to agree with each other 'pour nous attribuer les heureux succès de la maladie, et rejeter sur la nature toutes les bévues de notre art' ['in order that we should take credit for any successful treatments and blame nature for all the mistakes of our art']. As the doctors reach an agreement, all pretence of medical exactitude is abandoned as Fonandrès asks Tomès to submit to his method on this occasion, promising that they will follow Tomès' method the next time. It is significant that this most revealing of scenes should take place between the doctors and the theatre audience alone, and not within earshot of any of Molière's other onstage characters. Here the art of medicine is stripped of all its mystique and revealed to be as fraudulent and manipulative as we had suspected all along. The fact that the truth is exposed not by an opponent of medicine but by an insider makes its satirical impact all the greater. The medical profession relies on man's fear and ignorance, and all doctors must unite in order to preserve the illusion of their art and to keep themselves in business.

Differences of opinion among Molière's doctors are not solely for purposes of comic satire. They also refer to contemporary debates regarding different medical traditions and tendencies, notably the respective merits of humoral medicine as opposed to chemical medicine. By alluding specifically to the authority of Hippocrates and Galen, Sganarelle in *Le Médecin volant*, for example, refers to the precepts of classical humoral medicine, according to which any physical illness is a manifestation of an imbalance of the four elemental fluids: blood, yellow bile, phlegm and black bile. The principal treatments offered as means of restoring the desired balance were enemas, bleeding and purging. This old-style medicine was still favoured in Molière's time by the Faculty in Paris, while a new alternative had been found in the chemical approach, promoted particularly by the Faculty in Montpellier, whose favourite remedy was antimony (or *vin émétique*). Antimony was banned by the Parisian Faculty until 1666, the year that Molière produced *Le Médecin malgré lui*. The great majority of Molière's doctors are avid proponents of humoral medicine, which seems to have offered the playwright more comic – and specifically scatological – opportunities. It should be noted, however, that those who favour antimony (notably Des Fonandrès in *L'Amour médecin*) are depicted as being equally vain and inflexible, and just as likely to kill their patients.

Many of the features found in Molière's earlier medical plays are taken up again in *Le Malade imaginaire*, in which the playwright's interest in medicine and in medical satire is awarded unprecedented comic and thematic importance. The conservatism of certain doctors (notably at the Parisian Faculty), for example, is embodied by Diafoirus *père* and, especially, *fils*. In II, 5, M. Diafoirus proudly extols his son's virtues, which include the fact that 'il s'attache aveuglément aux opinions de nos anciens, et que jamais il n'a voulu comprendre ni écouter les raisons et les expériences des prétendues découvertes de notre siècle' ['he sticks blindly to the opinions of the ancient authorities and has never wanted to understand or listen to the reasons or the evidence of the alleged discoveries of our century']. Thomas' thesis, which he presents to Angélique, argues precisely against one such discovery: the circulation of blood. Although Harvey's discovery of the circulation of blood around 1615 had met with considerable opposition in the decades following, it was by the time of *Le Malade imaginaire* unusual for a doctor not to accept it as fact. With the pair of Diafoirus doctors, Molière also pursues his satire on the inefficacity of medicine and the unaccountability of doctors. M. Diafoirus' explanation in II, 5 of why he is reluctant for his son to become a doctor at the royal court is particularly revealing:

> Le public est commode. Vous n'avez à répondre de vos actions à personne; et pourvu que l'on suive le courant des règles de l'art, on ne se met point en peine de tout ce qui peut arriver. Mais ce qu'il y a de fâcheux auprès des grands, c'est que, quand ils viennent à être malades, ils veulent absolument que leurs médecins les guérissent.

> [The general public is accommodating. You are not accountable to anybody and providing you follow the rules of the art, nobody makes a fuss whatever happens. But what is tricky with the great and good is that, when they fall ill, they really want their doctors to cure them.]

As Toinette comments with delightful irony, the doctor's job is to prescribe medicine, but it is up to the patient to get better.

In addition to its development of familiar satirical gestures, *Le Malade imaginaire* also represents a significant shift in emphasis from Molière's earlier medical plays. By placing the hypochondriac firmly at the centre of the work, Molière highlighted the interplay between doctor and patient, and probed the fascinating phenomenon of the man who is obsessed with his own state of health. With Argan, he successfully combined the figure of the monomaniac with the theme of medicine in a joyful, carnivalesque *comédie-ballet* which culminates in the (temporary) triumph of folly over reason as Argan is received as a doctor. Argan's experience of medicine, rather than medicine itself, is Molière's prime concern here.

Argan's extraordinary opening speech in I, 1 immediately establishes him as an eccentric, caught between his doctor and his apothecary, and lovingly obsessed with his own health and his various treatments. Medicine is not just Argan's passion, it is his religion. In III, 3, he asks his brother, Béralde, if he believes in medicine as though he were asking if he believes in God; Béralde embraces the religious metaphor in his reply, commenting that he doesn't believe that a faith in medicine is necessary for one's salvation. Béralde's views on the subject form an intriguing counterpart to Argan's. Because Argan is so plainly deluded, it is tempting to assume that Béralde's opposing position is entirely balanced and reasonable, but this is not necessarily the case. Argan's questions and comments in this scene (at least until he becomes angry at the very thought of Molière and his medical plays) are not in themselves unreasonable. He asks, for example, what one should do when one is ill and Béralde replies 'Rien. Il ne faut que demeurer en repos' ['Nothing. One must simply rest']. Echoing Montaigne, Béralde declares that Nature is the only effective doctor and that human doctors, for all their learning and rhetorical skill, have no practical ability whatsoever. Argan comments (again, not unreasonably) that certain people who are just as intelligent as Béralde have recourse to doctors when they are ill, to which Béralde (recalling the words of the cynical Filerin in *L'Amour médecin*) offers the disdainful reply, 'c'est une marque de la faiblesse humaine, et non pas de la vérité de leur art' ['it's a sign of human weakness and not of the truth of their art']. While Béralde's views on medicine turn out to be almost as extreme as Argan's, what sets the brothers apart is their treatment at the hands of the playwright: where Argan provides the comic focus of the work and is thoroughly ridiculed, the portrait of Béralde is neither comic nor ridiculous.

In comedy, the deviant character is often made to see reason in order for the play to reach a satisfactory conclusion, but Argan, typical of Molière's comic protagonists, undergoes no conversion to reason. Recognition of his folly is not possible (it is too entrenched) and he and it must be accommodated in some other way. As one critic has pointed out, Argan's 'imaginary malady ... can only be cured by an imaginary cure'.[3] Realising this, Béralde proposes to work *with* Argan's mania rather than *against* it, or, as he puts it, to 's'accommoder à ses fantaisies' ['go along with his fantasies'] (III, 14). In this sense, folly has the last word in *Le Malade imaginaire* as the Troisième Intermède takes us into a world in which the deluded hypochondriac can become his own physician. This medical ceremony recalls two important theatrical precedents: the Docteur en Anerie entry from a court ballet by Isaac de Benserade, entitled *L'Amour malade* (1657),[4] and the Turkish Ceremony of Molière's own *Bourgeois gentilhomme* (1670). In the first, eleven dancing doctors receive a candidate who submits his theses dedicated to the farcical figure of Scaramouche; in the second, Jourdain's obsession with becoming a nobleman is indulged as he is elevated to the rank of Mamamouchi (or so he thinks). In historical terms, the ceremony of *Le Malade imaginaire* corresponds remarkably closely with John Locke's description of an authentic graduation ceremony for medical doctors which he witnessed in Montpellier in 1676.[5] Locke's ceremony included a processional entry in special costume, music and speeches from the candidate and the chair, all of which feature here. Molière's solemn oath, on the other hand, seems to have been modelled on the equivalent ceremony in Paris.[6]

When reading the text of the Troisième Intermède, it is particularly important to have a sense of its onstage impact as music, dance and costume (among other elements) combined to create a truly carnivalesque spectacle. In what was to be Molière's final medical scene, we find extended versions of many of the same jibes featured in *Le Médecin volant*. The satirical implication of Argan's certification as a doctor is that all doctors are charlatans anyway and that Argan is therefore no better or worse than his lawful colleagues. He eagerly subscribes to the precepts of humoral medicine, prescribing enemas, bleeding and purging ('Clysterium donare, Postea seignare, Ensuitta purgare'), whatever the illness, and swearing that he will use only those remedies that are countenanced by the Faculty, whether the patient lives or dies. Death even features in the Faculty's song as the ultimate exploit of the medical doctor: significantly, the last phrase of the work is 'Et manget et bibat, Et seignet et tuat!' ['May he eat, drink, bleed and kill!']. But the main point of this Intermède lies elsewhere, in celebration, and from this perspective, *Le Malade imaginaire* is very different from its early medical predecessors. The end of *Le Malade imaginaire* is a celebration of several things: it is a celebration of comic theatre, of music and dance and of human creativity; it is a celebration of the escape from reality afforded by those arts; it is a celebration of another imaginary world in which folly has triumphed over reason and which the spectator can enjoy for a few moments. The medical ceremony of *Le Malade imaginaire* is thus a reminder of the therapeutic properties of theatre and specifically of Molière's *comédie-ballet* genre.

The prologue to *L'Amour médecin*, which features the allegories of Comedy, Music and Ballet, is often cited as an exposition of the *comédie-ballet* aesthetic: led by Comedy, the three arts agree to cooperate in their common and higher goal of pleasing the King (Louis XIV). The reappearance of the three allegories at the end of the same work is equally revealing, as they sing the following text:

> Sans nous tous les hommes
> Deviendraient mal sains,
> Et c'est nous qui sommes
> Leurs grand médecins.

[Without us all men would become unhealthy and it is we who are their great doctors.]

Similarly, in *Monsieur de Pourceaugnac*, the singing doctors of I, 10 evoke quite specifically the therapeutic effects of song, commenting that madness is none other than melancholy which in turn can be cured by 'divertissement' ('entertainment'). The fact that these sentiments are sung in Italian has sometimes allowed us to overlook them, but they represent a significant step towards the idea of art as a cure for psychological illness, including mania (at least within the world of comedy). The medical theme of these works provides the perfect opportunity to comment in various ways on the healing qualities of the arts, a feature which bestows upon *Le Malade imaginaire* a strong thematic (if not structural) unity. The pretext for introducing the Second Intermède of *Le Malade imaginaire*, for example, is that it will calm Argan down and prepare him for the delicate discussion that is to follow. Béralde even comments explicitly that 'cela vaudra bien une ordonnance de Monsieur Purgon' ['it's at least as good as one of Monsieur Purgon's prescriptions'] (II, 9). It is not at all clear precisely what effect the music and dancing of the Second Intermède has on Argan, as immediately afterwards he hurries offstage, presumably to attend to the results of his latest enema. But we do know that it is the musical, dancing entertainment of the Third Intermède that will finally exert its own particular healing powers on Argan. Béralde explains in III, 14, that the material for the Third Intermède is in fact an entertainment that has been prepared in advance by a troupe of actors and in which his brother will play the lead role. In justifying his ruse, Béralde explains to Angélique that at carnival time it is perfectly acceptable to behave in this unorthodox way (carnival being a period of lively festivity prior to the sobriety of Lent). *Le Malade imaginaire* was indeed premiered during the carnival period of 1673 and it is in this celebratory, carnivalesque context that the work's finale is best understood.

While it received its premiere at the anticipated time, *Le Malade imaginaire* was not given its first performance in the anticipated location or before the anticipated audience. This fact is more significant than might first appear and is closely bound up with the intricacies of the theatrical environment of Paris and of the French court. With the exception of the first (*Les Fâcheux*, 1661) and the last (*Le Malade imaginaire*), all of Molière's *comédies-ballets* were collaborative efforts with the court composer Jean-Baptiste Lully (1632–87) and were written specifically for performance before Louis XIV and his court.[7] Molière's famous break with Lully occurred when the composer turned away from *comédie-ballet* with its extensive spoken dialogue and towards the embryonic genre of French opera, which was sung throughout. Lully took over the Académie Royale de Musique in March 1672 and rapidly set about establishing his monopoly on French music theatre in collaboration with his librettist, Philippe Quinault (1635–88). Molière in the meantime needed a new composer with whom he could collaborate and settled on Marc-Antoine Charpentier (?1643–1704), who wrote new incidental music for several existing plays and who composed the original score for *Le Malade imaginaire*. Lully was the most important and most favoured composer at Louis XIV's court, and it is likely that he refused to countenance the court premiere of a *comédie-ballet* by his former collaborator with music by a young and talented rival. And so it was that *Le Malade imaginaire* was premiered not before King and court in one of Louis XIV's châteaux, but at the Palais-Royal theatre in Paris, before a paying public.

The uncertainty surrounding the premiere of *Le Malade imaginaire* goes some way towards explaining why we find two alternative prologues to the work in most modern editions. The first prologue is an extensive musical pastorale in praise of Louis XIV, while the second is a brief dig at the medical profession sung by a solitary shepherdess. Charpentier composed the music for both. Thematically, the second prologue clearly fits better with the work's medical bias, but the first is a valuable reminder of Louis XIV's influence on the theatre of the day and specifically of the developing taste for the encomiastic prologue (which was to flourish in Lully's tragic operas). While the first prologue was clearly written with Louis XIV in mind, there is plenty of evidence to indicate that it was nevertheless performed during the work's first performance run in town (from which the King was absent).[8] The second prologue, on the other hand, may not even have been written by Molière at all. Changes in the theatrical climate also affected Charpentier's score for *Le Malade imaginaire*, which underwent several revisions in the 1670s and 80s as Lully continued to tighten his grip on musical productions in rival theatres.[9]

In 1674, *Le Malade imaginaire* was eventually given a lavish performance (with the second prologue) before Louis XIV and his court at Versailles, where it was enthusiastically received. By this time the climate of music theatre had changed considerably: Molière had been dead for a year and Lully's monopolistic operatic enterprises seemed secure. We can only wonder what direction French comic theatre might have taken had Molière not died when he did. But Molière's legacy lives on, and *Le Malade imaginaire* continues to speak to modern audiences as a work in which our dual themes of medicine and entertainment turn out to be more intertwined than might first appear. Not only do they rub shoulders, they intersect, assuming, at times, each other's conventional role. Molière's comic depiction of medicine is entertaining for his theatre audience, while the arts of comedy, ballet and music are seen to have positive healing effects on some of his characters. When attending the production of a Molière play (and especially a *comédie-ballet*), we in turn should expect to be entertained and thereby, perhaps, to receive some therapy for the human condition.

NOTES

1 See David Shaw, 'Molière and the Doctors', *Nottingham French Studies*, 33, 1 (Spring, 1994), 133–42, p. 135. Interestingly, in his third Placet to Louis XIV (written apropos of his *Tartuffe*), Molière mentions his own doctor, Mauvillain,

and asks the King to make Mauvillain's son a canon of the royal chapel at Vincennes.

2 Certain characteristics of the doctors of *L'Amour médecin* seem to have been modelled on famous doctors of the day, and there is evidence to suggest that the actors playing them originally wore masks resembling those doctors (see Molière, *Œuvres complètes*, ed. Georges Couton, 2 vols. (Paris: Gallimard, 1971), II, pp. 1,320–1n). This should not necessarily be interpreted as a personal attack on the doctors in question as it was customary at the time to refer to – and often to satirise – familiar individuals in courtly entertainments, especially in ballets.

3 Robert McBride, 'The Sceptical View of Medicine and the Comic Vision in Molière', *Studi Francesi*, 67 (1979), 27–42, p. 31.

4 For the text of *L'Amour malade*, see Marie-Claude Canova-Green (ed.), *Benserade: Ballets pour Louis XIV*, 2 vols. (Toulouse: Société de Littérature Classique, 1997), I, pp. 327–81.

5 See Lord Peter King, *The Life and Correspondence of John Locke*, 2 vols. (London, 1830), I, pp. 118–19.

6 For more details regarding these similarities, see Maurice Raynaud, *Les Médecins au temps de Molière* (Paris: Didier, 1863), p. 234.

7 Many of them were then subsequently transferred to Molière's public theatre in Paris, often in a scaled-down version.

8 See Julia Prest, 'The Problem of Praise and the First Prologue to *Le Malade imaginaire*', *Seventeenth-Century French Studies*, 23 (2001), 139–49, p. 140.

9 See John Powell, *Music and Theatre in France, 1600–1680* (Oxford: Oxford University Press, 2000), pp. 384–97, for details of these revisions.

I I

RALPH ALBANESE, JR

Molière and the teaching of Frenchness: *Les Femmes savantes* as a case study

Public education in nineteenth-century France was charged with the responsibility of ushering the nation into an era of modernity marked by reconstruction, and the militant republicanism of the 1880s valorised the pedagogical dimension of the State. The Republican School was, first and foremost, an ideological construct, public instruction being one of the chief objectives of French policy-makers during this period.[1] A socio-critical approach to Republican schooling in France during this period will allow us to examine the cultural dynamics inherent in the educational process, that is, the transmission of knowledge or, more specifically, the role of traditional literary education, particularly as it sheds light on the critical reception of Molière. By propagating a series of cultural models, the Republican School sought to shape French youth according to a particular strategy. An analysis of this process clearly raises various ethical, anthropological and ethnological issues. We will attempt to demonstrate the breadth of these issues by briefly examining the Republican School in light of the socio-cultural and ideological forces at work in nineteenth-century France: 1) nationalism, or the role of ethnic identity; 2) the rise of the bourgeoisie; 3) the politics of *laïcité*, or the secularisation of French society; 4) the history of the teaching of French and the formation of school discourse; and 5) the influence of literary education and humanism.

1) *Role of nationalism.* The extraordinarily popular history manual of E. Lavisse presented to generations of French children a highly idealised image of the national past predicated on the cult of nationhood, resulting in an affective attachment to mythical figures of the patrimony such as Joan of Arc, Napoleon and Pasteur.[2] The patriotic fervour of the Right, on the other hand, manifested itself in a nostalgic desire to recapture the national greatness of the past, notably the monarchical traditions of the *Grand Siècle*. The traditionalist Brunetière linked the ethnic survival of the nation to the valorisation of French classical culture: that is, the French language

and literature of the seventeenth century. He relates the canonical works of seventeenth-century French literature to:

> the most interior qualities of the national soul … a comedy of Molière … is the source, the changeless mirror, in which succeeding generations of French people have recognised themselves and taken pleasure … It is, in my opinion, with the laughter of Molière, so candid, so broad and so healthy (as compared to the sneer of Voltaire), that we abandon ourselves among equals to that spirit of mockery known as *l'esprit gaulois* [*gallic wit*].[3]

2) *Rise of the bourgeoisie.* Secondary education accorded privileged status to classical studies (Latin in the first half of the century and, increasingly, French during the latter part), and the *baccalauréat* became the principal defining experience in the new division of labour operative in post-revolutionary France. In its educational mission, the bourgeoisie attempted to legitimise its social pre-eminence vis-à-vis the working class by identifying itself as the incarnation of proper ethical values; it also attempted to teach the lower classes obedience, docility and respect for the social hierarchy. Finally, secondary education might be seen as a fundamental instrument of socialisation of the nineteenth-century French middle class, a way of inculcating its core behavioural norms and values.

3) *Politics of laïcité, or the secularisation of French society.* In order to win over a conservative bourgeois clientele, Jules Ferry, chief architect of the Republican School, needed to assure this clientele that state-run secondary education would contain a rigorous moral component. He advocated an ethics which was ecumenically correct, drawn from the common denominators of all religions, 'the good old morality of our ancestors'.[4] Of particular significance here is the new conception of knowledge implied by the philosophy of *laïcité*: the sacralisation of national culture as the legitimate replacement of religious truth. Secularisation meant nothing less than a symbolic transferral of cultural values into the realm of the sacred. The key figures of the curriculum – Corneille, Racine, Molière and La Fontaine – were to function as the lay saints of the new canon, appropriately commemorated by the Republican School and transformed into the most authentic teachers of France's moral conscience.

4) *The teaching of French and school discourse.* The teaching of French at the secondary level was equally dogmatic: instructors promoted the linguistic ideal of good usage by encouraging writing skills through frequent dictation (*dictée*), and speaking skills through recitation (*récitation*). By inculcating mastery of and attachment to the mother tongue, French instructors felt they were contributing to the moral development of their students; *une faute de français* [a grammatical impropriety] showed a

conspicuous lack of taste [*une faute de goût*], or a clear instance of moral inelegance. The pedagogical virtues of French classicism – order, clarity, and harmony – became the major characteristics of a national culture which projected itself as a universal model for other nations. More importantly, perhaps, linguistic acculturation in French served as the foundation for the development of both socio-cultural and ethical norms throughout the Third Republic. This *lingua franca* was instrumental in the creation of a public discourse allowing for the reproduction and circulation of Republican values.

5) *Influence of literary education and humanism.* The publication of Lanson's famous manual in 1895 was perceived by French literature professors at the time as an appeal to them to recycle themselves by abandoning their traditional rhetorical methodology, and adopting a new positivist methodology based upon the acquisition of concrete facts leading to the discovery of irrefutable objective truths.[5] French literature was to be elucidated by the scientific method and invested with an intellectual, formative and civilising value. As in the teaching of history and philosophy at this time, the Lansonian notion of literary history implied the existence of a national literature capable of transmitting consensus-oriented values of French culture on the basis of Republican civics and ethics. Literature was envisioned as a branch of French civilisation and 'packaged,' so to speak, in an academic lay pantheon of 'great writers' who, in varying degrees, incarnated the specific qualities of France's genius. In Lanson's ideological reading of French literature in terms of a vast national characterology, each writer contributed in his particular way to the construction of French national identity: the 'glorious' Corneille, the 'tender' Racine, the 'lovable' Molière, and the 'good' La Fontaine were all parts of an institutionalised myth of French cultural unity.

It is in the light of these broad ideals that we can understand the elaboration of the academic and cultural myth of Molière during the nineteenth century. The successive visions of the playwright – as romantic, academic and positivist – not only have historical and ideological significance, but also reveal the extent to which the bourgeoisie canonised the dramatist in order to transmit the fundamental principles of its value system through the Republican School. Hugo and Michelet, who shared the romantic and highly subjectivist interpretation of the comic poet, emphasised in Molière a free-thinking spirit, denouncing moral and socio-political forms of imposture.[6] Their reflections were inspired by social humanitarianism and anti-clericalism alike.[7] During the July monarchy, Nisard and Saint-Marc Girardin contributed significantly to the codification of the myth of Molière.[8] They pointed to Molière as the great advocate of the *juste milieu* (the ideal of moderation, as articulated by the *raisonneurs* in his plays, who defined the comic norm), and saw him as counselling prudence, modesty and conformism. These qualities lay at the heart of the nineteenth-century *morale du boutiquier* [shopkeeper's ethics]. Thus, Nisard drew from seventeenth-century French classicism a moralistic concept of literary criticism, while Saint-Marc Girardin sought in his criticism to privilege virtue and the ideal of good taste. Sainte-Beuve's laudatory discourse on Molière focused on the multiple reasons underlying his immense popularity.[9]

Positivist readings of the dramatist begin to appear in increasing numbers in the 1860s. In their attempt to identify the 'true' Molière, scholars such as Bazin, Soulié and Compardon developed a strictly biographical approach.[10] Their 'scientific' criticism was rigorously conceived and sought to demystify various misconceptions propagated by popular legend. Their research ultimately gave rise to the *Moliériste*, a journal which promoted the national cult of Molière during the period of militant Republicanism (1879–89).

With the advent of the Third Republic, and after the humiliation of the Franco-Prussian war, France embarked upon a search for national regeneration, and scholars highlighted the therapeutic value of Molieresque laughter. Their hero-worshipping of the playwright was linked to the cultural nationalism of the time as well as to the efforts of both the Catholic and secular bourgeoisie to establish a new 'Moral Order' predicated upon the idealisation of the *Grand Siècle*, a nostalgic return to a somewhat fantasised past, hence the valorisation of the *Siècle de Louis XIV* initiated by Voltaire. With the creation of the Republican School, the bourgeoisie attempted to transform Molière into the incarnation of the *génie français*, a veritable teacher to the nation, from whose works a fundamental moral authority could be drawn in defence of the national patrimony.

Much of the potency of Molière as symbol remains in contemporary France. It can be felt in his continuing immense popularity at the Comédie-Française and other national and regional theatres and, more importantly perhaps, in his constant presence in secondary-level curricula throughout France today. Molière remains the most relevant *classique scolaire* [canonical writer] in the eyes of the current generation of French youth. The laughter produced by his comic heroes appeals to the individualistic, anti-authoritarian strain in the French personality. He enjoys a privileged position in programmes of French studies in virtually every American university. The remarkable success of his plays abroad testifies to the strength of the Republican notion of French culture as an exportable commodity: the author of *Le Misanthrope* remains unmistakably France's greatest cultural ambassador. His comedy has become an integral part of the cultural lexicon in France, both through the numerous aphorisms and proverbs taken from the plays and through the psychological depth and ambiguity of such creations as Tartuffe (whose name has come to designate a religious hypocrite or indeed any kind of impostor), Monsieur Jourdain (a social climber and 'culture vulture'), Harpagon (a grasping miser) and Dom Juan (the eternally dissatisfied seducer of women).

By valorising the institutional significance of Molière's work, its specific investment in a field of reception, as well as a strategy designed to programme a particular reading of this work, it can be demonstrated that his comedy serves as a foundational text in French culture. The role of Sainte-Beuve, who transformed French writers into 'national products', is crucial: he highlighted the ideal of Frenchness within an organic vision of the national culture. As the first professional French critic, Sainte-Beuve was instrumental in defining the canon underlying the official literary programmes of the Republican School. Literary education played an integral part in the constitution of a cultural identity linked to the emergence of 'modernity' in France, in much the same way that the Panthéon, the first centenaries of Voltaire and Rousseau and the national funeral of Victor Hugo contributed to the building of a specifically French consciousness.[11] Furthermore, school discourse on Molière derives from perceptions of the formative value of French classicism, which sought both to acculturate and edify the student/subject by means of discursive practices which were markedly normative and corrective in scope. Hence, the radical disaffection experienced by the French, from Descartes to Renan and Lavisse, and up to twentieth-century French men and women vis-à-vis a school experience perceived as overly dogmatic, constraining and sterile. What we are witnessing here, in the canonisation of Molière, is the emergence of a Republican vision of modernity generating the fundamental values of reference for the French identity (moderation, reason, and order). In conformity with the educative mission of the bourgeoisie, the playwright served as the principal lay saint of a newly formed religion of culture which instituted its own canon, prophets and high priests. By analysing the institutional practices of secondary and university education, then, we can shed light on the workings of an archeology of knowledge in nineteenth-century France: we can observe the organisation of a literary corpus, considered the only 'legitimate' knowledge at that time, whose transmission was justified by a delivery system known as Republican schooling.

If the formation of the Molière myth, along with the creation of the concomitant notion of 'Frenchness', can be attributed to the mediation of those discursive practices inherent in education, then Foucault's implicit view of education as a correctional undertaking, stressing the disciplinary value of correction, is pertinent here.[12] Just as medical discourse constitutes, in the eyes of the patient/subject, a form of power, critical discourse, as institutionalised in school texts, represents an 'exercise in power' intended to form the reader/subject. As participants in the elaboration of the notion of truth, teachers strive to transform school discourse into absolute, reified truth. Moreover, the construction of the student's identity is grounded in an awareness of his or her active participation in the 'creation' of knowledge. Within this perspective of a corrective pedagogy of French, academic exercises function, then, as enterprises in linguistic and moral normalisation. The Republican School serves, in the final analysis, to regulate deviant behaviour, just as Molieresque comedy – by virtue of the power of the ancient principle of correcting morals through laughter (*castigat ridendo mores*) – aims to ridicule all forms of pathological excess [*démesure*] or immodesty [*impudeur*].

As cultural referent, Molière is recuperated both by partisans of the Republican Left, who view in him an ancestor of progressive, secular values,[13] and by defenders of the monarchical Right, who consider him a spokesman for traditional moral values such as moderation, reason and order.[14] As part and parcel of the classical humanism informing nineteenth-century secondary education, the dramatist also incarnates the ideal of consensus and those values of continuity fundamental to the aesthetics of comedy. Above all, his theatre projects an image of fictitious cultural unity in a nation torn by irremediable political conflict. Molière is the ultimate teacher of Frenchness since his comedies have played a major role in shaping French cultural identity. The example of the comic playwright clearly illustrates the efficacy of cultural models and the ethnological function of the Republican School system.

Les Femmes savantes offers an excellent illustration of the moral and ideological strategies underlying French secondary education during the Third Republic. Not only do Republican values shape the vision of the family, but they define cultural perceptions of the status of women in French society from 1880 to 1914. The establishment of French secondary education for girls in 1882 allowed the Republican School to socialise and acculturate French girls by the transmission of values which promoted a particular conception of women.[15] As the designated representative of the comic norm, Clitandre adheres to a restrictive view on women's education. In presenting his intellectual ideal that women should possess 'des clartés de tout' ['general knowledge'] (218), he implies generalised knowledge, since their social role requires acquisition of only the rudiments of learning. To the extent that it was viewed as 'unnatural' for a nineteenth-century woman to be professionally oriented, Clitandre's ideal suggests above all that women should only be exposed to the fundamental principles of liberal education without developing a particular area of specialisation. Thus, Republican school discourse focused on *Les Femmes savantes* in order to warn young women of the dangers of pedantry. Addressing the issue of women's education, Mlle Aline C., a fifteen-year-old (*classe de troisième*) at the Collège de la Fère, contends that an overly educated woman tends to lose her feminine identity:

> This claim to learning ... takes away from women those charming social qualities by which they are *truly* women [my italics] ... 'Je consens qu'une femme ait des clartés de tout' ['I'm happy for a woman to have all kinds of knowledge']. But [Clitandre] does not want this learning to go too far, since it is harmful for a woman to know too many things because she forgets those things that she must know.[16]

Along similar lines Mlle M. P., a thirteen-year-old (*cinquième*), establishes in her composition an antithesis between the egotistical pursuit of knowledge undertaken by the *femme savante* and the authentic knowledge of the modest, educated woman.[17] Both examples illustrate the widespread belief during this period that a woman's knowledge base must not go beyond what is considered gender appropriate. The Republican ideal for women was clearly an education in letters grounded on the traditional principles of humanism: truth, beauty and ethics (*le vrai, le beau et le bien*). Molière's efficiency as a moralist was valorised in order to encourage high-school girls to prepare themselves for the responsibilities of adulthood.

Wide-ranging in its socio-cultural implications, *Les Femmes savantes* dramatises the role of women within the family unit and in society at large. If Chrysale espouses the ideal of female domesticity, it is because his family is inscribed within the patriarchal social order of seventeenth-century France, an order which stressed a woman's reproductive function. Postulating the incompatibility between learning and marriage (590) as well as between learning and domestic affairs (586), this bourgeois father is, like Arnolphe, convinced that women should remain devoid of intelligence. Bordering on misogyny, his retrograde outlook holds that formal education tends to strip women of their natural qualities which allow them, under normal circumstances, to function as good mothers and heads of households (II, 7). Hence his complaint that Philaminte has failed to manage the household and, more importantly perhaps, to fulfil her maternal role as nurturer. In as much as he emphasises earthly values such as food and eating – his mind is perpetually on pots, roasts and good soup – Chrysale wants wife, daughters and servants to contribute to his domestic well-being.

The opening scene of the play has both dramaturgical and ideological significance. Centred on the desirability of marriage, the debate between Armande and Henriette invites the reader/spectator to decide whether the marital institution degrades or fulfils women.[18] Whereas Henriette lives in accordance with the laws of nature, Armande attempts to escape from the natural order of things by dint of her intelligence. The refusal of the *femmes savantes* to assume their traditional family duties constitutes a radical rejection of the domestic role conferred upon them by a long-standing social tradition. Thus, in Grenaille's *Honeste marriage* (1640), open opposition to marriage was perceived as an act of treason against the established order.[19] In this light, *Les Femmes savantes* not only addresses the dangers of pedantry to the family, but also its destabilising impact on the established social order. Pedantry is viewed as an intellectual vice which strips women of their natural charm in prompting them to adopt unnatural modes of behaviour.

Henriette represents the perfect role model for French girls at the turn of the last century: she is naturally modest, exhibits solid common sense, and exemplifies the classical ideal of moderation. By occupying the moral high ground of the play, she serves to devalorise the sexual pretensions of the learned ladies. First of all, by willingly submitting to the laws of nature, Henriette symbolises the reasonable counter-model to the *femmes savantes*, indeed, the very image of normality. Personifying normal instincts, she gladly accepts the conventional duties of marriage and adheres to a view of natural love which incorporates physical desire. It should also be noted that her realistic attitude towards sex and marriage is consonant with that of Clitandre. Moreover, her decisiveness and strength of character are evident in the manner in which she systematically fights for her own happiness. More importantly, perhaps, Henriette manages to retain her good nature despite the precarious situation in which she is placed. Through her behaviour, then, the play appears to suggest that women should be naturally inclined towards marriage and the preservation of family values.

On Henriette as the ideal sex role model for young French women during the Third Republic and beyond, Lanson writes: 'Molière wants women to know about life, to be reasonable, balanced, clear-thinking, determined, and faithful, like Henriette in *Les Femmes savantes*.'[20] J. Roger agrees, drawing attention to the 'lesson of bold simplicity and naturalness implicit in Henriette's attitude'.[21] S. Chevalley highlights her modernity: 'her common sense, her realistic knowledge of life, and her freedom of expression make of her, in my view, a particularly modern young woman'.[22] From 1880 to the First World War, academic exercises tended to defictionalise Molière's characters in order to construct tendentious models of social correctness:[23] hence, the frequent recourse to Henriette as a heroic illustration of feminine character in French high schools during this period.[24] Composition topics included, in addition to Clitandre's already cited observation, 'Je consens qu'une femme ait des clartés de tout' (*Revue universitaire*, 1892), an exercise asking students to confer upon Henriette an imaginary existence beyond the end of the play and to speculate on her ability to raise her own daughters: 'How do you imagine that Molière's Henriette, now married to Clitandre and a mother, would raise her own daughters, in view of her deep-seated memory of the antithetical theories of Chrysale and Philaminte?' (*Revue universitaire*, 1908). M. Dugard contends, finally, that so exemplary is Henriette as a role model for French womanhood in general that she can serve to acculturate all high-school girls by prompting them to personify the principal traits of the national genius; he calls upon the *lycée* to take on the responsibility of mass-producing, as it were, 'the Henriettes of the twentieth century'.[25]

If Henriette and Clitandre project an image of naturalness and authenticity, the *femmes savantes*, in contrast, exemplify affectation and imposture. The unnatural Philaminte, Armande and Bélise appear wilfully to distort the social values of reciprocity and compromise.[26] Molière's play raises the question of the extent to which the love of knowledge might preclude the very existence of femininity. The pursuit of knowledge, of course, can lead to error as easily as to truth, to say nothing of vanity and pretentiousness; learning is seen as a potential route to self-aggrandisement. As L. Riggs has aptly demonstrated, learning serves as a mediating force for the sheer desire for power.[27] The comic imposture of the learned ladies resides in the fact that they utterly fail to acknowledge that their love of knowledge is in truth a love of power.

Philaminte, Armande and Bélise all violate normative standards of feminine behaviour operative in seventeenth-century France. Whether they display forms of radical pedantry, in the case of Philaminte and Armande or, in the case of Bélise, pathological erotomania, all three betray a lack of sexually codified 'natural' feminine qualities. As a result of her vanity, Philaminte has abandoned the traditional responsibilities of wife and mother, and has nothing but disdain for household matters. Governed by the principle of maternal power, she pushes her feminist agenda to the extreme. Her aggressive brand of intellectualism perverts her maternal instincts and turns her into a bullying, intellectual snob. Persuaded of her unparalleled intellectual standing, and of her infinite moral superiority, this domestic despot exerts sovereign power over her household and her learned society. Her tyranny is predicated on linguistic norms, hence her attempt to regulate the discourse of others. Thanks to Chrysale's weakness, Philaminte assumes the paternal responsibilities of the household. Not only does she betray a singular lack of judgement in her endorsement of Trissotin, but she refuses to extend to Henriette her own high notion of a woman's freedom. Finally, this matriarch relinquishes none of her ascendancy over Chrysale and undergoes no conversion at the end of the play.

In her search for personal independence, Armande is perhaps the most authentic prototype of the *femme savante*. Inspired by an empty Platonic idealism, she appears to pay deep-rooted allegiance to the tenets governing the *Carte de Tendre* (the map which the *précieuses* used to guide them on their hazardous journeys through the different states and stages of love). In addition to denigrating the social status of the wife in a bourgeois family (I, 1:4, 12, 26), she denounces marriage as an institution, notably the baseness of its physical dimension. She also speaks scathingly of child-rearing and the pleasures of the hearth (29–30). In short, the sexual and domestic servitudes of marriage are anathema to her. Postulating the superiority of mind over body, Armande is convinced that corporeity constitutes the ultimate trap for women intent upon fulfilling their intellectual ambitions;[28] she thus values intellectual (linguistic) over physical (sexual) exchange. She rejects outright the natural 'calling' of women by attempting to suppress the workings of the laws of nature. Thus, in her effort to negate the reality of her sexual desire, she is a victim of self-deception. Despite her misplaced sense of moral and intellectual superiority vis-à-vis her younger sister, Armande is constantly brought to task by Clitandre and Henriette as she tries to sublimate her libidinal drive (I, 2, III, 5 and IV, 2). Suffering from repressed sexual desire, she seeks to discourage her sister from marrying Clitandre yet wants to marry him herself. Nature thus gives the lie to her feminist pretensions and, in her refusal to acknowledge her love for Clitandre, Armande shows herself to be petty and disdainful, as well as malicious and vindictive. Having rejected her feminine impulses, she is condemned to a life of lonely celibacy at the end. Finally, the negative perception of Armande in Republican School discourse is also based on the fact that, as opposed to the respectful daughter embracing family values, she symbolises the overly assertive daughter who is openly contemptuous of her father.

In comparison with other characters in the play involved in real-life conflicts within a middle-class household, Bélise, a somewhat farcical figure who inhabits a fantasy world of her own making, suffers the fate of the Molieresque *imaginaire*. As the victim of an amorous pathology, this outdated *précieuse* is not taken seriously by other family members. Her mythomania situates her in an illusory, romanesque mode of existence where she believes herself to be endowed with an irresistible charm and surrounded by innumerable lovers who all yearn to capture her heart. Like the other *femmes savantes*, Bélise also represents superficial intellectuality. More so than Philaminte and Armande, however, she spouts poorly digested scientific and philosophical knowledge.

Les Femmes savantes reflects an aspect of social reality in seventeenth-century France and offers us a caricatural image of life within a wealthy bourgeois family. More specifically, it addresses the socio-cultural implications of the projected marriage of Henriette and Clitandre grounded in middle-class values.[29] As in *Tartuffe*, Molière is focusing on a rather affluent family with several maids, numerous material possessions, and its attendant financial obligations, most notably the provision of Henriette's dowry. The learned ladies take their life of leisure as a given and, from this comfortable base, Philaminte denounces bourgeois values and appears unconcerned about financial matters (669 and 1,706). Chrysale, on the other hand, remains steadfast in his attachment to these values and, when Ariste brings (false) news of the loss of both Philaminte's and his own wealth, he is distraught (1,705). Henriette's pragmatism leads her – on hearing the same news – to conclude that marital bliss and poverty are incompatible (1,749–54): she agrees to marry Clitandre only when sure that her dowry has not been lost. It is clear, then, that as a wife 'la charmante Henriette' would manage her budget and household with care. Clitandre is a somewhat impoverished nobleman forming a *mésalliance* [mismatch] with the daughter of a wealthy middle-class family. The unscrupulous Trissotin is a threat to the family order in that he tries to seize Henriette's dowry. The denouement highlights the unmasking of this parasite as a mercenary 'coureur de dot' ['dowry hunter'] (V, 4).

If *Les Femmes savantes* dramatises the institutional opposition between marriage and the salon, it was ultimately seen as valorising the triumph of bourgeois common sense and ethics over values associated with a more worldly society. It clearly asserts the superiority of Clitandre's ideal of *honnêteté* [civility] over the pedantry of Trissotin and Vadius. To the extent that seventeenth-century French salons were female-dominated institutions, they raised issues of social stratification and mobility among women.[30] Thus, Molière appears to be satirising the public role of women in French society and the manner in which the salons served to expand social elites in early modern France. A significant part of the comic imposture of Philaminte, Armande and Bélise is that they are attempting to imitate the learned women at court. In effect, they are three middle-class women who ape the intellectual pretensions of the aristocracy. They simply fail, in a word, to escape the constraints of both their social and sexual status.

The canonisation of *Les Femmes savantes* in the secondary curriculum from 1880 to 1914 has great socio-cultural importance, since the play deals directly with the contemporary issue of women's education. Traditional school discourse, with its highly normative approach to women and French society, used the play as a moral treatise to prepare high-school girls for their future roles as wives and mothers. Yet it should be noted that even recent (post-Republican School) discourse continues to project stereotypical views on the female characters in the play. The Classiques Larousse edition of 1990 still holds to the anti-feminine bias which envisages Philaminte's quest for knowledge in pathological terms and extols Henriette ('a traditional, natural and intuitive woman') as a positive role model for young French girls.[31] The dramatist functioned as a sort of lay director and intellectual guide for generations of French girls during the first half of the Third Republic.

NOTES

1 For this and related issues, see my *Molière à l'Ecole républicaine: De la critique universitaire aux manuels scolaires (1870–1914)* (Saratoga, CA: Anma Libri, 1992).

2 E. Lavisse, *Histoire de France depuis les origines jusqu'à la révolution* (Paris: Hachette, 1900–11).

3 Ferdinand Brunetière, L'Idée de patrie (Paris: Hetzel, 1896), p. 20.

4 Senate, 1881; quoted by A. Prost in *Histoire de l'enseignement en France (1800–1967)* (Paris: Colin, 1968), p. 196.

5 Gustave Lanson, *Histoire de la littérature française* (Paris: Hachette, 1895).

6 See my 'Lectures critiques de Molière au XIXème siècle', in *Revue d'Histoire du Théâtre*, 36 (1984), 341–61.

7 See also O. Fellows, *French Opinion of Molière (1800–1850)* (Providence: Brown University, 1937) and J.-P. Collinet, *Lectures de Molière* (Paris: Colin, 1974).

8 Saint-Marc Girardin, *Œuvres complètes de Molière*, ed. C. Louandre, 3 vols. (Paris: Charpentier, 1858); Sainte-Beuve, *Nouveaux lundis* (Paris: Calmann-Lévy, 1884); *Port Royal* (Paris: Hachette, 1901).

9 *Œuvres complètes de Molière*, ed. Louis Moland, 12 vols. (Paris: Calmann-Lévy, 1884), V, pp. 277–8.

10 A. Bazin, *Notes historiques sur la vie de Molière* (Paris: Techenor, 1851); E. Soulié, *Recherches sur Molière et sur sa famille* (Paris: Hachette, 1863); E. Compardon, *Documents inédits sur J-B. Poquelin Molière ...* (Paris: Plon, 1871).

11 See P. Nora, *Les Lieux de mémoire* (Paris: Gallimard, 1984).

12 M. Foucault, *Surveiller et punir* (Paris: Gallimard, 1975), p. 185.

13 A. Vinet, *Poètes du siècle de Louis XIV* (Paris: Chez les Éditeurs, 1861); P. Souday, 'Le Tricentenaire de Molière', *Revue de Paris*, 2 (1922), 195–202; and P. Hazard, 'Ce que Molière représente pour la France', *Nouvelle Revue d'Italie*, 19, 2 (1922), 91–113.

14 D. Nisard, *Histoire de la littérature française* (Paris: Firmin-Didot, 1849); F. Brunetière, *Les Époques du théâtre français* (Paris: Hachette, 1906); and E. Faguet, *En lisant Molière* (Paris: Hachette, 1914).

15 See F. Mayeur, *L'Enseignement secondaire des jeunes filles sous la Troisième République* (Paris: Presses de la Fondation des Sciences Politiques, 1977).

16 See the journal *L'Enseignement secondaire des jeunes filles* 4 (1885), p. 9.

17 *L'Enseignement secondaire des jeunes filles* 2 (1883), pp. 111–14.

18 For a discussion of the various perspectives on marriage in the play, see J. Molino, 'Les Nœuds de la matière: L'Unité des *Femmes savantes*', *XVIIIe Siècle*, 113 (1976), 23–47.

19 'Opposition to marriage and the refusal to bear children were worse than immoral: they were treasonous. And it was precisely the *précieuses* who not only rejected the necessary maternal role but loudly preached against it'; see C. Lougee, *Le Paradis des Femmes. Women, Salons, and Social Stratification in Seventeenth-Century France* (Princeton, NJ: Princeton University Press, 1976), p. 90.

20 Lanson, *Histoire de la littérature française* (Paris: Hachette, 1953), p. 270.

21 J. Roger, *Histoire de la littérature française*, I (Paris: Colin, 1969), p. 395.

22 P. Gaillard, *Les Précieuses ridicules et Les Femmes savantes* (Paris: Hatier, 1978), p. 64.

23 Viewing Henriette as a paragon of feminine virtues, G. Reynier offers this laudatory appraisal of her character: 'How healthy and reasonable Henriette is! She doesn't ask too much of life. She incarnates the realistic, innocent wisdom of the middle class'; see *Les Femmes savantes de Molière* (Paris: Mellottée, 1962), p. 89. Also, see my 'Images de la femme dans le discours scolaire républicain (1880–1914)', *French Review*, 62 (1989), 740–8.

24 R. Doumic and L. Levrault, *Études littéraires sur les auteurs français* (Paris: Delaplane, 1900) and A. Ditandy, *Analyse explicative et raisonnée de cent morceaux choisis* (Paris: Belin, 1882).

25 M. Dugard, 'L'Henriette du XXème siècle', *Revue universitaire*, 22 (1913), pp. 294 and 298.

26 See, on this point, J. Gaines, 'Ménage versus Salon in *Les Femmes savantes*', *L'Esprit Créateur*, 21 (1981), 51–9.

27 'Reason's Text as Palimpsest: Sensuality Subverts "Sense" in Molière's *Les Femmes savantes*', *Papers on French Seventeenth Century Literature*, 28 (2001), 93–103.

28 C. Kintzler, '*Les Femmes savantes* de Molière et la question des fonctions du savoir', in *XVIIe siècle*, 211 (2001), 243–56.

29 S. Dosmond sees in *Les Femmes savantes* a dramaturgy anticipating that of the eighteenth-century *drame bourgeois* [bourgeois drama], where a middle-class audience can readily identify with some of the serious social problems depicted on stage. In her view, the play analyses social conditions, raises domestic issues dividing a bourgeois family and presents a rather moralising tone (due in great measure to the unnatural refusal of marriage and motherhood on the part of the learned ladies); see '*Les Femmes savantes*: Comédie ou drame bourgeois?', *L'Information littéraire*, 44 (1992), 12–22.

30 Lougee, *Le Paradis des Femmes*, p. 5.

31 Edited by E. Bessière, p. 19.

12

ROXANNE LALANDE

L'École des femmes: matrimony and the laws of chance

Mon Dieu, ne gagez pas, vous perdriez vraiment.

L'École des femmes, II, 5, 474

[Good Lord, don't bet! You're bound to lose!]

When Molière married the actress Armande Béjart in 1662, he was forty years old and exactly twice her age. It remains unclear to this day whether Armande was the daughter or the younger sister of Madeleine Béjart, Molière's former mistress and co-founder of the Illustre Théâtre, but she was born in 1642, during the same year that Madeleine and Jean-Baptiste became lovers. Some speculation arose as to whether the actor had married his own daughter and his rival Montfleury went as far as to present a written accusation of incest to Louis XIV. Although the scandalous rumours eventually subsided, Molière's marriage to a much younger woman was fraught with predictable infidelities and strife. In examining *L'École des femmes* (1662) with regard to the circumstances surrounding its creation, its reception and its literary value, it is impossible to avoid some speculation regarding the conflation of life and text. For one thing, Molière's marriage to Armande was conspicuously staged in early 1662, framed by the June 1661 production of *L'École des maris* and the December 1662 production of *L'École des femmes*.

Of equal significance to our understanding of the play is the polemical quarrel that followed the tremendous success of Molière's first major opus. *L'École des femmes* was the author's eighth play and his first five-act comedy in verse. The play marked a turning point in Molière's career, away from traditional farce and toward a new type of comedy that dared to bridge the gap between the comedic and tragic genres. With this comedy, the author openly subverted the aesthetic order by rivalling and challenging the superiority of tragedy. Molière would pay dearly for his triumph. The elevation of comedy to a higher rank made it subject to more rigorous critical scrutiny founded upon conformity to the Aristotelian unities. Erudite critics and *précieux* circles condemned the play for its vulgarity and

165

its lack of adherence to the classical rules of playwriting, rules that hitherto had been applied principally to the *nobler* genre of tragedy. Molière responded to these attacks in *La Critique de L'École des femmes* (1663), a clever apology disguised as parodic criticism, which explores the challenges of reconciling artistic freedom with literary strictures. As an artist, Molière felt deeply conflicted about the need to adhere to the rules and the desire to bend them, between the dream of creative self-determination and the drive for success and public recognition. Considering the circumstances surrounding his recent marriage, it is not surprising that in 1662 Molière's conflicted attitude toward aesthetic conformity should reveal itself in gendered discord. This conflict translates into a metaphorical engagement between the male protagonist, eager to comply with and to enforce ideological protocols and historical precedents, and the heroine's recalcitrance to embrace the rules of the reigning ideology.

Within the context of *L'École des femmes*, matrimony is defined as a game of chance, in which the relationship between men and women is intrinsically adversarial. The play begins with a spirited debate between the protagonist Arnolphe and his friend and confidant Chrysalde concerning the perils of wedlock. Arnolphe views it as a game of deception and trickery, in which morally unscrupulous women have the upper hand. If marriage is to be considered analogous to a game, a form of playful activity, then it must by its very nature include a set of rules and conventions to be accepted freely and willingly by all participants: in other words, a contractual agreement between players. From Arnolphe's perspective the rules of matrimony, which he tenders as a written canonical text entitled *Les Maximes du mariage ou Les Devoirs de la femme mariée* [*Marriage Maxims or The Duties of the Married Woman*], are the foundation of patriarchal hegemony and serve to subjugate the recalcitrant Other, who is continually striving to break free of the bonds of wedlock. Since ludic activity implies voluntary acceptance of the social contract, Arnolphe's perception of Agnès's role in relation to conjugal play remains at best peripheral. Her obedience can be ensured only through sequestration or persuasion. She must either internalise her own subservience through a process of indoctrination and domestication in order to participate 'freely', passively accept her alienation, or resort to deception.

Chrysalde is quick to remind his friend that although rules are an essential component of all games, the element of chance remains an equally pivotal concept. When Arnolphe makes a mockery of cuckolded husbands, his friend elucidates the role of fate:

> Ce sont coups du hasard, dont on n'est point garant,
> Et bien sot, ce me semble, est le soin qu'on en prend. (I, 1, 13–14)[1]

[No one is immune to such chance events and any attempt to evade them seems like a foolish waste of time to me.]

Thus, successful participation in the game, which is by nature voluntary, implies not only the player's acceptance of a code of conduct, a set of rules and restrictions, but also of the risk factor involved. Arnolphe's insistence on the rules leaves him persistently blind to the role of chance, which in turn increases his vulnerability to a reversal of fortune.

Arnolphe has set out to guarantee his honour, predicated on his future wife's fidelity, by selecting and sequestering the four-year-old orphan, Agnès, in order to mould her to his specifications. The education she receives is essentially negative, for the pedagogical objective is oxymoronic: the teaching of ignorance. Arnolphe's mission is founded upon the notion of preserving Agnès's natural innocence, but the paradoxical nature of his endeavour, based upon the equation of goodness and ignorance, escapes him. The ingénue's inexperience is an ideal breeding ground for vice as well as virtue, and Chrysalde admonishes him for overlooking the incompatibility of virtue and foolishness. True moral character is always a function of wilful and rational choice. When decisions are not the result of conscious self-determination, chance predominates over reason:

> Une femme d'esprit peut trahir son devoir,
> Mais il faut, pour le moins, qu'elle ose le vouloir;
> Et la stupide au sien peut manquer d'ordinaire
> Sans en avoir envie et sans vouloir le faire. (I, 1, 113–16)

[At least when a clever woman goes astray, it is because she dares to do so deliberately; but a stupid one may fail in her duties while remaining utterly oblivious of her transgression.]

By sequestering Agnès spiritually as well as physically, by barring her path to knowledge, Arnolphe has virtually destroyed his own authority to regulate her behaviour. Devoid of the ability to think autonomously and analytically, she is driven by pure, unmediated instinct and has remained a totally amoral, spontaneous being, unable to internalise rules and strictures. As such, she is the pure incarnation of chance: nature's revenge over man's best-laid plans. Thus, Arnolphe's precautionary measures are by definition paradoxical: in order to eliminate the element of surprise, the chance factor, he has created a purely impulsive creature, receptive to even the slightest urge. As Patrick Dandrey succinctly phrases it, Arnolphe's biggest mistake is to misunderstand the nature of nature.[2]

Arnolphe bases his smug sense of superiority not on any positive, heroic qualities he might possess, but on what he is *not*: a cuckold. Accordingly, as

Chrysalde points out, the comic manifestation of the heroic project is defined in the negative:

> On est homme d'honneur quand on *n'est point* cocu,
> A le bien prendre au fond, pourquoi voulez-vous croire
> Que de ce cas *fortuit* dépende notre gloire (IV, 8, 1,235–7)

[Our honour depends on *not* being cuckolded? All things considered, how can you believe that our reputation depends on such a *chance* circumstance?]

Arnolphe's honour is indeed predicated upon fortuity, in this instance upon the unpredictability of his future wife's faithfulness. What he has not foreseen, yet is subliminally aware of, is that he has unwittingly forged a relationship of dependency, in which ironically Agnès has the upper hand. As creator, Arnolphe cannot escape responsibility for his creation: the smallest flaw will inevitably reflect back upon him, tying his destiny to that of Agnès and reversing the order of empowerment. His personal freedom will thus be limited by the need to limit that of his pupil:

> Songez qu'en vous faisant moitié de ma personne,
> C'est mon honneur, Agnès, que je vous *abandonne*. (III, 2, 723–4)

[Remember that by allowing you to share my life, Agnès, I *am abandoning* my honour to your care.]

Unbeknownst to Arnolphe, the die has been cast before the action of the play begins, and fate has already foiled his carefully constructed plans. While he was away on business, a fortuitous encounter has taken place between Agnès and a young suitor by the name of Horace, who happens to be the son of one of Arnolphe's best friends, and the two have fallen in love. Arnolphe attempts to limit the damage by imposing a more restrictive set of rules on his pupil, placing her under house arrest, to be guarded by his ineffectual servants, Alain and Georgette. Chance occurrences, however, cannot be countered by unyielding authoritarianism; they can only be circumvented by versatility and adaptability. Chrysalde attempts to explain this fundamental principle of successful gamesmanship to his friend, likening marriage to a game of dice, but his advice falls upon deaf ears:

> Mais comme c'est le sort qui nous donne une femme,
> Je dis que l'on doit faire ainsi qu'au *jeu de dés*
> Où, s'il ne vous vient pas ce que vous demandez,
> Il faut *jouer d'adresse* et, d'une âme réduite,
> Corriger le hasard par la bonne conduite. (IV, 8, 1,281–5)

[But since we owe our choice of wives to chance, we should behave as in *a game of dice*, where, when you do not get the roll you want, you have to *play with great finesse* by lowering your stakes to change your luck through caution and delay.]

Instead of heeding his friend's admonitions, Arnolphe endeavours to direct every aspect of Agnès' conduct, thereby attempting to make her a mirror image of himself. His narcissism is coterminous with complete self-absorption and his fascination with the tantalising image of a perfect, self-sufficient, god-like whole, in which the desires of the Other are the una-dulterated reflection of his own. In Arnolphe's view, Agnès's value is not intrinsic, but derivative of his own identity:

> Je vous épouse, Agnès, et cent fois la journée
> Vous devez bénir l'heur de votre destinée,
> Contempler la bassesse où vous avez été,
> Et dans le même temps admirer ma bonté,
> Qui de ce vil état de pauvre villageoise
> Vous fait monter au rang d'honorable bourgeoise. (III, 2, 679–84)

[Agnès, I'm marrying you; and you should bless your lot a hundred times a day, while contemplating your former deprivation and marvelling at the benevolence of a man like me, who raised you from the state of humble village girl to that of honourable middle-class wife.]

Thus, the first stage in Arnolphe's strategy is to make Agnès aware of her lack. Without him, she is nothing, a nonentity and a dim and faithful shadow of the only positivity in the world according to Arnolphe: himself. In the opinion of the feminist critic Luce Irigaray, the exclusion of a female imaginary puts woman in the position of experiencing herself only frag-mentarily, in the margins of a dominant ideology, as waste, or excess, what is left of a mirror invested by the masculine subject to copy himself.[3] Agnès can become Arnolphe's wife on condition that she accept the void that masculinity needs to find in a woman.

Implicitly, then, the ideal wife is also the perfect child: the child-bride, the woman-child, the sex kitten. Man is both husband and father (creator) to this creature, whose presence allows him to supplant the mother by usurping the role of life giver and creator. By replacing the mother with the father as embodiment of reason and structure, the harmony of the civilised patriarchal order remains intact. However, the paternal figure's attraction to the woman-child is troubling, for it borders on the incestuous, as well as onanistic desire.

As she is initially depicted, Agnès is situated at an ambiguous moment that predates the onset of her sexual awareness. Her enlightenment will coincide with her first encounter with the young suitor Horace. The coa-lescence between nascent sexuality and intellectual enlightenment is an immediate consequence of this event. Agnès readily admits that she owes this awakening to her male counterpart:

> C'est de lui [Horace] que je sais ce que je puis savoir,
> Et beaucoup plus qu'à vous [Arnolphe] je crois lui *devoir*. (V, 4, 1,562–3)

> [It is from him that I have learned what little I know; and I believe I *owe* him much more than I do you.]

Despite her growing awareness, Agnès will never bypass the stage of obligation to achieve full autonomy. Her indebtedness will mark her dependency throughout the play. Furthermore, her maturation demonstrates a correspondence between sexual desire and the intellectual identity of women. It conveys the impression that, unlike men, women cannot separate their ability to reason from their emotional state or their reproductive function and that their thinking is accordingly muddled and confused by sensations, in other words by their materiality.

Woman's identity is so closely linked to her sexuality in *L'École des femmes* that it is not surprising that adultery is her principal weapon in combating the patriarchal order. The hordes of adulterous wives whose ever-present danger haunts Arnolphe's overactive imagination seek out sexual gratification and flaunt their affairs in public, empowered by the arrogated freedom to give and take rather than to be given or taken. Within the confines of the patriarchal order, economic exchange and bartering are the prerogatives of men. The only form of giving permissible to women is the act of generous self-sacrifice, in which personal pleasure is entirely sublimated and subsumed by the political order. Thus, these unfaithful women, whose peripheral presence Arnolphe repeatedly invokes, are a subversive threat to the masculine hegemony, which is founded upon bourgeois proprietary notions that are foreign to women. Indeed, when the servant Georgette has difficulty understanding Arnolphe's jealous rage, her male counterpart Alain stresses the consumerist economy inherent in the strictures of matrimony:

> La femme est en effet le potage de l'homme;
> Et quand un homme voit d'autres hommes parfois
> Qui veulent dans sa soupe aller tremper leurs doigts,
> Il en montre aussitôt une colère extrême. (II, 3, 436–9)

> [Well, in actual fact a woman is like a man's bowl of soup; and when one man sees others about to dip their fingers into his serving, he immediately flies into a terrible rage.]

Through her sexual awakening, Agnès's femininity asserts its prerogatives, all the more forcefully as she lacks the intellectual tools necessary to comprehend and internalise social conventions. Will G. Moore correctly contends that *L'École des femmes* portrays a struggle between Arnolphe and the forces of nature,[4] for the hero's frustration stems from his incessant endeavours to impose the strictures of symmetry – Agnès will be his mirror image – on a woman who is simultaneously an object of fear and desire. This sexual opposition within marriage (a microcosmic reflection of society itself) serves as a metaphor for the irresolvable conflict between Nature and Culture, between the Law and Chance. In these camps the natural is associated with a feminine essence, whose history in metaphysics is bound to matter, just as culture is connected to the masculine order, a concept manifest as 'form' or 'ideal'. Arnolphe's misguided attempt to mould Agnès into the perfect wife is predicated on his belief that the ideal can shape matter:

> Ainsi que je voudrai, je tournerai cette âme:
> Comme un morceau de cire entre mes mains elle est,
> Et je puis lui donner la forme qui me plaît. (III, 3, 809–11)

[I'll shape her soul at will. She's like a piece of clay between my hands and I can fashion her in any way.]

The inevitability of the reaffirmation of nature is structurally parallel to the inescapability of fate, for despite man's attempts at creating order out of chaos and symmetry out of randomness, part of the game remains unpredictable and beyond his control. In *L'École des femmes* these ungovernable forces of fate are always associated with the feminine principle. It seems appropriate, therefore, that it is Agnès who warns Arnolphe of the impossibility of harnessing chance. When the latter wants to wager that the rumours he has heard about Horace and Agnès are false, she exclaims: 'Mon Dieu, ne gagez pas, vous perdriez vraiment' ['Good Lord, don't bet! You're bound to lose!'] (II, 5, 474).

It is interesting to note that initially Agnès does not wilfully disrupt Arnolphe's carefully instrumented plans; rather she does so unknowingly. Her presence alone constitutes a disruptive force. Furthermore, strategically Arnolphe has the upper hand, as Horace, who remains unaware of the former's true identity, unwittingly and repeatedly alerts his rival to his tactics. This advantage notwithstanding, the older man is unable to prevent the action and is subsequently informed of each of Horace's victories as a *fait accompli*. This is what the critic Myrna Zwillenberg refers to as the 'retroactive reality principle' at work in the play.[5] It serves to further accentuate the absurdity of Arnolphe's attempts to anticipate and master the situation through the application of logic and undermines the very concept of rationality. Each of his efforts to shape events, objects and people has the opposite effect of the one anticipated. Arnolphe's parodic echoing of Pompée, the Cornelian hero's command – 'Je suis maître, je parle: allez, obéissez' ['I'm master: when I speak, obey'] (II, 5, 642) – not only underscores the futility of his endeavour to master the situation but also refers obliquely, on a meta-theatrical level, to Molière's own rival, Corneille, the patriarch of the theatre, whose tragedies, unlike Molière's comedies, generally obeyed the rules and conventions of playwriting.[6]

Although Agnès never achieves full autonomy, she emerges progressively as an assertive force, and this development would seem to be causally linked to each new external constraint Arnolphe attempts to impose on her. Thus, a pattern of action and reaction is established, in which each new law is met by its transgression. However, since the transgression frequently *predates* the constraint, it appears less deliberate than fated.

Although Arnolphe eventually does admit that the best defensive strategy would be to let fate play itself out, thereby allowing Agnès to fall prey to her own fate, he cannot give up his compulsion to control destiny and to impose order on an increasingly chaotic situation. By Act IV he has at least acknowledged the force of fate without, however, understanding its inevitability: 'Il se faut garantir de toutes les surprises' ['I must protect myself against any surprises'] (IV, 2, 1,044). As proof thereof, each new precaution is met with predestined failure. This backfire principle is at the very heart of his own growing passion for Agnès. Arnolphe comes to the painful realisation that his passionate obsession with the young woman is directly proportional to her growing autonomy. In his proprietary desire to possess Agnès, he sees her value increase as she escapes his grasp. This gendered conflict, in which both the risk of possessing and the desire to possess woman intensify as she gains autonomy, is the bane of Arnolphe's existence. Once Arnolphe has accepted this paradox, his only possible alternative is one of non-intervention and the humble acceptance of adversity.

> Ciel, faites que mon front soit exempt de disgrâce;
> Ou bien, *s'il est écrit* qu'il faille que j'y passe,
> Donnez-moi tout au moins pour de tels *accidents*,
> La constance qu'on voit à de certaines gens. (III, 5, 1,004–7)

[Heaven, keep my forehead free from disgrace; or if it is *written* that I must endure such trials, grant me at least the fortitude of some whom I could name to face such *accidents* of fate.]

In coming to grips with the notion of predetermination, Arnolphe uses the term 's'il est écrit' ['if it is written'], a phrase that implies textual authority of the type that he himself has tried to impose upon Agnès. He refers to fate by using the terms 'destin', 'destinée', 'hasard', 'surprise' and 'accident' interchangeably; however only the first two suggest the presence of a universal order or organising principle, in contrast to the random nature of chance. As Zwillenberg points out, despite the illusion of fortuitous surprises, an underlying structural principle seems to be operative within the play. Each successive tactical move results in the opposite effect. Ironically, Arnolphe's resistance to risk shapes his own destiny: he is ultimately, like Oedipus, the architect of his own fate.

These considerations alone do not solve the problematic nature of fate, nor do they explain the fundamental dichotomy between destiny and happenstance that the play attempts to expose. The feminine concept of *fortuna* (fortune, chance, surprise, accident) is essentially a destabilising principle. Due to its random and capricious nature, it rocks the very foundations of the reigning hegemonic order: patriarchal law. The fear it inspires is founded upon man's disturbing inability to anticipate or control it. Ultimately, *L'École des femmes* strives to replace this feminine force with the neuter/neutral concept of *fatum* (destiny, fate). *Fatum* in Latin means 'what has been spoken', from the verb *for, fari* (an *in-fans* can't speak), and it denotes the sovereign word of some great power higher even than divinity. Interestingly, in French, which unlike Latin has no neuter, the word for fate has two variations: the feminine *destinée* and the masculine *destin*.

Although fate, like chance, is perceived as an ungovernable force, the very notion that it is preordained by some higher power is reassuring, for it eliminates the idea of absurdity and chaos by reaffirming a masculine order founded upon a rational and comprehensible, if not foreseeable and controllable, governing principle. Quite to the contrary, chance is inherently unreckonable and irrational; it is disturbing because its randomness defies anticipation. Within the play's rhetoric, there is a progressive substitution of terms such as 'coups du hasard' ['blows of chance'], 'accidents', 'jeu de dés' ['game of dice'], with 'destin', 'astre' ['star'] and 'fatalité'. Act V is a staged demonstration of the laws of fate: ultimately an underlying and preordained structuring principle was in operation from the outset: Horace's betrothal to Agnès, a prior agreement between their two fathers, Enrique and Oronte. This principle can be applied to Molière's playwriting itself. Although at first glance, *L'École des femmes* appears to fall short of the third rule of classical dramaturgy, the unity of action or plot, it is kept from random wandering by the retroactive operations of fate. Thus, although on one level *L'École des femmes* portrays the disturbing failure of one man's attempt to counter destiny, the comedy is ultimately comforting in its re-establishment of patriarchal law and order based upon a rational principle to which the protagonist was simply blind.

Within this framework, Agnès remains a symbolic representation of chance. Initially, her alienation is the result of her lack of moral or rational governing principles. Due to this lack, her actions are essentially random and unforeseeable, and her being is receptive to uncontrollable and instinctive urges. She responds to Arnolphe's admonishments with the reply: 'Le moyen de chasser ce qui fait du plaisir?' ['Tell me the means to resist the source of such pleasure!'] (V, 4, 1,527). Her unwillingness to control her natural, physical impulses through self-denial or repression marks her, for the masculine, as the embodiment of a dangerous inde-terminacy. Within the patriarchal order, she is an unsettling commodity, even though her situation is one of dependency and indebtedness to others. Unable to control her in an alternative manner, society's solution will be to turn her into an object of economic barter. Arnolphe will turn her over to his rival, but in the process he will exact repayment of Agnès's debt:

> ARNOLPHE: ... est-ce qu'un si long temps Je vous aurai pour lui nourrie à mes dépens?
> AGNÈS: Non, il vous rendra tout jusques au dernier double. (V, 4, 1,546–8)

> [ARNOLPHE: ... do you think that it is for his benefit that I have fed you for so long at my expense?
> AGNÈS: Not in the least! He'll pay you back to the last penny.]

Agnès seems to passively accept the inevitability of her transferral and her appropriation. Her incipient autonomy seems to coincide with her recog-nition of indebtedness to Horace, and therefore her total liberation from a male tutor is never fully achieved. She not only owes her sexual and intellectual enlightenment to him, but her reputation as well. He takes full credit for controlling his carnal desire for Agnès despite his awareness of her receptivity and vulnerability. However, subtending Horace's chivalrous attempt to suppress his own impulses lies the fear of unleashing Agnès's unbridled libidinous desire. In many ways, Horace's anxiety with regard to women is similar to that of Arnolphe himself. In his excellent study of the dynamics of fear in Molière's comedies, Ralph Albanese comments on Horace's acute awareness of Agnès' reputation and his respect for paternal authority.[7] Following in his father's footsteps, he is a bourgeois in the making and already aware of his future position in society and the intrinsic value of an untarnished bride.

As this study has attempted to demonstrate, the male protagonist's efforts to retain control of a rational order by barring women from the realm of knowledge is motivated by an underlying desire to keep the masculine play world exclusive and intact. Ironically, Agnès will thereby become the embodiment of chance, thus disrupting the patriarchal order even more effectively. This is the ultimate paradox subtending the play's structure and the reason that every one of Arnolphe's strategic actions is followed by an adverse reaction. Although he continually endeavours to summon Agnès to orthodoxy by reminding her of the limits that circumscribe and define her, he has provided her with no frame of reference and is therefore unable to co-opt her into internalising and accepting her servitude as a natural condition. It is Horace who will achieve this goal when Agnès openly recognises him as her teacher and master.

Thus, Arnolphe's efforts to impose external constraints on the ingénue, be they physical or moral, are totally ineffectual in contrast to the internal constraints that Agnès eventually places upon herself. His departure from the stage marks this failure and coincides with the arrival of the real father figure. Arnolphe's sexually equivocal role as father-lover is reintegrated into the sexual norms of society by being redistributed and assumed by two characters: Horace and his father Enrique, the patriarch of the new order. Enrique can uphold the paternal law because, unlike Arnolphe, he is no longer swayed by the feminine. Thus, symbolic infringement of the incest taboo is avoided, and the threat of destabilisation is circumvented as well.

The ending re-establishes the permanence of the Law and Horace stresses the balance between chance and reason, in which Enrique's wisdom takes precedence over happenstance:

> Le hasard en ces lieux avait exécuté
> Ce que votre sagesse avait prémédité. (V, 9, 1,766–7)

[In all this chance has carried out exactly what your wisdom had in mind.]

Although much has been written about Molière's advocacy of the natural order, the final reconciliation is ultimately founded on the subservience of feminine chance to masculine reason. The play's finale rests upon the reassuring (for some) reaffirmation of the pre-eminence of patriarchal law, whose authority is sustained by Christian values '(le) Ciel, qui fait tout pour le mieux' ['Heaven, which does all for the best'] (V, 9, 1,779).

As an artist striving for creative freedom, Molière would be naturally suspicious of his century's urge to centralise and standardise language and culture by silencing unorthodox voices. As an actor he would also be naturally distrustful of textualism: the authority of the written document. As a playwright, he would chafe under the restrictions imposed by the three Aristotelian unities and the rules of *bienséance* [decorum]. However, as the husband of an attractive and capricious younger woman, he would undoubtedly have felt a natural inclination to assert patriarchal authority within his own household and quite possibly a disinclination to entirely discredit the patriarchal paradigm. In *L'École des femmes* Molière teaches us to treasure surprise and to value happenstance, of which Agnès is the embodiment, which undermine rigid categories and closure. Nonetheless, in his desire for literary legitimacy, he understood the risks of unorthodoxy. As stated earlier, *L'École des femmes* is his first 'regular' comedy, the first to attempt to rival the cultural authority of tragedy. It is in this sense that this play reflects his conflicted attitude toward his craft. In *La Critique de L'École des femmes* he attempts to deflect criticism by arguing for creative freedom, while at the same time defending the legitimacy of his text and its adherence to the rules. In *L'École des femmes*, the final reconciliation between nature and culture, chaos and order, woman and man, chance and reason, is an uneasy alliance, a metaphorical enactment of Molière's struggles as an artist and only secondarily of his trials and tribulations as the husband of a woman half his age.

NOTES

1 In his book entitled *Molière: The Theory and Practice of Comedy* (London and Atlantic Highlands, NJ: Athlone Press, 1993), pp. 52–4, Andrew Calder reminds us that Molière makes an explicit textual reference to Rabelais' *Tiers Livre* as a source for *L'École des femmes*. Like Arnolphe, Panurge is obsessed with the prospect of cuckoldry. When he resorts to divination to avoid such a fate, his friend Pantagruel exhorts him to simply accept whatever is in store for him, reminding him that any precautions are essentially useless.

2 Patrick Dandrey, *Molière ou l'esthétique du ridicule* (Paris: Klincksieck, 1992). Chapter II, Part III ('L'Éthique de l'élégance: l'intuition et la règle', pp. 221–30) is of particular relevance to my argument.

3 Luce Irigaray, *This Sex Which Is Not One*, trans. Catherine Porter (Ithaca: Cornell University Press, 1985), p. 30.

4 Will G. Moore, *Molière. A New Criticism* (Oxford: Clarendon Press, 1949), pp. 38 and 107.

5 Myrna K. Zwillenberg, 'Arnolphe, Fate's Fool', *Modern Language Review*, 68 (1973), 292–308, pp. 304 and 293.

6 In his *Dissertation sur la condamnation des théâtres* (1666), the abbé d'Aubignac accused Corneille of having out of jealousy fuelled the ire of Molière's enemies.

7 Ralph Albanese, Jr, *Le Dynamisme de la peur chez Molière: une analyse socio-culturelle de Dom Juan, Tartuffe et L'École des femmes* (University, MS: Romance Monographs, 1976), pp. 167–76.

13

NOËL PEACOCK

Molière nationalised: *Tartuffe* on the British stage from the Restoration to the present day[1]

The notorious difficulty of reproducing Molière on the British stage has been a commonplace disclaimer in prefatory statements by translators and in programme notes by theatrical directors. The dramatist's verve and comic spirit, steeped in Gallic culture, were perceived as 'foreign' within the British theatrical tradition. Translating Molière's work, as George Meredith warned when analysing the *vis comica* of *Tartuffe*, was 'like humming an air one has heard performed by an accomplished violinist of the pure tones without flourish'.[2] Until recently, Molière has not enjoyed the success on the British stage which his status warrants. As John Fowles lamented, Molière has been consigned to a theatrical limbo in Britain, to the status of a study dramatist: 'on the whole, we don't know what to do with him so we leave him alone'.[3] This perceived 'foreignness' has led even to a questioning of Molière's status as a comic dramatist,[4] and of his accessibility beyond the Hexagon.[5]

There is an additional level of 'foreignness' with regard to *Tartuffe*, which is of all Molière's comedies perhaps the most rooted in seventeenth-century French *mores*. The concept of the *directeur de conscience*, introduced by the Counter-Reformation Church in France at the beginning of the seventeenth century, has no equivalent in the British ecclesiastical tradition. This essay will seek to analyse attempts by translators and directors, from Molière's times to the present day, to make *Tartuffe* accessible to British audiences.

Some translators have opted to retain the notion of a 'foreign text'. These have included, for the most part, the academically orientated translations, intended more for publication than for performance. Some of these are contained in translations of complete works.[6] The dramatic effectiveness of most of these versions has been called into question.

The most significant translations and productions, however, have attempted to relate the Otherness of *Tartuffe* to British culture. The first translation of the play in 1670, by the actor Matthew Medbourne, has been curiously neglected in standard works of reference on Molière and Restoration Comedy.[7] It has recently been argued that Medbourne's version sheds unexpected light on the earliest version of Molière's play; it is proposed that the last two scenes of Medbourne's Act III, one between Tartuffe and Laurent 'at their most villainous' and one between Madame Pernelle and Flypote 'at their most duped', are reflections of the 1664 version.[8] The two scenes heighten the emphasis on the corrupting power of hypocrisy in religious communities like Orgon's household. The notion of part of the bowdlerised *Tartuffe* appearing in England, where the intellectual climate was more favourable, is an exciting one. But there is insufficient historical evidence for concluding that Medbourne might have had access to Molière's original script. What is certain, however, is that Medbourne turned *Tartuffe* into a satire against Puritanism, calculated to appeal to Charles II and the court. The new satirical focus is blurred by Medbourne's prudential claim that the emendations to the original had been prompted by cultural and theatrical considerations: 'What considerable Additionals I have made thereto, in order to its more plausible Appearance on the English Theatre ...' Critics have tended to take Medbourne at face value.[9] It is true that Medbourne adheres more closely to Molière than other Restoration dramatists, most of whom saw in the French texts a source for plots and stage tricks. In fact, Medbourne's literal-mindedness often leads to serious mistranslations.[10] The major thrust in the anti-Puritan satire is seen in the recontextualising of the religious conflict and in the creation of a sub-plot. Tartuffe is portrayed as a 'canting' Puritan, and, in fact, called 'his canting worship'; Madame Pernelle has traits of the dissenters, attending conventicles during the night with other 'Brethren', singing hymns of thanksgiving at Tartuffe's success; Orgon's language is also steeped in Puritan jargon.[11] The sub-plot offers what Gardiner has termed a satire on land-acquisition during the interregnum. The love-relationship between Tartuffe's servant Laurence (who does not appear in Molière's play)[12] and Dorina may be seen as Medbourne's attempt to prepare a denouement which many directors and critics have found to be too contrived and embarrassing, penned by Molière as an expression of gratitude to Louis for his part in helping Molière stage his play in 1669, after nearly five years of political and religious opposition. Medbourne's addition does, however, make the final act an anticlimax, even if it allows for a contrapuntal relationship between Tartuffe/Elmira and Laurence/Dorina. The main import of the sub-plot lies elsewhere. In the demonstration of the loyalty of two servants who restore to Orgon and his family what is rightfully theirs, and for which they are rewarded with a pension of a hundred pounds a year for life and a change of status,

Medbourne provides an ironic comment on the plight of Catholics who had faithfully worked to save their Stuart master from Puritan appropriation of title, land and possessions, and who, despite the Restoration of the Monarchy, had gone unrewarded and had failed to regain what had been handed over to Parliament during the interregnum. Medbourne's ending includes a brief eulogy to the King (that is, Charles) for his exemplary handing-over of the lost estate to Cleanthes, who returns it to his brother Orgon.

Medbourne's *Tartuffe*, which, according to the *London Stage*, was performed both in 1670 and in 1671, made him a target of the Whig faction at the start of the plot concocted by Titus Oates, a bogus convert to Catholicism, who had Medbourne imprisoned for treason in the Newgate on 26 November 1778 for being 'Captain in the Pope's imaginary army in England'.[13]

Other early attempts to 'nationalise' Molière's *directeur de conscience* were less recognisable. Similarities may be discerned in Dryden's hypocritically fanatic landlady, Mrs Saintly (*Limberham*, 1678). Tartuffe was thought to have been the theatrical source for John Crowne's Finical (*The English Friar or the Town Sparks*, performed in 1689 and published in 1690), a prior of the convent of St James. The real-life model, Father Petre, the Jesuit adviser and confessor to King James II, who was considered untrustworthy and opportunistic, was believed to have attempted to have the King establish Popery in England and fled during the Glorious Revolution of 1688. Crowne's play is, as he has himself acknowledged, an exposure of the fraudulent behaviour of the Catholic priesthood and the gullibility of bigoted papists captured in his Sir Thomas and Lady Credulous. In a dedication addressed to William, Earl of Devonshire, Crowne complains of the dangers to which the Protestant faith had been exposed under Charles' successor:

> It has been our misfortune to live in a vicious, degenerate age ... When men were thought the best divines, and truest sons of the Church, who were for delivering up the English Church which has neither faith nor mercy, but boasts of infidelity as a virtue. And we have fal'n into the same miserable mistakes; virtue has been so strange and unknown amongst us, vice has pass'd for virtue. Treachery to our country was called fidelity to them: baseness of spirit was called Christian fortitude: and therefore men did all they could to dispirit us, in order to improve us.[14]

The challenge to the Catholic orders was immediately recognised by the Jacobite faction. Like Molière before him, Crowne defended himself against the severity of their attack in his *Preface to the Reader*. An edulcorated version, which appeared in 1717 under the name of *The Nonjuror*, without any acknowledgement by its author, Colley Cibber, to Molière or to Crowne, had a more favourable reception, no doubt on account of the dedication to George I, for which the dramatist received 200 pounds. Nevertheless, violence was occasionally associated with the play. An actor from a production at Lincoln's Inn Fields in March 1718 was reputed to have killed an Irish Catholic in a tavern swordfight. The *London Stage* also cites serious disturbances at London's Haymarket Theatre during two performances in November 1749 by 'the Company of French Comedians'.

The satirical edge of the seventeenth-century versions of *Tartuffe* is generally somewhat blunted in eighteenth-century adaptations. Martin Clare, whose *Tartuffe* was first performed in 1726 and published in 1732,[15] aware of the play's subversive potential, adds a prologue by a young gentleman protesting the moral import of Molière's work and an epilogue by another young gentleman in the character of Madame Pernelle abortively counselling her maid to avoid the snares of men's deluding tongue. Isaac Bickerstaffe's *The Hypocrite* (1769), an adaptation of adaptations by Crowne, Cibber and Medbourne, gentrifies the play: Tartuffe becomes Dr Cantwell; Orgon and Elmire, Sir John and Young Lady Lambert; Cléante, Colonel Lambert; and Madame Pernelle, Old Lady Lambert. The emphasis on theatricality is given by Bickerstaffe's invention of Maw-Worm, a petty shopkeeper who fancies himself as a preacher, and whose hyper-spirituality makes him even more credulous than Old Lady Lambert, refusing, even after the exposure of Dr Cantwell's hypocrisy, to believe that his own wife's position could have been compromised: 'It's unpossible … I says its unpossible … [Dr Cantwell] has been lock'd up with my wife for hours together, morning, noon and night, and I never found her the worse for him'.[16] The new character, suggested by Robert Garrick for the comic actor Mr Weston, is indicative of the creative collaboration between dramatist and director in the production of *Tartuffe*, a development which was to be crucial to the success of modern productions.

England seems to have missed out on the mythologising of Molière which took place in France in the nineteenth century, which led to the renaming of streets, the erection of statues and the publication of magisterial editions of Molière's complete works. Thomas Constable in his translation of *Tartuffe* in 1898 resumes the century's lack of familiarity with Molière, Corneille and Racine: 'It is little to say that the masterpieces of the greatest French dramatists are not *acted* in England; except in schools they are hardly read.'[17] Though Tartuffe's name and character were better known, he was, for Constable, by no means as celebrated as Dickens's Mr Pecksniff.

However, one highly successful production premiered on 25 March 1851 at the Haymarket, featuring the actor/manager Ben Webster in the title role, claimed to be the first rendering in English of Molière's complete 1669 version.[18] If this be true (all of the translations examined above, which are essentially adaptations of *Tartuffe*, would confirm the authenticity of this claim), for nearly 200 years London audiences would have encountered Molière's 'entire' text only in the performances by French companies at Lincoln's Inn Fields, Goodman's Fields and the Haymarket (1669, 1671, 1721, 1734, 1735, 1749).

The upswing in the play's fortunes has come only in the period following the Second World War. The Comédie-Française brought *Tartuffe* to Britain in 1945 as a token of gratitude for support during the war and returned with another acclaimed production of the play six years later. It may be that the new *entente* at government levels and the changed religious climate after the war provoked greater interest in this play. However, the most significant development was in the approach to the play by translators and directors, in particular in their efforts to reproblematise the play for English-speaking audiences. Two main trends have underpinned the new approach.

(1) *Theatricalist interpretations, in which the translator and director have explored aspects of illusion and mimesis in the text.*

The success of postwar translations of *Tartuffe* has been due largely to the fact that these have been commissioned by theatres or have been written with performance in mind. With the amount of critical apparatus available, particularly through reviews of performance, it is easier to chart the stage fortunes of *Tartuffe* in the last five decades. Miles Malleson was the first to restore theatrical practitioners' confidence in Molière, which had been undermined by flat, stilted, workmanlike translations, in a series of adaptations which as actor/director he performed at the Bristol Old Vic in the 1940s and 1950s. In 1950, Malleson attempts to situate the problematic French text in a theatrical and historical context with his *Tartuffe* taking the form of a play within a play, a hybrid of *Tartuffe* and *L'Impromptu de Versailles*. When the audience enters the curtain is up, revealing a simulated reconstruction of the Théâtre du Palais-Royal in 1664. The actors and actresses arrive for a rehearsal of a new play but are asked, by the royal command, to stage *Tartuffe* instead. In Malleson's Prologue, Louis XIV's carriage is reported to be drawing up: fanfares attend the King's entry to the royal box; the King moves to the front of the box and acknowledges the reception from the actors (and the audience). The stage direction indicates that from time to time during the performance of *Tartuffe*, the King's hand and the white lace ruffles of his sleeve can be seen on the edge of the box.

The adaptation of *L'Impromptu* is very free. Malleson omits Molière's professional attacks on rival actors and introduces (anachronistically) some of the comments on the first performance of *Tartuffe* (which took place some seven months after the premiere of *L'Impromptu*): an Aristocrat informs the troupe that *Tartuffe* has given offence in very influential quarters; Molière defends himself against the charge of writing about real people. The Prologue draws attention to the King's influence during the *querelle* and helps prepare the audience for the panegyric to Louis at the end of *Tartuffe*. The transition between Malleson's Prologue and his *Tartuffe* reinforces the audience's awareness of the presence of the Supreme Spectator. At the same time, by means of what might otherwise appear to be gratuitous stage business, Malleson establishes a comic framework for *Tartuffe*: the Stage Manager and a Stage Hand bump into the Aristocrat while removing a skip from the stage; the stage curtains hit the Stage Manager and envelop him in their folds; the Stage Manager and the First Stage Hand bump into each other while lighting the candles representing the footlights (and glance apologetically towards the royal box).

While reminding the audience of the historical context of *Tartuffe*, Malleson's Prologue does, paradoxically, focus on the theatrical and illusory quality of Molière's art and encourages the audience to suspend disbelief. The main drawback is that the preliminaries further delay the appearance of Tartuffe, which Molière had held back until the third act. Malleson's text was in the English theatrical repertory for three decades and was a standard point of reference for future adaptations.[19]

Richard Wilbur, whose translation was given an all-star British premiere in Tyrone Guthrie's production at the National Theatre in 1967 (with John Gielgud as Orgon, Richard Stephen as Tartuffe and Joan Plowright as Dorine), and which has been performed frequently since (for example, BBC Television, 1971, Almeida Theatre, 1996), has had an uneven reception from the British press (which has given insight into the marked difference in taste between American and English audiences). In the USA, Wilbur's *Tartuffe* was awarded a share of the Bollingen Translation Prize in 1963 and was regarded as the 'nearest thing to Molière that we have'. As James Gaines and Michael Koppisch have observed, Wilbur has become Molière's voice in English, particularly in the USA, and has become the anthological text par excellence (his *Tartuffe* appearing regularly in American collections).[20] Reviewers in Britain, however, were initially scathing, evoking, for example, 'the uninspired jog-trot translation ... apt to sound like the doggerel which used to be reeled out by the hack-writer who used to sling together the "books" of Victorian pantomimes',[21] and calling it a 'trumpery translation'.[22] Recent productions of the play, however, have given Wilbur the accolade of 'Prince of Translators'.

Christopher Hampton's *Tartuffe*, which the author described as a 'neutral' translation, was used by the Royal Shakespeare Company (at the Barbican in London in 1983, and on BBC television in 1985). The subversive political context of *Tartuffe* was restored in the intertextual coupling of the play, in production and TV schedules, with Bulgakov's fictional biography, *Molière or the Union of Hypocrites*, which traced Molière's downfall to the persecution by the Church and to Louis XIV himself. Anthony Sher's Tartuffe oscillated between pantomimic victim and villain, at times sinister, menacing, animalistically sensual, snorting like a pig in his overtures to Elmire and lifting his cassock and dropping his trousers in one of the seduction scenes, at other times, exaggeratedly pious and sanctimonious, chanting prayers, using a rosary as an instrument of mortification and daubing his hands with jam to simulate stigmata. Some of the French in the audience were annoyed by the manic dimension of Sher's villainy, which led the critic of *The Spectator* to wonder whether the actor were filming *Carry On Rasputin*,[23] but for Irvine Wardle, the senior literary critic of *The Times*, this was the greatest Molière production he had ever seen.[24]

In Ranjit Bolt's *Tartuffe*, the self-conscious rhyming, quite foreign to Molière's dramaturgy, created a signifying process on stage which appealed to Anglophone taste. In Sir Peter Hall's production at the Playhouse Theatre in London in 1991, the actors, particularly John Sessions, Paul Eddington and Felicity Kendall, were encouraged to end-stop each line, thus calling attention to unconventional juxtapositions:

> I must say my [pause]
> Erotic tinder isn't half so dry.
> What earthly happiness is equated to [pause]
> The happiness of being loved by you.
> Look at him he's totally besotted [pause]
> If there's Tartuffo-mania he's got it![25]

Bolt's text has been further popularised in his revised version for Lindsay Posner's National Theatre production in 2002 (which starred the television sitcom comedian Martin Clunes in the title role). Critics drew attention to coarse expressions like 'big fat arse', 'bugger me sideways', 'bugger that', 'bugger off', 'prat', 'git' and updated references to topical affairs, for example, to New Labour. Though Molière juxtaposes high and low registers, his lexis does not descend to levels of vulgarity which have characterised Bolt's and other English translations of Molière in the last twenty years.[26] In a programme note to the 2002 production, Bolt gives expression to the overwhelming dilemma facing any Molière translator. The solution he advances lies in 'acceptance' and 'creativity': 'Run with the paradox of untranslatability, go with the flow, and dare, within the confines of basic accuracy, to be a little creative'.

The extra jokes, the new rhymes, the updating were seen by Bolt, not as improvements but, paradoxically, as a means of preserving the character of the original. While such rationalisation might be disowned by French purists, some of the leading Molière sceptics in the British press (notably, Charles Spencer[27] and John Peter[28]) found both the translation and the production among the best they had seen on the English stage.

(2) *Intercultural experiments: the 'foreignising' of Molière's play.*

In recent years, one of the most significant developments has been the translation of *Tartuffe* into a minority idiom as, *inter alia*, a means of challenging the standard cultural idiom of the majority of the audience. Liz Lochhead's *Tartuffe*, commissioned by the Royal Lyceum Theatre in Edinburgh in 1985, pitches Molière into the twentieth-century Catholic/ Protestant divide, particularly prevalent on the west coast of Scotland. The emphasis is shifted away from religious hypocrisy to sectarianism and power structures in what was regarded as a marginalised annex of the UK. In fact, one of the most comic pleas from a distraught Marianne to a father determined to marry her off against her will ('Let me turn Catholic!') highlights the religious bigotry underpinning the Scotticised version. The Scottish Kirk, the Presbyterian denomination (established in 1650) which exerted until recent times a powerful influence over the nation, is a means of social-climbing for Orgon and Pernelle. The political backcloth provides both historical and contemporary resonance. Set against the General Strike of 1926, the satire is directed less against monarchy than at ways in which political power was misappropriated by the upper classes. Created and performed at a time when Margaret Thatcher dominated the political landscape and nationalism was in the ascendant, Lochhead's *Tartuffe* was seen as a blow struck against the Westminster government's disregard for the social problems affecting Scotland. From the linguistic standpoint, the play invited audiences to rediscover the rich resources of their own language. As Lochhead comments in her introduction to the published text, most of the characters are at least bilingual, an invention which generates comedy not in the original. Standard English is used to show 'kirkish' superiority, particularly when, in accordance with Lochhead's stage direction, delivered in a 'Bearsden voice', an accent found in one of the most chic suburbs of Glasgow. Lochhead strips away the pretentiousness of the bourgeois family in causing them under pressure to abandon their anglified tones and to lapse into colloquial Scots. The new linguistic norm is set by Dorine's consistent exploitation of the full range of Scots diction, replete with its phonetically suggestive lexis like 'whidjies' and 'houghmagandie'.[29] With its redefining of the satiric target and the play's intellectual and cultural agenda, Lochhead's *Tartuffe* contributed to the Scots' theatrical adoption of Molière as their own 'Wullie Shakespeare', and helped shape the distinctiveness of modern Scottish theatre.[30]

The Asiaticised version of *Tartuffe* by Jatinder Verma, performed at the National Theatre in London in 1990, is both a rereading of Molière's play and a critique of British national identity. A *mise en abyme* of Molière's text, Verma's *Tartuffe* is framed in the Indian story-telling tradition and set to the musical accompaniment of the sitar. Molière's play is performed in an Indian translation as a commission by the seventeenth-century Moghul Emperor Aurangzeb to an out-of-favour Hindu poet to mark the visit of the seventeenth-century traveller François Bernier to the Emperor's court. Tartuffe is transformed into a self-flagellating, faking fakir. The addition to the cast of two roles, the translator and the Emperor, paradoxically allows Verma to interrogate, through another culture, the complex genesis of Molière's *Tartuffe*. The poet-translator's recasting of *Tartuffe* stops with the eviction of Orgon and his family by a triumphant Tartuffe, an ending which probably, if we accept the speculation of academic detectives, corresponds to the first *Tartuffe*, the three-act version of the play. The revised ending is attributed by Verma to the Emperor, Aurangzeb, who becomes slowly aware of a satirical intention on Molière's part, intervenes on stage in person to complain about the insult which the ending implied to divine and earthly justice, to Islam and to himself. The fact that the Emperor appears as Orgon in a mask (the same actor playing both roles) reinforces the link between absolute power and bigotry. The actors are then required to improvise a *rex ex machina* – a flattering denouement which approximates to Molière's introduction of the Sun King's representative. Within the context of Verma's adaptation there is a tight link between politics and religion, reflecting particularly those countries in which absolutism is upheld by fundamentalist religious practice. Verma brings out the parodic potential in Molière's eulogistic postscriptum and offers a new reading for this contrived ending. Seventeenth-century audiences would most probably not have taken the Exempt's speech at face value, being only too aware (even if unable to articulate it in public) of the gap between the ideal of kingship depicted by Molière and the historical reality.

However, in addition to this rereading, Verma explores Molière's text as part of a quest for national identity and as a plea for recognition of ethnic minorities and a defence of multiculturalism. Verma's choice of *Tartuffe* at the national shrine of culture in London was, in part, a statement with regard to the multicultural society in Britain, in part, a migrant's search for identity through a post-colonialist critique of a colonial situation which threatened to reaffirm itself. Verma had emigrated to Britain as a boy from Nairobi, where he was born. His use of ethnicity is not ghettoised but a point of connection between three cultures. The fact that the actors spoke a variety of mother tongues, and some interspersed their speech with words of Gujarati, added to the cultural diversity of the auditory experience.

With the dissolution of the binary opposition between original and translation, the theoretical shift from source-oriented to target-oriented replacing the quasi-fetishistic concern for the text, a new dialectical relationship is, we have seen, being established between Molière's *Tartuffe* and modern British audiences. The prestige and polemical force of the French version is being restored, paradoxically, through works which seek to remove the play from its original context, and, in fact, to denationalise or renationalise it. These recent experiments take us full circle, however, back to early essays, however flawed, by the play's first translators and adaptors, which ruffled the feathers of the religious and political establishment, rehearsing, on the British stage, the outcry following the first performances in France, which gave rise to the most robust defence from its embattled author: 'It is a crime which they could not pardon me, and they have all risen up in arms against my comedy with a terrible fury.'[31]

The offence caused by recent translations is, however, no longer regarded as criminal in a changed intellectual climate. The new hostility has, somewhat ironically, come largely from critics denouncing the betrayal of the original. These 'transtextualisations'[32] of *Tartuffe*, however, have proved a major success at the box-office, testimony itself to the power of Molière's play to transcend boundaries of time, language and nationality.

NOTES

1 Tony Harrison used the title 'Molière Nationalised' (*Revue d'histoire du théâtre* (1973), 169–86) as a punning commentary on the production of his version of *The Misanthrope* at the National Theatre.

2 George Meredith, *An Essay on Comedy* (New York: Doubleday Anchor Books, 1956), p. 28.

3 *The Times*, 6 April 1981.

4 Charles Spencer, *Daily Telegraph*, 31 March 1990: 'there was nothing wrong with Molière that a sense of humour wouldn't have put right'.

5 John Peter, *The Sunday Times*, 18 October 1987: 'If we are not careful, Molière could become one of the obstacles to a united Europe. How can you trade freely, let alone merge with a nation whose best comedy does not travel.'

6 For example: H. Baker and J. Miller, 2 vols. (1739), whose translation, in an eighteenth-century idiom, survived until recently in the Everyman Series; Henri Van Laun (1875–6), whose version, though written in a language which was

neither modern nor archaic enough to pass for seventeenth-century usage, is being reprinted as a single text by Dover Publications; A. R. Waller (1902–3), whose *Learned Ladies* was rehabilitated by Stephen Pimlott's use of it for his production at Stratford in 1995; John Wood's translation for the Penguin series, which has been the standard text in schools and colleges.

7 Such as H. C. Knutson, *The Triumph of Wit: Molière and Restoration Comedy* (Columbus: Ohio State University Press, 1988).

8 Lori Sonderegger, 'Sources of Translation: A Discussion of Matthew Medbourne's 1670 Translation of Molière's *Tartuffe*', *Papers on French Seventeenth-Century Literature* (2000), 553–69.

9 Including, for example Allardyce Nicoll, *A History of English Drama*, 6 vols. (4th edn, Cambridge: Cambridge University Press, 1952), I, p. 259, cited in Anne Barbeau Gardiner, 'Matthew Medbourne's *Tartuffe* (1670): A Satire on Land-Acquisition During the Interregnum', *Restoration and Eighteenth-Century Theatre Research*, 9, 1 (1994), 1–16, p. 1.

10 For example Cléante's ironic description of Madame Pernelle as 'cette bonne femme' is rendered as 'Alas! good woman'; 'avoir raison' is frequently translated as 'have right'.

11 See Gardiner, 'Matthew Medbourne's *Tartuffe*', pp. 6–7.

12 Medbourne's Laurence is introduced at the end of Act I, Scene 4, where he arranges to meet Dorina; in I, 5, Laurence's declaration of love to Dorina, dressed up in religious terminology, anticipates Tartuffe's seduction of Elmira and indicates his preparedness to betray his master out of love for Dorina; in II, 5, Laurence sings a song and dances a jig to distance himself from his master and to persuade Dorina of his own less than holy pursuit of her; Laurence also mentions his master's interest in Elmira, an insight provided by Dorine in Molière's text; in IV, 2, Laurence reveals Tartuffe's acquisition of Orgon's fortune and suggests a meeting be set up between his master and Elmira (with Orgon under the table), a scenario devised by Orgon's wife in the original, and suggests that the King and the Council be apprised of Orgon's former services; in IV, 8, Laurence hands over to Dorina the cabinet and the deed entrusted to him by Tartuffe.

13 See Gardiner, 'Matthew Medbourne's *Tartuffe*', p. 12.

14 *The Dramatic Works of John Crowne* (Edinburgh: William Paterson, 1874), IV, p. 15.

15 *Tartuffe, or the Imposter* (London: J. Watts, 1732).

16 *The Hypocrite* (London: W. Griffin, 1939).

17 Thomas Constable, *The Great French Triumvirate* (London: Downey and Co. Ltd., 1898).

18 I am very happy to acknowledge the work of John Buckingham on the 1851 production, which was part of his submission for an M. A. for Royal Holloway University of London, and to David Bradby for drawing my attention to it.

19 For a fuller account of the Malleson version see my *Molière in Scotland* (Glasgow: University of Glasgow French and German Publications, 1993), pp. 9–10 and 69–75.

20 See Jim Carmody, 'An American Molière: Richard Wilbur's Translations', *Le Nouveau Moliériste* IV–V (1998–9), 270–93, pp. 271–2.

21 W. A. Darlington, *Daily Telegraph*, 22 November 1967.

22 Harold Hobson, *The Sunday Times*, 25 August 1974.

23 See James Fenton, *The Sunday Times*, 31 July 1983.

24 *The Times*, 29 July 1983.

25 See my 'Translating Molière for the English Stage', *Nottingham French Studies*, 33, 1 (1994), 83–91, p. 88.

26 Notably translations by Jeremy Sams and Nick Dear.

27 *Daily Telegraph*, 6 March 2002.

28 *The Sunday Times*, 10 March 2002.

29 See Randall Stevenson, 'Triumphant Tartuffication: Liz Lochhead's Translation of Molière's *Tartuffe*', in Bill Findlay (ed.), *Frae Ither Tongues: Essays on Modern Translations into Scots* (Clevedon, Buffalo, Toronto and Sydney: Multilingual Matters, 2004), 106–22.

30 See Peacock, *Molière in Scotland*, particularly pp. 13, 90–7 and 230–7.

31 Molière's Preface to the first edition published in 1669.

32 A term used by Haroldo de Campos to describe a new kind of post-colonial translation (see Susan Bassnett and Harish Trivedi, *Post-Colonial Translation: Theory and Practice* (London: Routledge, 1999), p. 15.

14

JIM CARMODY

Landmark twentieth-century productions of Molière: a transatlantic perspective on Molière: *mise en scène* and its historiography

If over the course of the last half-century or so the majority of Molière scholars have become increasingly convinced of the value of studying the plays in the context of their performance in the theatre, the task of analysing Molière in performance has itself grown considerably more complex during the same period, particularly with the proliferation of Molière productions following the Second World War.[1] This proliferation was especially evident in France, where the decentralisation of state-supported theatre led to the creation of what has become, in effect if not always in name, a network of national theatres – a network in the sense that many productions tour from one state-supported theatre to another, and also in the sense that companies from time to time pool resources to make certain projects possible. Over roughly the same period, a decentralisation of theatre occurred in the United States, although not as a result of a consciously promoted government policy. The institutions that were created in the American process of decentralisation came to be called regional or resident theatres, although four decades or so after the majority of those decentralised institutions came into being, given the remarkable homogeneity of their season planning and the very small number of resident companies of actors these theatres house, they are now 'regional' and 'resident' in name alone. Despite this homogeneity of taste, however, there is very little networking of productions in the American theatre – touring remains the province of the commercial theatre.

With more and more productions to study, how can Molière scholars most productively negotiate this wealth of performance? Further complicating any attempt by Molière scholars to come to grips with the abundance of theatrical data are the increasingly sophisticated models developed by theatre scholars in an attempt to study theatrical performance and indeed

the concept of performance itself. This essay explores some of the historiographical problematics encountered in the effort to identify and discuss
landmark twentieth-century productions of Molière's plays.

Writing in the late 1980s, Alfred Simon offered a brief survey of Molière
production as a postscriptum to his biography, *Molière ou la vie de Jean-
Baptiste Poquelin*, that neatly divides the history of Molière's plays on stage
into two periods: the 200 years or so preceding the emergence of the
modern director in the late nineteenth century and the slightly more than
100 years that followed.[2] In the first of these periods, Molière production in
France was virtually exclusively the domain of the Comédie-Française, and
new ideas about how to perform Molière originated with actors.[3]

Such new ideas emerged in the context of an evolving tradition of performance within the Comédie-Française company, with each new generation of actors in turn learning the roles from the preceding generation and
establishing its own artistic identity by how well it differentiated itself from
the older, model generation. Within this tradition, and the clearly circum-
scribed practices of the Comédie-Française, it is difficult to decide the
extent to which a given actor's performance marks an original contribution
to the construction of the role, and it becomes even more difficult to do so
when one considers Molière performances outside the Comédie-Française.
As Molière's plays came to be performed by more and more companies in
more and more varied locations – a practice that developed in tandem with
the rise to power of the modern stage director and expanded exponentially
with the decentralisation of French theatre following World War II – it
becomes more and more difficult to establish lines of influence from one
actor to another, largely because actors are no longer asked to learn roles
from those who have played them before but are, instead, asked to create
roles in the context of a new *mise en scène*. Such *mises en scène* are 'new' in
the sense that they offer ways of staging classic plays that are different from
those already in the repertoire. In time, the innovations of the director
replace those of the actor; indeed, they do so to the extent that all innovations, whether in acting or scenography, come to be attributed to the
director, who eventually rises, like his or her counterpart in the world of
film, to the status of *auteur*.

There are, however, some crucial differences between the *auteur* director
in film and the *auteur* director in the theatre. Perhaps the most important of
these differences as far as Molière production studies are concerned arises in
the different relationship the director has to the text – the playscript or the
screenplay. Generally speaking, the film director refashions the screenwriter's text at will, discarding, adding or altering images, dialogue,
even major elements of the dramatic structure during pre-production and

production to an extent that the screenwriter's work is often obliterated. Later, during post-production, the director reworks the raw footage with the editor and others – again discarding, adding, altering almost at will – to make the finished film. Given the often very numerous changes and interventions between the screenplay and the finished film, it is hardly surprising that film directors' work is not examined in terms of their interpretation of a text. In the theatre, however, and in particular where classical authors like Molière are concerned, the *auteur* director's work is virtually always examined with a view to understanding its relationship to the original text, and when we speak of Planchon's *Tartuffe*, for example, or Vincent's *Misanthrope*, or Chéreau's *Dom Juan*, or Vitez's Molière tetralogy, we are calling to mind a complex cultural artefact that comprises both a unique work of theatrical art – a performance, a production, a *mise en scène* – and an exploration of a play written over three centuries ago by Jean-Baptiste Poquelin. We consider these directors *auteurs* not because we find their exploration of Molière persuasive, although we may of course find it so, but because of their ability to fashion compelling works of theatrical art; it is precisely because of this extraordinary artistic ability that we pay special attention to their explorations of Molière. On those relatively rare occasions when a superbly gifted director creates a genuinely new way of staging a particular Molière play – my emphasis here is on innovation, not novelty – the resulting work of theatrical art is significant both in terms of its theatrical innovation and in terms of its innovative exploration of Molière. Such a work of art also immediately becomes a potential landmark production.

During a conversation in early June 2002, I asked Marcel Bozonnet, currently Administrateur Général of the Comédie-Française, which were the twentieth-century productions of Molière he considered the most important, the most influential.[4] Almost immediately, he mentioned Copeau, Jouvet and Vilar, and a few seconds later, Planchon. In the course of our conversation, he also named a dozen or more directors who had, in his estimation, staged persuasive and/or provocative productions of Molière's play, some of them his predecessors at the Comédie-Française. He expressed a particular fondness for the productions of *Dom Juan* by Jacques Lassalle and *Amphitryon* by Anatoli Vassiliev, both of which were in the repertoire at that time (the *Dom Juan* was a reprise of Lassalle's *mise en scène* of 1993; the *Amphitryon* was a new production). Lassalle's *Dom Juan* was an old audience favourite, still drawing almost full houses; *Amphitryon* was very unpopular with audiences – a substantial number of spectators left during the performance I attended. Bozonnet was not at all unpleased with the response to the *Amphitryon*. While he hoped that audiences would come to appreciate Vassiliev's *mise en scène*, Bozonnet felt the production had already been a success as far as its beneficial effect on the company was concerned. For Bozonnet, the most important contribution Vassiliev made was to bring fresh ideas about performing Molière to the company.

Like most practising artists, Marcel Bozonnet views theatre from the perspective of his own practice, so it is not surprising that he would value Vassiliev's contribution to the development of the institution he is charged with administering. Nor it is surprising that I, too, would view Vassiliev's work in the context of my own work, although my perspective is necessarily quite different from Bozonnet's. There is, however, one important way in which our two perspectives largely come together, and that is our professional interest in Molière *mise en scène* and its developments: we are both interested in learning what different *mises en scène* can bring to our understanding of Molière. Consequently, we are interested in perceiving and understanding how new *mises en scène* add to our evolving comprehension of Molière in the context of stage performance; almost but perhaps not quite as important, we are interested in finding productions of Molière that provide both aesthetic and intellectual pleasure, even if in many cases that pleasure derives from a source other than a genuinely innovative *mise en scène* or a genuinely innovative performance. The question of landmark productions, however, has a great deal more to do with innovation than with pleasure – perhaps it has everything to do with innovation. After all, quite a few landmark productions were criticised, even rejected or condemned, by their first audiences, and yet, for one reason or another, these same rejected and despised productions came to be seen as important far beyond their initial impact.

Given the multiple points of view on any single production already mentioned, and given the very wide range of personal tastes both within and across cultural boundaries (I have mentioned only French productions so far, but I turn to transatlantic work later), how can there be any agreement with respect to the identification of landmark productions? To answer that question, we will have to look more closely at the potential range of meanings and the potential use value of most of the terms in which the question is posed.

The title of this essay contains a number of words commonly used both in theatre studies and in Molière studies assembled in a sequence that most readers immediately understand as promising that the accompanying discussion will name some influential or otherwise significant stagings of plays by Molière between the end of the nineteenth century and the beginning of the twenty-first. In a similar manner, the subtitle makes an equally clear promise, namely that the discussion will also be concerned with some methodological issues related to the subject named in the principal title. For a variety of reasons, however, the contract with the reader implied by the title and subtitle is a contract virtually impossible to fulfil.

The difficulty in fulfilling this implied contract begins to arise the moment one moves beyond the obvious reading of the title already sketched out to interrogate some of the terms employed, only to find that even the most apparently banal element of the title is more evocative and slippery than it might first have appeared to be. Among the more slippery of these elements, perhaps, is 'landmark'. What, it might reasonably be asked, constitutes a 'landmark' production? On what cultural landscape is this landmark prominent, who identified it and, perhaps the most complex attendant question, who mapped the landscape and for what purpose? Assuming it were possible to provide satisfactory responses to those questions, other, perhaps even more vexed, questions remain, such as what exactly does the practice of making 'productions' of 'Molière' imply? Is what 'Molière' means in the context of a discussion such as this clear? Does 'Molière' indicate the historical person, the actor, director, company manager and playwright? Not exactly, for 'Molière' in this context obviously indicates the texts he composed, the published œuvre; but that, too, is not quite right, for 'Molière' simultaneously indicates the texts themselves, the physical objects, and what those texts have been understood to contain, to suggest, or to mean. But to borrow Marvin Carlson's useful application of the Derridean theory of supplementarity to the text/*mise en scène* relationship, 'Molière' has morphed with each successive production to include (embrace, subsume?) the images, ideas and meanings that generations of actors and directors have created in performances that used Molière's texts.[5] Given the amorphous nature of 'Molière', the theatrical production of a play by Molière – what might be termed (accurately, if somewhat flippantly) the *mise en scène* of a 'Molière' by 'Molière' – immediately assumes a high level of complexity as an object of study, a complexity that is only further intensified by the notorious difficulty presented by either *mise en scène* or the work of an actor as objects of study.

It is clearly beyond the scope of this brief essay to undertake an extensive discussion of the reasons why *mise en scène* and the work of the actor constitute such intractable objects of study, but a brief mention of one or two of the factors involved may help illuminate the historiographical difficulties presented by the study of Molière productions. Perhaps most important among these factors is that acting and directing are both intensely culture-specific. At the most basic level, this means that the work of French actors and French directors must be understood in the context of the institutions that support and house their work and in the context of the audiences that come to their performances with the expectations and experiences of whatever generation of French residents they happen to belong to. 'Molière', in all the meanings of the terms suggested above, is part of the shared expectations and experiences of all involved – actor, director, spectator, critic, teacher, etc. – regardless of age, but 'Molière' also means something different to people of different ages. Thus, a French actor, director or spectator who is in his or her mid-twenties in 2004 cannot have seen any of the arguably landmark productions of the sixties, seventies, eighties, or even early nineties; the productions of *Dom Juan* by Chéreau, Vitez and Planchon, for example, are no more a part of that person's experience and expectations than those of Jouvet or Vilar. But a French actor, director or spectator in his or her fifties or sixties in 2004 may very well have seen one or more of the productions by Chéreau, Vitez and Planchon, and that theatrical experience might have become an integral part of 'Molière' for such a person. In short, 'Molière' can very well mean something very different to members of different generations of the same culture at any given moment in history.

In the same way, to return for a moment to the questions with which I began, 'landmark' must be understood (or at least considered) in generational terms – what might be a landmark production for a director of an older generation may no longer seem relevant to his or her younger counterpart. Indeed, 'landmark' may be a term that implicitly, if not explicitly, belongs always to the older generations, for its metaphorical use in the context of theatre studies and Molière studies is exclusively retrospective. By contrast, in its more frequent and less obviously metaphorical geographical meaning, landmarks are useful both prospectively and retrospectively, salient elements of a landscape that orient both the outward- and homeward-bound traveller equally.

While it is important to bear in mind the different perspectives of members of different generations with regard to their understandings of both 'Molière' and 'Molière' production, it is no less important to take account of the generational evolution of theatrical institutions and the other cultural and political institutions from which they draw support or against which they are obliged to struggle. The Comédie-Française, for instance, the Maison de Molière itself, is no less subject to the forces of history and culture than any other, and although it has often been criticised as a bastion of conservatism in the theatre, it has, especially in the last half-century or so, shown itself willing to experiment. Certainly, the Comédie-Française has had its share of artistically and politically conservative Administrateurs Généraux and sociétaires in its long history, but like many other French institutions in the post-Second-World-War period, and especially in the years following the cultural revolution of the late 1960s, it has become on the whole less reactionary and more adventurous. The new production of *Amphitryon* in 2002, directed by Anatoli Vassiliev, might serve as a useful landmark of the degree to which the present Administrateur Général, Marcel Bozonnet, is willing to open up the classic repertory to relatively fresh, even foreign approaches (relatively fresh, because Vassiliev is hardly the first director to borrow from Japanese performance traditions). On the other hand, Vassiliev is by no means the first foreign director to stage a Molière play at the Comédie-Française – Andrei Serban, the Romanian director who has lived and worked in the United States for over thirty years, staged *L'Avare* at the Comédie-Française in 2000, a production that can be considered a revised version of the production of *The Miser* that he had staged at the American Repertory Theatre in Cambridge, Massachusetts, in 1989. Within the context of the Comédie-Française, these two productions might very well serve as landmarks of the institution's evolution, but that in itself is not a sufficient reason to name them as landmark productions of Molière in a different context. A similar argument might be made with respect to every other major theatre company or producing entity, such as a theatre festival, in France and in other countries as well.

A production that marks a salient moment of evolution or revolution in either a company or a festival can obviously serve as a landmark for those interested in the work of such institutions, even if such a landmark production may hold no special value to those interested in the historiography of Molière *mise en scène* in particular. Nevertheless, prominent companies and festivals play an extraordinarily important role insofar as they provide a privileged forum for the exploration and exchange of ideas about subjects such as 'Molière'. Such forums are privileged in a number of ways: they enjoy a high degree of cultural visibility on the national and even international scale; they tend to employ either the most experienced artists or the most interesting emerging artists (sometimes both); and they tend to attract, largely on the basis of their visibility and the calibre of artist they present, the best-informed spectators. Indeed, it is difficult to imagine a landmark production being staged in the absence of well-informed and discriminating spectators, for it is precisely such spectators who are most likely to be appreciative of the contributions such a production is making to 'Molière'. They are, in fact, the only spectators who have seen enough productions of Molière to be able to form a sufficiently broad and heterogeneous sense of 'Molière' to enable them to perceive the ways in which a new production adds to their growing understanding of 'Molière'.

For the purposes of identifying landmark productions, the most important subset of those well-informed and discriminating spectators is comprised of the critics, scholars and artists who assume the task of articulating the importance of a production's contribution. It is the critics, scholars and artists who record and disseminate their reactions to and reflections of the 'Molière' that emerges from each noteworthy production of one of the plays, who perform the invaluable cultural work of identifying potential landmarks and explaining how these emerging landmarks might be understood as redrawing the 'Molière' map. Subsequent generations of critics, scholars and artists may either ratify or challenge the landmarks nominated by this first group, and the question of ratification may not be settled for a generation or two, but no production can become a landmark that has not received a significant level of attention from the critics, scholars and artists who first encountered it and who embraced the new 'Molière' it created. In short, no production can become a landmark if those critics, scholars and artists who experienced it did not publish their responses in some way – in newspaper and magazine articles, essays, books, interviews, photographs, or on the stage or screen.

Many Molière productions in France in the twentieth century did, indeed, provoke most, if not all, of those possible published responses, and it is relatively easy to find published accounts of contemporaneous analysis and evaluation. The fact that many French actors and directors have been willing to publish their reflections on their own work and on the work of other artists has only added to an ever-accumulating discourse. Carlson's suggestion that we consider *mise en scène* as a Derridean supplement to the playwright's text opens up a useful perspective on this accumulating discourse, for it encourages us to appreciate the extent to which the successive generations of commentary on the work of the innovative directors of the first half of the twentieth century has come to appear to be virtually indistinguishable from the work itself. Indeed, for scholars like myself who were born too late to see the work of Copeau, or Jouvet, or Vilar, for example, the discourse to which I refer is the only remaining trace of their *mises en scène* – as a potential object of study, the discourse is the *mise en scène*. When we study the landmark *mises en scène* of Copeau, Jouvet and Vilar, we study the discourses they inspired, and as Molière production study develops, the discursive field is likely to continue to expand.

Theatre artists, critics and scholars working in France are fortunate that their cultural context provides them with a wealth of experience of Molière in performance and of the reception of Molière in performance that greatly facilitates the comparative discussion of the work of different directors with Molière texts. But the situation is quite different in the United States. Even though Molière was one of the classic authors most frequently staged in the early years of the regional theatre movement, forty years or more later,

Molière production remains relatively rare and even the most widely experienced theatre artists have seen only a handful of the plays. The most frequently performed plays are *Tartuffe*, *The School for Wives*, *The Miser*, *The Misanthrope* and *The Imaginary Invalid*. (Molière is also taught in American universities, but *Tartuffe* and *The Misanthrope* appear in text-books more frequently than all the other plays combined.) Curiously, *Dom Juan*, one of the plays that has most frequently attracted directors in France since Jouvet's 1947 production, is not at all well known in the United States.[6]

Given the relative infrequency of performances of Molière's plays in the United States, the relative poverty of the responsive discourse from theatre artists, critics, and scholars is hardly surprising.[7] Even productions that were presented in contexts that otherwise attracted a good deal of attention have failed to provoke much discussion. An especially eloquent example of this general neglect of Molière production is the production of *The Miser* that was one of four in the inaugural season of the Guthrie Theater in Minneapolis. While the production was reviewed (favourably) by the press along with the others, it inspired very little additional commentary and appeared to exercise little influence on the following seasons – a fate quite different from the productions by the other two classic authors featured in the first season, Shakespeare and Chekhov (the fact that the study of how to perform Shakespeare and Chekhov is a key component of American actor training is not irrelevant here). Even Tyrone Guthrie, founding artistic director of the theatre that bears his name, virtually ignores *The Miser* in his book about the creation of the theatre and the preparation for the first season.[8]

This poverty of response to Molière is exacerbated by another kind of poverty: the lack of an analytical discourse dealing with the work of the director in the last half-century – the period in which the majority of American productions of Molière were staged. Consequently, there are very few American directors who have either written about directing or who have been the subject of extensive commentary, and of this relatively small number, few have been interested in Molière. Even those who, at one time or another in their careers, had been interested in staging plays by Molière neglected to write about that aspect of their work. William Ball, for example, founding artistic director of the American Conservatory Theatre (a first-rank regional theatre that also houses a widely respected actor training programme), at the end of his career produced a book in which he tried to explain his work as a director.[9] The book mentions Molière only in passing, yet the inaugural production of the ACT was Ball's *Tartuffe*, generally acknowledged as one of the most important American produc-tions of a classic play of the 1960s.[10] Given the prevailing poverty of response to productions of Molière's plays in the United States, and the relatively small number of such productions, especially in relation to productions of plays by Shakespeare and Chekhov, the criteria for establishing which productions can be considered landmark productions that I offered in the context of French theatre cannot be embraced without some qualification in the context of the American theatre.

An additional element that must enter any discussion of the difference between American and French *mise en scène* of Molière is, of course, translation.[11] Indeed, the selection of the translation employed in a given production may itself be sufficient to argue for the landmark status of a given production. Thus, for example, Robert Falls' production of *The Misanthrope* in 1989 at the La Jolla Playhouse in La Jolla, California (the production was mounted later that season at the Goodman Theatre in Chicago, where Falls is artistic director) might qualify as a landmark production solely because it was the first major American production to use a translation of the play by somebody other than Richard Wilbur, the translator who, more than any other, has become 'Molière' for Americans. Falls adapted Neil Bartlett's British translation for an American audience by moving the action from Bartlett's British media environment to a more America-accessible Hollywood.[12] It would be more difficult, on the other hand, to argue on the same basis for the landmark status of the first British production of Bartlett's translation and adaptation because Wilbur's translations have never achieved the canonical status in Britain that they have received in the United States.[13] While the American version of Bartlett's *Misanthrope* has been produced at only two other regional theatres in the United States, three major theatres have, following the example of Falls, abandoned Wilbur's translation. The Classic Stage Company (CSC) in New York used Martin Crimp's translation in the 1998–9 season; ACT in San Francisco used a new American verse translation of *Le Misanthrope*, commissioned from playwright Constance Congdon in the 2000–1 season; and the Arena Stage in Washington, DC, used Ranjit Bolt's British translation in the 2002–3 season.[14] Nevertheless, however the influence of the Falls/Bartlett collaboration (or any other American translation) is calibrated, such influence remains relatively local, for it serves to enlarge only the American sense of 'Molière', a feat it accomplishes by giving 'Molière' a fresh vocabulary and rhythm, replacing Wilbur's familiar, superficial, literary wit and predictably rhymed iambic pentameter with Bartlett's supple rhyming alexandrines and larger frame of cultural reference.

While Richard Wilbur has been regarded as the American translator of Molière's verse par excellence, Wilbur has, until quite recently, refrained from translating Molière's prose plays.[15] The most prominent American translator of Molière's prose plays in the last quarter century or so has undoubtedly been Albert Bermel, a prominence that is in large part the result of two collaborations with Andrei Serban. (Like Wilbur's, Bermel's translations are available in inexpensive paperback editions and are widely used in American universities.) The first of these collaborations was a programme of Molière one-acts entitled *Sganarelle: An Evening of Molière Farces* that was first produced at the Yale Repertory Theatre in 1978 and later in New York. When Robert Brustein left Yale in 1979 to create a new company and a new professional theatre training programme at Harvard, the Bermel/Serban *Sganarelle* was among the early productions of the new American Repertory Theatre (ART). ART toured the production extensively in the United States and Europe, and even performed at the Festival d'Avignon. Consequently, this *Sganarelle* may well be the most widely seen American production of a play by Molière, surpassing even Ball's *Tartuffe*. Bermel's other collaboration with Serban was a production of *The Miser* in 1989, also at ART. While Bermel's translations today seem a little fresher than Wilbur's, it is only because he belongs to a slightly younger generation, and his language does not yet seem as dated.

Already almost fifteen years old, Bartlett's American *Misanthrope* is clearly a product of its time, just as Wilbur's many translations are products of Wilbur's time, the late 1950s and 1960s. True, Wilbur has published many translations of Molière's texts since the 1960s, but his approach to translation has evolved little since then. Clearly, new American stagings of Molière will emerge only when new translations become available to facilitate their emergence. In the absence of such new translations, it makes little sense for a director to attempt a radical reconsideration of Molière's text using an old, outdated translation, for that old, outdated translation belongs exclusively to the already familiar 'Molière', *déjà lu*, *déjà entendu*.

NOTES

1 Although the value of studying Molière's plays in the context of their production is generally acknowledged, the number of such studies remains very small, especially with respect to studies of modern and contemporary *mise en scène*. Book-length studies include: Albert Bermel, *Molière's Theatrical Bounty: A New View of the Plays* (Carbondale, IL: Southern Illinois University Press, 1990); Michel Corvin, *Molière et ses metteurs en scène d'aujourd'hui: Pour une analyse de la représentation* (Lyon: Presses Universitaires de Lyon, 1985); Noël Peacock, *Molière in Scotland* (Glasgow: University of Glasgow French and German Publications, 1993); David Whitton, *Don Juan* (Cambridge: Cambridge University Press, 1995); and my own *Rereading Molière: Mise en Scène from Antoine to Vitez* (Ann Arbor: University of Michigan Press, 1993).

2 Alfred Simon, *Molière ou la vie de Jean-Baptiste Poquelin* (Paris: Éditions du Seuil, 1995). This book was first published in 1988 under the title *Molière, une vie*.

3 The most detailed discussion of the contributions of various actors from the time of Molière up to the early years of the twentieth century can be found in Maurice Descotes, *Les Grands Rôles du théâtre de Molière* (Paris: Presses Universitaires de France, 1960).

4 Personal interview, Paris, June 2002.

5 Marvin Carlson, 'Theatrical Performance: Illustration, Translation, Fulfillment, or Supplement?', *Theatre Journal* 37, 1 (1985), 5–11.

6 *Dom Juan* may be in the process of becoming better known in the United States as a result of a new, still unpublished translation by Stephen Wadsworth, whose translations of Marivaux were largely responsible for the popularity of Marivaux in the 1990s. Unfortunately, Wadsworth's version of Molière's play contains a number of Wadsworth's own interpolations, some of which radically alter the meaning of Molière's text.

7 In her book, *The Revisionist Stage: American Directors Reinvent the Classics* (New York: Cambridge University Press, 1994), Amy S. Green devotes a brief chapter to the plays of Molière. Such is the dearth of context for a discussion of such work in the United States that she introduces her reader to the directors she discusses via a rather basic overview of Planchon's work.

8 Tyrone Guthrie, *A New Theatre* (New York: McGraw-Hill, 1964).

9 William Ball, *A Sense of Direction* (New York: Drama Book Publishers, 1984).

10 For an account of the founding of the American Conservatory Theatre and the importance of *Tartuffe* in the company's early repertoire, see John R. Wilk, *The Creation of an Ensemble: The First Years of the American Conservatory Theatre* (Carbondale: Southern Illinois University Press, 1986), especially pp. 27–53.

11 Another critical factor that needs to be considered in this context – doing so is beyond the scope of this essay – is the considerable difference between American and French acting practices and American and French acting training. While virtually all French actors are trained in the performance of Molière, Molière's plays are virtually completely ignored in American theatre schools.

12 For an analysis of this production, see my 'Alceste in Hollywood: A Semiotic Reading of *The Misanthrope*' in Janelle Reinelt and Joseph Roach (eds.), *Critical Theory and Performance* (Ann Arbor: University of Michigan Press, 1992), pp. 117–28.

13 For an investigation of Wilbur's canonical status in the United States, see my 'An American Molière: Richard Wilbur's Canonical Translations', *Le Nouveau Moliériste*, 4–5 (1998–9), 269–93.

14 Bartlett's *Misanthrope* was produced at the Dallas Theatre Center in Texas (1992–3) and at the New Repertory Theatre in Newton Highlands, Massachusetts (1994–5). Bartlett's adaptation of *L'École des femmes*, reworked to locate the action in Washington, DC, was produced by the Arena Stage in 1991–2.

15 Wilbur published a translation of *Dom Juan* in 2001 (San Diego: Harcourt).

15

DAVID WHITTON

Dom Juan the Directors' Play

Until the middle of the last century, *Dom Juan* was one of Molière's least valued plays. Withdrawn – possibly suppressed – after its initial run, and sidelined during nearly three centuries of critical and theatrical neglect, it came into its own during the twentieth century, when it featured prominently in the experiments of major theatre artists throughout Europe. In France it came to be seen as a touchstone of directorial art and, with *Le Misanthrope*, became one of the two most frequently performed works of the entire repertoire.

The ubiquity of *Dom Juan* is such that to recount its performance history would effectively be to describe the most significant directorial tendencies of the twentieth century. This essay, which can only hint at the richness of the play's stage life, has a twofold purpose. First, to account for its singular place in the history of the stage. Second, to evoke a sample of modern productions. By comparing some stage interpretations in their respective contexts it is possible to see how, by being constantly reactualised, a text composed in 1665 to meet a specific need can resonate profoundly in different and varied cultural contexts.

To elaborate on the last point: contemporary culture is saturated with cultures of the past to the point where they become naturalised and virtually invisible. Al Pacino directs Shakespeare, Claude Chabrol films *Madame Bovary*, John Lennon sings on the radio every day. However, not all the past is of equal interest or value to us. The texts, artefacts and practices inherited from earlier cultures comprise those which people living in previous eras considered worthy of preservation and transmission. Similarly, when we employ cultural products from the past, we do so according to our own priorities, privileging elements which serve some particular purpose and ignoring those which do not seem useful or relevant.

Cultural amnesia is thus the necessary corollary of cultural memory, and *Dom Juan* has been an object of both. The successive disregard and enthusiasm shown for Molière's play has the appearance of a fashion, but the term 'fashion' merely refers to an effect without explaining what needs it fulfils. In general, materials produced by earlier cultures are actively present in contemporary culture only if they are regularly employed and if they impinge on current consciousness in a form that makes them utilisable in some way. To describe the situation that prevails when these conditions are met, Marco De Marinis uses the term 'synchronous': 'The word synchronous does not apply to everything *that belongs chronologically to the same period*, but rather to everything that is *validated* by the given culture.'[1]

The notion of cultural synchronicity takes up the observations of semioticians of the Tartu school who argued that a given culture may recognise as its own (and hence may consider culturally contemporaneous, or synchronous) texts which 'belong' to foreign cultures or to earlier historical periods. For example, Thomas Dekker's play *The Shoemaker's Holiday* and Shakespeare's *Hamlet*, both written and performed in London around 1599–1600, belong to the same historical culture. But while Shakespeare is often considered as 'Our Contemporary' (to quote the title of Jan Kott's influential study), the present culture obviously does not accord an equivalent degree of contemporaneity to Dekker. Although his play exists materially as a text, it does so towards the periphery of most people's awareness and with little cultural actuality, albeit with the potential to be reactivated at any time. In that sense (though in a more extreme form) it resembles the status of Molière's *Dom Juan* for most of the time the text has been in existence. What, then, allowed *Dom Juan* – unlike Dekker's play, and unlike Molière's own *Dom Garcie de Navarre* – to be recovered as a synchronous text for European cultures in the twentieth century? And what accounts for the relatively marginal place to which it was formerly assigned in Molière's work?

The immediate causes of *Dom Juan*'s years in exile are bound up with the quarrel which engulfed the author of *Tartuffe* in 1664. His audacious response was to take a popular Spanish morality play and, relocating the action to contemporary France, turn it into a dangerously ambivalent study of a powerful nobleman riding roughshod over Christian morality. Even for a playwright who consciously treated comedy as a forum for serious social and philosophical debate, it was a bold move. In the event it proved to be miscalculated. When *Dom Juan* opened, it was met with amazement and outrage in equal measure. 'Tout Paris s'entretient du crime de Molière' ['All Paris is talking about Molière's crime'], began one anonymous sonnet circulating in the salons.[2] In an effort to save the play Molière made cuts before the second performance, but to no avail. Despite good box-office figures *Dom Juan* disappeared from the playbills in circumstances which have never been properly explained. It would not be performed again during Molière's lifetime, nor indeed for nearly 200 years thereafter. After his death, Molière's widow commissioned a bowdlerised version set in verse. This substitute for *Dom Juan* was performed intermittently by the Comédie-Française during the following two centuries, conferring on the play a shadowy half-life. Even after Molière's text was restored in 1841, contemporary accounts show that until Jouvet's 1947 landmark production, revivals in France tended to be mounted half-heartedly, more out of obligation than conviction, and were given a lukewarm reception.

These historical facts – the initial resistance to the play and its prolonged absence from the stage – go some way towards explaining the low opinion that developed of *Dom Juan*. But the deeper reasons for its persistent marginalisation and its eventual recovery must be sought in the text's singularity and in the changing cultural values against which it is evaluated.

Dramaturgically, the play disregards the classical unities in favour of an alternative model derived from the baroque machine-play. Typically for this genre, the plot is episodic, featuring a somewhat discontinuous succession of incidents and locations. Compared with the tightly plotted action of classical drama, this produces an apparently looser, more variegated dramatic form. The exposition appears tangential and incomplete, and the denouement lacks all credibility. There are sensational onstage actions and supernatural occurrences which were disallowed in classical drama by the rules of *bienséance* [propriety] and *vraisemblance* [verisimilitude]. The text is composed in prose not verse, and the tone is an unusual amalgam of serious drama, farce and moral discussion.

Given the subject of *Dom Juan*, the choice of a baroque aesthetic was inevitable, and it had the advantage of capitalising on the public's appetite for the spectacular effects which machine-plays could supply. A negative consequence, however, was to set the play apart from works conceived in the culturally more prestigious aesthetic of classical drama. In classical theory's hierarchical perspective, regular comedies such as *Le Misanthrope* towered over entertaining but supposedly inferior genres such as *comédie-ballet*, farce and machine-plays. According to classical theory, the dramaturgical features mentioned above were classified as irregularities, from where it is only a short step to mistaking them for poor craftsmanship. By the twentieth century it was unquestioned orthodoxy that *Dom Juan* was a hastily written and not entirely coherent gap-filler, an opinion which contemporary productions never really sought to challenge.

Ethically and philosophically, moreover, *Dom Juan* is one of the most provocative plays in the repertoire. Molière's intention may have been to show an aristocratic egotist borrowing the language of a free-thinker to give a spurious justification for his selfish behaviour. The distinctly positive aura the character sometimes evokes is a more modern perception, but his contemporaries already identified a disturbing ambiguity. One of the things that shocked them was the absence of effective countervailing voices within the play. Tellingly, the 'crime' which most scandalised the play's critics was not the plausibility of the atheist but the comic naivety of the believer Sganarelle. Ostensibly matters are resolved by a higher agent. The ending, in which the Statue takes Dom Juan to Hell, appears finally to give the lie to his rationalism and to satisfy the moralists' desire to see the miscreant punished. In reality it does nothing of the sort. Molière's enemies saw immediately that the recourse to a theatrical *deus ex machina* was a purely formal resolution which robs the ending of its plausibility and the play of any clear moral lesson. The passage of time has served only to deepen the ambiguity by enhancing the potential appeal of Dom Juan's charisma. Is this the story of a progressive thinker exposing ignorant superstitions and piercing the mask of petty-minded moralists, or is it about a callous, unscrupulous egotist? When, confronted with the supernatural apparition that will kill him, he rejects the evidence of his eyes and reaffirms his rationalist beliefs, is that intellectual courage or foolish obduracy? Is he a Promethean over-reacher or a shallow materialist? A Nietzschean Overman or a rotten egg? All these possibilities, and more, are entirely plausible.

The singularity of *Dom Juan* thus comprises both an 'inferior' aesthetic and a capacity to sustain radically divergent interpretations. Historically, the combination has proved capable of both repelling and attracting, according to the cultural expectations brought to bear on it. To the Enlightenment thinkers who regarded theatre as a school for virtue, to the nineteenth-century critics who found in Molière the virtues of middle-class common sense, and to all critics for whom Molière stands for the virtues of classicism, *Dom Juan* appeared literally as an aberration. Symptomatically, the adjective most often employed to describe its strangeness is 'shakespearienne', a mistake whose real meaning is to signify that the work has no place in the canon of a classical Molière.

Conversely, it is not hard to see how the same features elevate *Dom Juan* as a directors' play of choice. Jouvet, the first French director to take it seriously, claimed that when a play by Molière resists analysis, that is an infallible sign of its interest.[3] But less contrarian artists have also been drawn to it precisely because it departs from more familiar dramaturgical norms or because of the interpretive possibilities it suggests. In straightforward rendition, it readily appears amorphous, its dramatic focus unclear and its meaning obscure. On the other hand, its open-endedness positively demands a clear directorial line, whilst its complex and shifting dramatic interest allows directors exceptional freedom in formulating theatrical statements. The following examples will illustrate how divergently directors have exploited it.

The definitive modernist staging, a production of impeccable theatrical formalism and rigorous coherence, was Louis Jouvet's (Théâtre de l'Athénée, 1947). The play's reputation was such that it required a director who was capable of seeing it without preconceptions and who had confidence in its theatrical qualities. Jouvet was ideally qualified to supply this. He believed passionately in the play and the directorial method he had learned under Jacques Copeau facilitated a fresh approach to it. The method involved a *tabula rasa* and a return to theatrical first principles. In a deliberate challenge to the false traditions maintained at the Comédie-Française (the performance traditions supposedly handed down through generations of actors since Molière's own time), it involved dismissing everything that was known or thought to be known about a play, reading it as if it had just been written and placing total confidence in the text translated to the medium of the stage. At Copeau's Vieux-Colombier theatre, that had literally meant actors performing on a bare platform stage. Although Jouvet developed a more elaborately stylised theatricality, his starting point was always the text, which, he insisted, it was the director's role to interpret as faithfully as possible.

16. Louis Jouvet in 1947 as Dom Juan encounters the statue of the man he has murdered, Roger-Viollet.

In reality, even if the requirement to make interpretive and material choices did not make an impersonal rendition of a text a practical impossibility, Jouvet himself had a more personal agenda in exploring the religious dimensions of *Dom Juan*. His reading was based on a view of Dom Juan as a lapsed Catholic who becomes tormented by uncertainty but is proudly incapable of admitting to having made a wrong choice. Against this the other roles fell into place: Sganarelle as a simple but sincere believer, Dom Louis as the upright father and voice of conscience, Elvire (whom Jouvet described categorically as a saint) as the loving wife pleading with Dom Juan to attend to his soul. These characters served to focus attention more sharply on the central drama of Dom Juan's perdition.

Jouvet played Dom Juan as a defiant Spanish hidalgo with a scornful intellect. With his overweening hubris, he could not be other than a tragic character. The turning-point came with the meeting with the Statue. Until then, he had seemed distant and bored. Now spectators saw the trap that opened up when, confronted with a sign from beyond, he was incapable of backing down. It was no longer a matter of defying society but of defying God in a drama where what was at stake was Dom Juan's immortal soul. This may have been a personal reading, but it was rendered compelling by the technical mastery in Jouvet's own acting and the high theatricality of his production style. Another remarkable feature of the production was the solutions it brought to the text's supposedly problematic form. The need to engage spectators totally in Dom Juan's stage destiny meant that every element had to be moulded into a stylistic and narrative unity. Christian Bérard's sets were designed to play down the episodic structure and elide successive scenes with the continuity of an edited film.

This production had the effect of revealing the play in an entirely new light and finally gave the lie to the notion that it was dramatically inferior. It showed that, by looking beyond the incidents to focus on the underlying drama, it was possible to uncover a rigorous, ineluctable logic to the action. Despite relaunching the text for the stage, however, the production stands alone in its approach to the play. Directors who project an isolating spotlight on the central character form a minority. Ingmar Bergman, another modernist director who used Dom Juan to articulate a personal sense of existential despair in a series of productions (Malmö 1955, Stockholm 1965, Salzburg 1983) may be counted among them. More commonly, the non-classical form has been exploited by directors as a malleable material to a variety of ends. The episodic action lends itself to the stage equivalent of a 'road movie' (the term used by Marcel Bluwal to describe his 1965 television film adaptation and by Jacques Lassalle for his 1993 Avignon production), an approach which has the effect of putting the Dom Juan/

Sganarelle couple at the centre of the story. Alternatively, the unstable illusions conjured up by the baroque aesthetic have proved of great interest to directors who treat theatre as a metaphor for life and use theatricality as a device to interrogate the nature of reality. Another fruitful approach has been to deconstruct the mechanism of the machine-play to expose its ideological underpinnings, a concept brilliantly exploited in different ways by Patrice Chéreau and Bernard Sobel.

If Jouvet unleashed the power of a dark masterpiece, Vilar's production in 1954 set it on the brightly lit stage of the TNP and gave it a glaring contemporary resonance. The TNP (as the former Théâtre National Populaire was now called) occupied a unique position in the 1950s as the flagship of a movement intended to endow France with a cultural state comparable in importance to that created by Richelieu and Louis XIV but underpinned by the egalitarian rhetoric of the Republic. In the postwar reconstruction of France, one of the political priorities was to forge a new national unity. Culture was to play an important role in the process of cementing the so-called *union sacrée* [sacred union]. To this end successive governments since the 1940s have pursued a programme of state investment in cultural infrastructure of which the TNP, whose idea was rooted in earlier socialist-inspired movements to democratise theatre-going, became one of the first beneficiaries.

Its director Vilar subscribed explicitly to the policy of a more equitable distribution of what Bourdieu would call cultural capital, for example by making the classical repertoire and other works of high culture accessible and affordable to the masses. He also aimed to raise spectators' critical awareness, supposedly in a non-sectarian way, by programming plays which raised issues of contemporary relevance. Underlying all this was Vilar's humanist belief in the unifying potential of shared culture and a conviction that theatre could act as a civic forum where ordinary people could be both educated and entertained. It was in this context that he directed a *Dom Juan* which became the TNP's most popular production. Its 233 performances were seen by more than a third of a million spectators, almost certainly a record for a theatre production in France.

The interpretation, like Jouvet's, centred on the question of disbelief, but the approach to it could not have been more different from Jouvet's. Vilar stated it was obvious that Molière did not believe in God.[4] (In 1954, it should be remembered, the drift away from religion had hardly begun and more than half the French population were practising Catholics.) With Dom Juan's atheism given as a premise, the play's focus shifted from the personal drama of the central character to the social consequences of his atheism, making it a matter of direct relevance to every member of the audience. What are the limits of human freedom in an openly secular society? What are the constraints on individual actions in a society where humans are free to invent their own values? Those were the challenges thrown by Dom Juan to audiences at the TNP.

Vilar dressed the character as a swashbuckling cavalier and played him as a fearless free-thinker bestriding the world. This was a man of conviction who assumed responsibility for this thoughts and words. Even his silences were affirmative. At certain key moments, when questioned by Sganarelle or when the Statue nods its head, Dom Juan says nothing. These reticences, which contribute greatly to the text's ambiguity, may be resolved in performance in any number of ways. Jouvet treated them as moments of hesitation and doubt. In contrast, Vilar imbued them provocatively with the certainty of a man incapable of doubting. In a sense, the production vindicated his rationalist convictions. Dom Juan's fate was not to experience the flames of hell but to suffer a cardiac arrest. Vilar did not want spectators to understand his death as divine punishment but rather, he said, as a conjuring trick, that is, a contrived resolution. In ordinary lighting with no eerie effects or pyrotechnics, the lumbering plaster Statue was self-evidently artificial, and when Dom Juan took its hand he collapsed as if electrocuted.

This production participated in a key ethical debate of the 1950s, in which writers like Camus and Sartre were also engaged, by encouraging spectators to reflect on their own responsibilities as free agents. Dom Juan's intellectual emancipation and fearlessness undoubtedly conferred a heroic quality on the character. That was not to say he necessarily supplies a model to be emulated, Vilar cautioned in a private memo.[5] As well as accentuating his disdain for conventional morality, he exposed a flagrant indifference to the suffering he inflicts on others. The trait was made more appalling by being echoed in a minor key by Sganarelle, whom Daniel Sorano played as the master's alter ego. The performance thus aimed to trigger an ambivalent response in keeping with the TNP's policy of allowing plays to 'speak for themselves' without trying to direct spectators to a specific response.

Until the 1960s most French directors (at least in their rhetoric) regarded their role as subordinate to that of the playwright. Their system of values, originally laid out by Copeau, reflected the superior prestige of writing compared with performing, a commitment to the integrity of the text, and the respect that was felt to be owed to the classics. In Russia and Germany, where the concepts of directors as autonomous creators and of directing as an interventionist process gained acceptance earlier than in France, directors showed no such reticence. Brecht deliberately spoke about 'the old works' rather than 'classics', implying that they were there to be used by present-day artists like any other raw material. These directors also incorporated into their work a different sense of historicity. Going against the view of the classics as works of art that are somehow timeless (and therefore constantly contemporary), they maintained an awareness of a text's historical context and placed it in a dialectical relationship with the present-day context of their productions.

These emerging tendencies were behind Vsevelod Meyerhold's legendary production of *Dom Juan* in pre-revolutionary Russia (Alexandrinksy Theatre, St Petersburg, 1910). The most important revival since the initial run in 1665, it was not primarily dedicated to the play at all but was intended as a showcase for Russian theatrical modernism. It also served as a manifesto for the new approach to directorial theatre. Meyerhold's approach was dictated by his desire that the production should not simply perform the play but should reflect on the society that produced it. His creative reconstruction of Molière's stage in the gilded auditorium of the Imperial theatre was not only a demonstration of contemporary theatricalism but was also intended to suggest analogies between Louis XIV's absolutist France and Tsarist Russia.

The new concepts that Meyerhold was exploring in his *Dom Juan* – using stage design and acting as instruments to stimulate a critical understanding of the play – reached their logical conclusion in the Berliner Ensemble's *Dom Juan* (Theater am Schiffbauerdamm, 1954). Brecht's interest in the pedagogic value of 'old works' led to his choosing the play for the company's inaugural production at its new theatre in Berlin. In a theatre whose aim was to promote insights into social reality and provoke a desire for change by presenting negative and positive examplars, *Dom Juan* was an almost inescapable choice. According to Brecht's assistant Benno Besson, it was chosen in preference to *L'Avare* because 'it showed a better cross-section of society at the time'.[6]

Brecht's thinking was that modern perceptions which cast Dom Juan in a favourable light (as a tragic role, for example, or a revolutionary hero fighting the old order with militant atheism) would have been impossible in Molière's time, when he would have been seen clearly for what he was. Restored to a correct historical perspective, the character is self-evidently a social parasite and also self-evidently a comic figure. These formed the twin premises of the Berliner Ensemble's production. To reinforce them, the text was extensively adapted by Besson. Many of the alterations served to discredit Dom Juan comically. In the scene where he helps to fight off robbers who are attacking Elvire's brothers, he pushed Sganarelle into the fray instead and only stepped in to take the credit when it was safe to emerge from his hiding place. Other changes, such as the introduction of a raft of new characters, served to widen the spectrum of social roles. The speeches of Dom Juan's father were subtly altered so that when he rebukes his son, what was expressed was not moral outrage but self-interested annoyance that his conduct threatened to undermine the nobility's enjoyment of unquestioned hegemony.

An unusual and revealing feature was the emphasis placed on Dom Juan as a seducer. A man of no convictions and no occupation, neither an original thinker nor socially useful, his energies were channelled exclusively into sexual pursuit. It has often been observed that Molière's Dom Juan is not a very dedicated or effective seducer and in performance it is often treated as incidental. Brecht made seduction central to the role (and introduced a new character, the Commander's daughter, for him to pursue) but made clear that his conquests were entirely the result of the social power he wields and nothing to do with the amorous talents of Erwin Geschonneck's pompous and comically strutting Dom Juan. Sganarelle, in a total inversion of convention, became the straight foil to the comical master. Norbert Christian played him as a man of the people who, despite his bondage, knows how to enjoy the pleasures of life, an interpretation which was striking for the level of social realism it brought to a role conventionally defined in terms of comic tradition.

By the 1960s, the implications of Brechtian staging had been assimilated by directors in France – not as a specific methodology but as an understanding of the function of *mise en scène* which increasingly came to be seen as a critical language rather than a transparent window on to a text. There was also widespread acceptance of the need to historicise texts by incorporating into the performance what Bernard Dort called the 'supra-text' (in contra-distinction to Stanislavsky's insistence on sub-text).

A product of this approach was the *Dom Juan* directed in 1969 by Patrice Chéreau (Théâtre du Huitième, Lyon) whose hallmark was the theatrical transcription of an ideological reading of the text employing conceptually bold scenography. Work on the production was preceded by extensive documentary research to determine the meaning of the sociological supra-text. According to their analysis, the story reflects a society in crisis and shows the problems of individuals caught up in processes they neither control nor fully understand. The recent civil war (the Fronde), the last spasm of the old feudal order's resistance to monarchical power, has left the nobles struggling to come to terms with their disempowerment as absolutism becomes the new reality. Within their ranks, an individualist (Dom Juan) profits from the disorder to pursue his own hedonistic pleasures, undermining his own class from within but also, more dangerously, threatening the newly emerged absolutist order.

17. Patrice Chéreau's production of *Dom Juan* in 1969, Claude Bricage.

Chéreau's productions often employ an over-arching concept of the stage as a 'machine à jouer' [acting/playing machine]. In *Dom Juan* this held a literal meaning, since the work being performed was a seventeenth-century machine-play. Chéreau viewed the play's dramatic form as a metaphor for its ideological discourse whereby a troublesome enemy of the regime is disposed of. This machine-play was metaphorically and literally a machine for eliminating libertines, a point made very clearly by the way Dom Juan was pulverised by an automaton. In Richard Peduzzi's beautiful stage design, the machinery that produced the spectacle by turning the revolve, changing the scenery and operating the mechanical statue was exposed to view below the stage and in towers at either side of the stage. The machinists too were on full view, crouching beneath the stage to operate cranking handles and pulleys, or swarming over the stage to add finishing details to the sets. In this way, spectators were reminded of the anonymous workers and peasants of Louis XIV's France, their alienation made clear by the fact of them supplying the labour to drive the machinery of state control.

In the years around 1968 it was the prevailing orthodoxy for French theatre to be overtly political and interventionist. This tendency was reflected in other productions besides Chéreau's, such as Maurice Sarrazin's inspired by Foucault (Théâtre Daniel-Sorano, Toulouse, 1972) and Bernard Sobel's Marxist-inspired production (Théâtre de Gennevilliers, 1973). However, it should not be assumed that theatre is only political when it is explicitly ideological. In the former Soviet-bloc countries of Europe, where censorship made approaches of the sort just described impossible, artists developed more allusive approaches. In Russia there was an established tradition stretching from Bulgakov in the 1920s to Lyubimov in the 1960s of using Molière to approach political issues tangentially. The tradition was exemplified by Anatoli Efros's *Dom Juan* (Malaya Bronnaya theatre, Moscow, 1973) presented ostensibly as an apolitical morality tale but subtly hinting at the dangers that threatened artists who defy authority.

In former Czechoslovakia Jan Grossman, one of the country's leading dissident artists, used *Dom Juan* to stage a critique not so much of the communist authorities but of the corrosive effect of totalitarianism on a whole society (Na zábradlí Theatre, Prague, 1989–92). The production, Grossman's first in Prague since his expulsion in 1968, opened early in 1989, which in retrospect we can place a few months prior to the Velvet Revolution. At the time, however, few people could have imagined that the regime was about to come to an end, and the production provided a bleakly pessimistic assessment of the so-called 'normalised' society that the Soviet authorities had imposed after the failed Prague Spring of 1968.

The performance was remarkable for its atmosphere of almost intolerable cynicism. It was also unusual in making Dom Juan exempt from blame. In contrast to those productions which focus criticism on him, the intention here was to use him as the critical conduit to attack the other characters and through them the spectators' consciousness. Dom Juan was interpreted as a Camusian hero who is penetrated with an awareness of the absurd, of the meaninglessness of life and the certainty of death. One of his dramatic functions was to expose the inauthenticity of the other characters, each of whom was concealed behind a mask: Sganarelle's cowardice, Elvire's mask of the wronged wife disguising the spite of a rejected lover, the absurdly pompous social mask of her brothers, the peasants' acquisitive materialism, and so on. In all the encounters Dom Juan seemed to be testing the other characters, trying to find a genuine human response and, instead, always meeting manipulations of truth.

Grossman rewrote the ending in line with Camus's observation that, whilst Dom Juan would willingly accept punishment, his tragedy is to see clearly that there is no Commander. So there was no Statue in this version, implying the absence of moral order in society. Instead Dom Juan fell on a blade wielded by Sganarelle, possibly in an act of suicide or possibly killed by his inauthentic accomplice who had taken fright and hoped to reintegrate himself in society. In a disturbing coda, the rest of the cast closed ranks over his body. Moving like automata, they stared with dead eyes at the audience, challenging them to react.

As this last example reminds us, the function of performance is to actualise a text by rendering it meaningful for spectators in a particular society at a particular moment. It is not by accident that the modern ascent of *Dom Juan* coincides with the emergence of directors as the dominant creative agency in theatre, since the recovery of meaning from this formerly neglected text has been an essentially directorial initiative. Ignoring critical opinion which viewed the play as an aberration, it was they who identified the conceptual opportunities and theatrical challenges it presents.

Of necessity, the productions referred to above constitute an extremely limited sample. In France alone, the names associated with *Dom Juan* constitute a roll-call of notable theatre artists of the last fifty years. In addition to those already mentioned, they include the directors Maurice Bénichou, Antoine Bourseiller, Jean-Luc Boutt, Philippe Caubère, Francis Huster, Jacques Lassalle, Marcel Marchal, Daniel Mesguich, Jean-Luc Moreau, Roger Planchon, Jacques Rosner, Maurice Sarrazin, Jacques Weber and Antoine Vitez. These directors have staged the play with radically differing motives according to their own artistic priorities and in the process have unfolded previously unimagined dimensions of the text. The central character, for example, has appeared in countless guises: from tormented Catholic to bold atheist, from hedonistic nobleman to revolutionary standard-bearer, from sexual imperialist to liberated gay, from crude débauché to epicurean sensualist, from victim of existential soul-sickness to decadent aesthete in love with death. All of these, like the productions evoked above, also illustrate how a staging is simultaneously a liberating and a diminishing operation: it extends the play's life by actualising it, but narrows its focus by concretising a particular version of it. Cumulatively, they demonstrate the seemingly inexhaustible potential of *Dom Juan* as a text for directorial theatre.

NOTES

1 Marco de Marinis, *The Semiotics of Performance*, trans. by Áine O'Healy (Bloomington, IL: Indiana University Press, 1993), p. 135. My italics.
2 *Comédie-Française*, 79 (May–June, 1979), 38.
3 Louis Jouvet, *Témoignages sur le théâtre* (Paris: Flammarion, 1951), p. 46.
4 Jean Vilar, 'Réponses à un questionnaire sur *Dom Juan*', 1963 (unpublished).
5 Ibid.
6 Benno Besson, *Jahre mit Brecht* (Willisau: Theaterkultur-Verlag, 1990), p. 84.

16

DAVID BRADBY

'Reculer pour mieux sauter': modern experimental theatre's debt to Molière

The contributors to this volume have demonstrated the impossibility of approaching Molière without also reflecting on how we read and view his work, how we understand it and construct a model of what it means for us. For example, Ralph Albanese has shown how advocates of *laïcité* in nineteenth-century France found meanings in Molière's work to fit their educational project of building a modern secular French identity. Noël Peacock has demonstrated how *Tartuffe* has been appropriated by different British theatre companies as they develop their own cultural discourses – most notably in the case of Jatinder Verma's intercultural project with his 1990 production at London's National Theatre. Charles Mazouer has reminded us that a whole aspect of Molière's *comédies-ballets* (which represent almost half his output) has been neglected for centuries, only to be rediscovered in the wake of the classical music industry's promotion of baroque music. Like Shakespeare's œuvre, Molière's has a protean quality, and each succeeding generation discovers a new Molière in its own image. The purpose of this last chapter in the *Cambridge Companion* is to explore some of the ways in which theatre reformers of the twentieth and twenty-first centuries have rediscovered aspects of Molière that mirror their own preoccupations and have found that one of the most effective methods of researching and developing new approaches to the art of theatre is through productions of his plays.

The twentieth century was the period in which the role of the theatre director was recognised for the first time as an art in its own right. From the prophetic writings of Edward Gordon Craig and of Jacques Copeau in its early years, to the achievements of great contemporary directors known internationally, such as Peter Brook or Ariane Mnouchkine, it was the century in which a new form of artistic discourse came to be generally recognised: that of theatre production, known in France as *la mise en scène*. The responsibilities of the *metteurs en scène* spread beyond the simple choice of play and supervision of rehearsals to the point where they assumed control of every aspect of the production: the choice of images – in scenery, in costumes, in the casting and directing of actors – the use of colour, light, sound, music, and the development of rhythms, groupings, etc., as well as the selection of the performance space and of the publicity and marketing methods. This is not the place to develop a history of the rise of *mise en scène*,[1] but the phenomenon is closely related to our understanding of Molière, since so many of the directors who shaped the theatre of the period in question, especially in France, invoked the authority of Molière in their support.

It is important to remember, of course, that theatre companies in Molière's day had no 'director' in the modern sense and their rehearsal process was normally very brief. Indeed, the members of Molière's company would not see the complete play before it was performed, each actor receiving only the words that they were expected to learn. More important still, in seventeenth-century France 'classic' plays were not staged in the professional theatre. To people of that time, the classics meant the plays of ancient Greece and Rome; these were studied and sometimes performed in schools, but were only seen on the professional stage in adaptations by contemporary writers. When Molière wanted to perform the classic comedies of Plautus or Terence, he had no compunction about making them into something entirely new.[2] When twentieth-century theatre directors such as Copeau spoke of returning to the classics, they envisaged a different approach to 'making new': not rewriting their texts but rediscovering their underlying principles of staging and performance that had been lost over the years.

As Jonathan Miller has argued (1986), our concept of the 'classic' is a complex one, related to intellectual developments in Modernism. In his discussion of what makes a 'classic' today, Miller establishes parallels with the ways in which we relate to paintings by the old masters. Roger Planchon, a major contemporary French theatre director, also sees the similarities between the work of the *metteur en scène* and that of the art gallery curator:

> The emergence of the classic brings with it the birth of a dubious character. He presents himself as a museum curator; leaning on Molière and Shakespeare, he levers himself into a position where he is running the whole show. We may lament the fact, but the two things are linked: the birth of the classic gives power to the theatre director. In his hands the great theatres of the world become museums and justify their existence by producing *Oedipus*, *Hamlet*, or *The Miser*. A museum curator 'restores' works and puts them on show. And this is where the ambiguities begin.[3]

The ambiguities alluded to by Planchon stem from the co-existence of competing discourses: today the *mise en scène* of a classic play has not one but two authors. The first is the theatre director, who, through his *mise en scène*, develops his own authorial voice;[4] the other is the original author, that is, the one responsible for the text of the play. The best-known directors of the past century have established their reputations largely through productions of classic texts, in which Molière's works rival those of Shakespeare as the most performed. The resulting process, for the production of plays by Molière, is well summed up by Jim Carmody, when he evokes:

> a kind of aesthetic compromise between a three-hundred-year-old play and a specifically contemporary theatrical practice ... Enveloped in the new *mise en scène*, the familiar script takes on a new array of possible meanings, meanings that are directly generated by the juxtaposition of the familiar script and its traditional interpretations with a new scenography. The new *mise en scène* alters the contours of what we imagine we know by creating a fresh set of scenic images that recontextualises the well-known characters and dramatic events of the classic play ... The contemporary *mise en scène* of a classic play may, therefore, be seen as an event in which the past is confronted by the present, the already known becomes the unknown, established interpretations are overturned, and familiar cultural and moral values are contested.[5]

Carmody's book *Rereading Molière* explores in detail this process through which Molière has been recontextualised by succeeding generations of French directors over the past century. His contribution to this Cambridge Companion takes that argument one stage further, showing how the discourses of scholars, reviewers and theatre artists intersect and overlap to contribute to an ever-changing understanding of what is meant by the single word 'Molière'. He observes that, 'on those relatively rare occasions when a superbly gifted director creates a genuinely new way of staging a particular Molière play ... the resulting work of theatrical art is significant both in terms of its theatrical innovation and in terms of its innovative exploration of Molière'.[6] It is because a number of these 'gifted directors' *have* succeeded in innovating in this way, that it seems important to conclude this Companion with a discussion of some of them.

The person usually credited with revolutionising French theatre in the opening years of the twentieth century, inaugurating the idea of 'art' theatre, was Jacques Copeau. Copeau railed against the extravagance and superficiality of the commercial theatre of his day; in its place he proposed a return to *le tréteau nu* [the bare stage] and invoked the example of Molière to justify this departure from current practice. In order to illustrate and

justify his *essai de rénovation dramatique* [attempt at dramatic renewal], he
directed a number of productions of classic plays, achieving particular
success in his first season at the Théâtre du Vieux-Colombier with *L'Avare*
by Molière (November 1913) and *Twelfth Night* by Shakespeare (May
1914). Later, one of his most successful productions was *Les Fourberies de
Scapin* by Molière (November 1917 at the Garrick Theatre in New York
and April 1920 in Paris at the Vieux-Colombier). His production of *Scapin*
provided an interesting demonstration of his theory of the bare stage: its set
was a multi-level space, involving an open stage with a central raised
platform. Steps led up to the platform from all sides; in Michel Saint-Denis'
account, 'the actors played both on the platform and around it. The
younger actors could leap onto the platform with exuberant wildness, while
the older characters were obliged to climb the steps laboriously.'[7] All
accounts of this production stress its inventive use of movement, and its
debt to the *commedia dell'arte*. It clearly had similarities with experiments
in physical and acrobatic theatre that were being carried out by Meyerhold
in Russia at this time. The two major directors who were part of Copeau's
company before setting up their own, Charles Dullin and Louis Jouvet,
both continued his habit of seeing Molière as the touchstone of their art:
Jouvet's greatest success in his middle years was with *L'École des femmes*
and his last great hit was with *Dom Juan*; Dullin had one of his biggest
successes with *L'Avare*.

Building on the examples of Copeau, Dullin and Jouvet, the directors of
the decentralisation movement that followed the Second World War also
found in Molière a fertile ground for developing new approaches to *mise en
scène*. Jean Dasté fitted naturally into this pattern. Inspired by the experiences of Molière's company, which spent the years from 1646 to 1658
touring the provinces before their first Parisian success, and by the example
of Copeau, who left Paris for Burgundy in 1924, Dasté chose to perform to
audiences hitherto deprived of theatre in the towns around Saint-Étienne.
His company performed in the open air, or in the ubiquitous *salles des fêtes*
or other improvised spaces. Hardly a year went by without a new Molière
entering the repertoire of his company; his concern was to rediscover a
genuinely popular form that would appeal to the audiences of peasant and
working-class people unused to theatre productions. With this aim in mind,
he was one of the first to understand the value of the *comédies-ballets*.
His production of *Le Bourgeois gentilhomme* (first performed in 1950 and
then revived in a circus tent in 1958) included all the danced interludes
usually omitted, and he went on to direct *Le Malade imaginaire* in 1955
and *Monsieur de Pourceaugnac* in 1963. His work prefigures the bold
innovations of Jérôme Savary's *Bourgeois gentilhomme* in 1980.

Roger Planchon was one of the first theatre practitioners to develop a theory of the director as *auteur*. He coined the term *écriture scénique* [scenic writing] to denote his claim that it is the director's responsibility to develop a discourse (using the vocabularies of the stage) in parallel to the textual discourse of the playwright. In so doing, Planchon was following Brecht, who had promoted what he called *Historisierung*, which means putting the world of the play into historical context so that lessons may be learned about contemporary society by comparison with the peculiarities of a historically distanced society. Also like Brecht, Planchon did not seek to hide his *écriture scénique*, but jolted the audience into recognition that he was providing a recontextualisation of the classic text, encouraging them to see the familiar play in a new light and to reflect on its historical period. His method was to accumulate stage action which showed the way life was lived and the way the different social classes related to one another. In 1958, he set *George Dandin* in a realistic farmyard, and instead of following the rhythm of a farcical entertainment, he introduced a new rhythm: that of the working day. The action was played out against the background of the regular workaday activities of country life, none of which are explicitly present in Molière's text. This production was much admired by Bernard Dort, an influential theatre critic, who wrote that, beneath the farce of a cuckolded husband, Planchon had revealed the cruelly humorous story of a nouveau-riche peasant wanting to escape his class origins by marrying a well-born lady. Dort went on to say that 'the way is open for a new usage of the classics', a usage which, rather than focusing on the depiction of characters, displays their whole situation, both their material circumstances and their ideological condition. As a result Dandin's conflict represented, in Planchon's production, the error of the whole class of entrepreneurs who had allowed themselves to be fascinated by the myth of aristocratic superiority.[8]

In 1962, Planchon took a similar materialist approach to *Tartuffe*, using the settings, costumes and actions of his performers to build up a detailed evocation of a society in transition from feudalism to a modern nation state in which a growing bourgeois class presents a challenge to the King's attempt to construct a centralised monarchy. The authority of the church, Planchon suggests, was the device employed by Louis XIV to maintain control, and the 'directors of conscience' who served as private chaplains to wealthy families operated in ways that suggest comparison with the secret police in a twentieth-century dictatorship. Viewed in this context, Orgon's fascination for Tartuffe, and his willingness to sacrifice his family to him, becomes more sinister than comical. In order to add plausibility to the plot and distance it from the seeming ridiculously farcical, Planchon hinted at an unacknowledged homosexual attraction in Orgon's relationship with Tartuffe. A second production, in 1973, brought out this interpretation much more vividly and this production has been analysed in great detail by Carmody.[9] Through the productions of *George Dandin* and *Tartuffe*, we can thus see how Planchon developed his Marxist-inspired materialist *écriture scénique*. He also applied this method to other classics, notably Marivaux and Shakespeare. And it is striking that, although he was also writing and staging his own plays during this period, it was through the productions of Molière and other classic authors that he was most successful in developing and achieving recognition for his own, personal style as an *auteur*. When he made his first major film (in 1988), it was of *George Dandin*, thus confirming the centrality of Molière to the development of his own style as *auteur*, both on screen and on stage.

In 1973 Planchon's theatre in Villeurbanne, a working-class suburb outside Lyon, was dignified with the title of Théâtre National Populaire, under the joint directorship shared between him and Patrice Chéreau. Chéreau was to go on to become one of the most high-profile directors of the decade, with internationally acclaimed productions of Marivaux's *La Dispute* (1973) and Wagner's *Ring* cycle at Bayreuth (1976–80). Like Planchon, he had forged his artistic vision through productions of classic texts – by Shakespeare and Lenz among others – and these included an iconoclastic *Dom Juan* by Molière (1969), in which he had cut and rearranged much of the dialogue to suit his production idea. This was to present the parallels between Dom Juan's social situation, as a petty aristocrat frustrated by the outcome of La Fronde, and the situation of the Parisian intellectuals frustrated by the failure of the near-revolution of May 1968. Many other less well-known directors have turned to Molière to explore how to stage a provocative contemporary message. Daniel Benoin, for example, in 1977 produced *George Dandin* in modern dress (mostly bathing costumes) around a swimming pool with an introductory 'voice-over' explaining that the characters are all at the 'Club Molière: Le club est là pour enrichir votre culture' ['The club is here to enrich your culture'].[10] The play's satire of social climbing was all played out in the context of the social mores of the 1970s.

Antoine Vitez, generally recognised as an influential innovator in French theatre of the late twentieth century, also defined his authorial 'voice' through productions of classic texts more than through contemporary ones. His staging in 1978 of four plays by Molière, treated as a tetralogy, is one of the 'landmarks' referred to by Carmody in his essay. The plays were *L'École des femmes*, *Le Tartuffe*, *Dom Juan* and *Le Misanthrope* and they were first presented at the Avignon Festival in July 1978. Rejecting the sociological-historical style of performance illustrated by Planchon, Vitez's production was a self-consciously theatrical exploration of Molière in which 'the theatre itself is the real subject'.[11] Rather than asking his audience to focus on historical or political realities through the production, Vitez invited them to set aside their normal expectations and to view the plays as fundamentally foreign to us, and rather frightening. The four plays were given on successive evenings on the same stage set, and the same twelve actors shared out the roles between them. All were young and athletic, and the performance was almost acrobatic at times. There was no attempt at verisimilitude in the imitation of real life, whether of 1978 or of Paris in the 1660s. The characters wore costumes of the 1660s, but their behaviour was out of keeping with their costumes, whose stiff formality only served to emphasise the acrobatic acting style – indeed the elaborate lace and ribbon frills were often damaged in the course of performance.

The effect was of a number of overlapping images or discourses which obstinately refused to resolve into a unified perspective. Every opportunity was taken to introduce a new level of play. For example, the frequent narrative passages were acted out as if they were a play within the play, and Michel Corvin suggested that 'we might say here that Vitez was using the methods of a cubist painter, simultaneously showing all aspects of the *jeu* in a spatio-temporal shortcut'.[12] Vitez was interested, as many before him, in the primitive farce structures that he felt underlay all Molière's comedy. But this was not because he wanted to reduce the comedies to the status of farce; rather, he wanted to jolt the audience out of its sense of recognising familiar stories or conventions of representation, and to liberate the playful anarchy of theatre from the conventions of realistic story-telling. He was convinced that the biomechanical experiments of Meyerhold offered a way forward for the theatre of his day. He included moments in the performance when the characters' relations to one another were expressed through physical manipulation: for example, a male character would simply pick one of the female characters up and tuck her under his arm, like a piece of property, or again, in *L'École des femmes*, Horace, escaping from the house, landed on Arnolphe's shoulders, and Arnolphe walked around carrying this burden for the space of several speeches. Carmody cites Vitez explaining the importance that Meyerhold had for him:

For Meyerhold, realism itself has nothing to do with the real; it is but one of the conventions, one of the codes that allows us to translate the real. The essence of Meyerhold's thought is that there is no such thing as a 'normal' *jeu*, that there are only various kinds of *jeu* ... Meyerhold tells us that *vraisem-blance* itself is nothing more than one kind of *jeu*, one kind of simulacrum.[13]

Through their work on Molière, Vitez and his actors were thus developing new experimental approaches to the arts of acting and theatrical representation. Their reading of the plays was essentially tragic, as in each of the four plays, 'the marginal hero, a kind of exalted fool, attempts to live out an impossible passion in a rigidly structured and passionless society'.[14] The disjointed, violent, erotic images of the performances pointed to a bleak, cruel world of rigid hierarchies, especially between the sexes. But rather than simply offering this reading as a résumé of Molière's worldview, the production entailed a reflection on the means available to theatre as a whole at the end of the twentieth century. It represented, in Carmody's words, 'a collage of post-Absurdist, post-Existentialist *farce tragique* and highly self-conscious postrealist scenography'.[15] Vitez pursued this kind of research through productions of other classic plays throughout his career as director and teacher and achieved notable successes with productions of Sophocles, Racine, Hugo and Claudel, but his Molière 'tetralogy' represented a high point in this process.

Directors, however creative, can achieve nothing until they persuade a company of actors to share their vision. In the years immediately following 1968, when all established hierarchies in French life were called into question, the right of the director to control all aspects of the creative process was challenged, and a number of companies adopted collective devising methods know as *la création collective*. These companies looked to the history and traditions of the performer rather than to those of the writer or director for inspiration. They found in the *commedia dell'arte* an especially fruitful resource because of its emphasis on masked acting and on what Jacques Lecoq termed the 'poetic body'.[16] Lecoq had set up a theatre school in 1956, with a curriculum that was original for the period in giving a large place to physical training, mime and mask. Many leading contemporary performers experienced the influence of Lecoq, either by attending the school, or by working with its graduates. He taught that the actor needs to develop a physically expressive style of performance which can range across tragedy, comedy, melodrama or grotesque farce as required. This principle of flexibility and *disponibilité* was foreign to most actor-training in France at the time and opened up new ways of thinking about performance, not dissimilar to the ideas of Vitez that we have just been examining.[17]

An outstanding example of an innovator who attended the Lecoq School is Ariane Mnouchkine, director of the Théâtre du Soleil since 1964. This company came to prominence in the early 1970s with a series of remarkable *créations collectives*, after which they went on to make a film about Molière, the purpose of which was to explore the creative life of a theatre company and to assess the various ways in which theatre can reflect on the society of its time.[18] The Molière film demonstrated the extent to which the company's working methods were inspired by Molière and the *commedia*, but it was not until 1995 that Mnouchkine first directed a play by Molière: *Le Tartuffe*. Though very different from the productions by Planchon or Vitez, the production by the Théâtre du Soleil provides another example of an experimental approach to staging and performance expressed through the production of a play by Molière.

The originality of Mnouchkine's method lay both in her improvisatory, collective system of rehearsal and also in the depiction of the world in which the action of the play takes place. Through the use of settings, costumes, movements and music, the production made it clear that the family of Orgon was to be seen as inhabiting an Islamic culture. The religious zealotry used by Tartuffe as a cover for his criminal designs was located within the context of Islamic fundamentalism and the production was dedicated to Cheb Hasni, an Algerian *Rai* singer murdered by extremists. Mnouchkine's reading of the play explored the politics of the family, showing how religious belief systems of any kind, when manipulated by unscrupulous men, can become aggressive instruments in asserting tyranny, especially the tyranny of men over women and of fathers over families. For her, as for other directors we have looked at, Molière's drama offered the chance to experiment in new directions, both theatrically and politically. The alternation between classic and modern plays was part of her 'repeated rhythm of exploring forms from other times and places as a pedagogic *reculer pour mieux sauter*, a way forward into representing contemporary histories with critical distance'.[19]

A very different approach to Molière's comedy was taken by Jérôme Savary and his company Le Grand Magic Circus, who scored a huge success with a production of *Le Bourgeois gentilhomme*, first performed in 1981 and revived several times throughout the following two decades. Le Grand Magic Circus was a company that emerged from the upheavals of 1968 as a counter-cultural group performing collectively devised shows which drew on the traditions of clowning, acrobatics and street performance. They self-consciously adopted the techniques of popular theatre, which tends to oppose the single-minded seriousness of 'high' culture by including a great variety of different styles of performance in the same show and by the use of musical interludes, song and dance routines, clowning and feats of skill or strength.[20] All of these were present in the performances of Le Grand Magic Circus, which took a broad satirical approach to well-known, myths or stories, such as their *Robinson Crusoe* (1972). *Le Bourgeois gentilhomme* was the first play from the repertoire that the company had attempted, and their unusual approach helped breathe new life into the form of the *comédie-ballet*, by making the play's interludes as significant as its dialogue scenes.

In their production the play was prefaced by the arrival of a group of street performers (dancers, jugglers, etc.) in front of M. Jourdain's elegant town house. As the action unfolded, these performers used a variety of tricks to invade the domestic interior. Their gags were sufficiently comic and their dance routines sufficiently dazzling for the audience to be delighted every time they interrupted the action, and this process culminated in the play's concluding 'mamamouchi' ceremony, which thus became a celebration of the triumph of popular culture over high culture. Jérôme Savary played the role of M. Jourdain, as well as directing the production; his interpretation presented Jourdain not as a fool, but as an ignorant man with a genuine thirst for knowledge. The succession of self-important teachers who try to exploit him come to represent the failure of high culture, and the triumph of the street players the vigour and appeal of low culture. The production divided the critics, some of whom were shocked by what they saw as the overthrowing of the classical Molière by the tradition of 'les bonimenteurs du Pont-Neuf et les turlupins de tréteaux' ['the stand-up comics of the Pont Neuf and fair-ground stages'];[21] others were persuaded by the wittiness of his interpretation: one wrote that 'Savary a réalisé ce miracle d'être, dans l'irrespect – un irrespect fraternel –, d'une fidélité sidérante à Molière' ['The miracle Savary has achieved is to be staggeringly faithful to Molière while maintaining a fraternal disrespect'].[22] Through this production, Savary and his company found the way to reconcile their own original brand of anarchic humour with the demands of the classic repertoire.

The company-centred approach to performance, with an emphasis on multi-skilled performers, effervescent use of music, dance and spectacle, has helped to reveal a new Molière, not amenable to being summed up in school textbooks: an impudent Molière of joyful celebration, who borrows the broad social satire and comic lazzi of the *commedia dell'arte*, using them to celebrate the victory of young love over old jealousy. It is fitting that the oldest theatre company in the world, the Comédie-Française, should have invited one of the most avant-garde performers of recent times, Dario Fo, to direct a production of Molière's *Le Médecin volant*. Fo is known for his left-wing politics, his irreverent challenge to all forms of authority and his innovative performance work drawing on the traditions of *commedia* and the medieval *giullare* or travelling jesters. The Comédie-Française has seldom placed itself in the forefront of theatrical experiment and has too often seen its role as essentially conservative. But in this case, with the 1990 production analysed by Steve Knapper in his essay in this Companion, it demonstrated the extraordinary opportunities Molière's plays offer to anyone seeking to explore experimental approaches to acting. The invitation to Fo came partly at the instigation of Antoine Vitez, then Administrateur Général, who also commissioned a short play on Molière from the leading contemporary dramatist Michel Vinaver. Destined to be performed at the annual Molière celebrations by the company, *Le Dernier Sursaut* is a witty skit on contemporary attitudes, both cultural and political, questioning the role of Molière as repository of French classical values and chief French cultural export to the world.

Other, much smaller, companies working in the same spirit have had similar experiences. The Footsbarn Theatre, for example, a small travelling company composed of actors who met at the Lecoq school, have been accused of irreverence. After a production of *Romeo and Juliet* making much use of clown routines, a member of their audience told them they could do what they liked with Shakespeare, but they should keep off Molière ('ne touchez pas à Molière').[23] The company adopted this phrase as the title of their following show, a triple bill of *Le Médecin malgré lui*, *Le Sicilien ou l'amour peintre* and *Le Mariage forcé*. Making use of tightrope

18. Footsbarn Theatre's production of *Ne Touchez pas à Molière* on the village square at La Bourboule, 1997, Jean Pierre Estournet.

19. Footsbarn Theatre's production of *Ne Touchez pas à Molière*, 1997, Jean Pierre Estournet.

artists, stilt walkers, marionettes and outsize phalluses, this production, in 1996, placed Molière firmly in the tradition of street performance. When the Footsbarn went on to perform *Dom Juan* in similar style in 1998, the critics complained that this approach was all very well for Molière's more farcical output, but that the major plays should be treated with more respect. Or, as the *sociétaires* of the Comédie-Française put it in Vinaver's satirical play, '*Touchez pas à mon Molière*'.[24]

This protective attitude towards Molière is borne out by the fact that the vast majority of modern productions of Molière, however bold and playful their theatrical devices, have shown scrupulous respect for the texts. Here is a striking paradox in the afterlife of Molière's works: whereas the seventeenth-century playwrights had protested reverence for their classic models, while using them in whatever way they wanted, the productions of post-Brechtian revolutionary directors, seeking to give immediacy and contemporary relevance to these plays, have not tampered with the texts.

Molière continues to provide a stimulus to new work in the theatre, and his plays have played a pivotal role in the major experimental movements of the period since the early twentieth century. The creative life of Molière's company remains an inspiration and a model to emulate for many of the most exciting new actors and directors in today's theatre, even if the ways of understanding and contextualising that creative life change from decade to decade. Each one of the chapters in this Companion has contributed, in one way or another, to building up a composite picture of the many reasons why the life and work of the man dismissed in his time as *le premier farceur de la France* should continue to have such resonance for us today.

NOTES

1 The reader is referred to the section of the bibliography on Directors and *mise en scène*.
2 This practice was even more common among tragic dramatists: see the large number of tragedies on classical themes by Racine and Corneille, the best known of all, perhaps, being Racine's *Phèdre*, a very free adaptation of Euripides' *Hippolytus*.
3 Roger Planchon, Preface to Molière. *L'Avare* (Paris: Livre de Poche, 1980), p. 7.
4 So, for example, commentators will often refer to 'Brook's *Hamlet*' or to 'Mnouchkine's *Tartuffe*'.
5 Jim Carmody, *Rereading Molière: Mise en Scène from Antoine to Vitez* (Ann Arbor: University of Michigan Press, 1993), pp. 14–15.
6 See p. 191 above.
7 Quoted in John Rudlin, *Jacques Copeau* (Cambridge: Cambridge University Press, 1986), p. 73.
8 See Bernard Dort, '*Dandin* en situation' in Bernard Dort, *Théâtre Public* (Paris: Seuil, 1967), 30–3, p. 33.
9 Carmody, *Rereading Molière*, pp. 55–87.
10 Quoted in Michel Corvin, *Molière et ses metteurs en scène d'aujourd'hui: Pour une analyse de la representation* (Lyon: Presses Universitaires de Lyon, 1985), p. 63.
11 Carmody, *Rereading Molière*, p. 141.
12 Corvin, *Molière et ses metteurs en scène*, p. 235. Corvin's is the most detailed published analysis of the Vitez tetralogy (pp. 189–249). Jim Carmody devotes twenty lucid pages to it in *Rereading Molière*, pp. 139–59; he also quotes this passage from Corvin on p. 147.
13 Carmody, *Rereading Molière*, pp. 151–2.
14 Judith Graves Miller, 'Vitez's Molière', *Theater*, 11, 3 (1980), 74–81, p. 74.
15 Carmody, *Rereading Molière*, p. 149.
16 Jacques Lecoq, *Le Corps poétique* (Arles: Actes du Sud, 1997); trans. David Bradby as *The Moving Body* (rev. edn, London: Methuen, 2002).
17 Vitez taught at the École Jacques Lecoq from 1965 to 1969 before going on to teach at the Conservatoire.
18 The film, entitled *Molière, ou la vie d'un honnête homme*, was first released in 1978. A remastered version entitled simply *Molière* was released on DVD by Belair classiques in December 2004.
19 David Williams, *Collaborative Theatre: The Théâtre du Soleil Sourcebook* (London: Routledge, 1999), p. xiii.
20 See John McGrath, *A Good Night Out: Popular Theatre: Audience, Class and Form* (London: Methuen, 1981; rev. edns 1984 and London: Nick Hern Books, 1996).

21 Pierre Marcabru, 'Le Bourgeois gentilhomme: Une énorme bouffonnerie', Le Figaro, 7 December 1981. Marcabru is referring to the farcical street performers of Molière's day who performed on the Pont Neuf.
22 Gilles Sandier, 'Le Bourgeois gentilhomme par le Grand Magic Circus: Un fantastique délire bouffon', Le Matin, 14 December 1981.
23 See Jean-Louis Perrier, 'Ne touchez pas à Molière', Le Monde, 14 September 1996.
24 Michel Vinaver, Le Dernier Sursaut (Arles: Actes Sud, 1990), p. 19. The phrase is a play on the slogan of the anti-racist movement of that time: 'Touchez pas à mon pote' ('Hands off my pal').

SELECT BIBLIOGRAPHY

This is a small selection from the huge volume of work on Molière. It includes brief sections on *mise en scène* and on *comédies-ballets*. For the many books and articles not listed here, readers are referred to the Molière bibliography on Gabriel Conesa's website (www.toutmoliere.net), where around 5,000 items are listed.

Editions

Œuvres, ed. Eugène Despois and Paul Mesnard, 13 vols. and album (Paris: Collection des Grands Écrivains, 1873–1900).
Œuvres complètes, ed. Georges Couton, 2 vols. (Paris: Gallimard, 1971).
Œuvres complètes, 2 vols., ed. Robert Jouanny (Paris: Garnier frères, 1962).

Bibliographies and documents

Gaines, James (ed.), *The Molière Encyclopedia* (Westport: Greenwood Press, 2003).
Grente, Cardinal Georges (ed.), *Dictionnaire des Lettres françaises. Le XVIIe siècle* (1951), revised Patrick Dandrey et al. (Paris: Fayard, 1996).
Guibert, A. J., *Bibliographie des œuvres de Molière publiées au XVIIe siècle*, 2 vols. (Paris: Centre National de la Recherche Scientifique, 1962, supplement 1977).
Jurgens, M. and E. Maxfield-Miller, *Cent ans de recherches sur Molière, sur sa famille et sur les comédiens de sa troupe* (Paris: Imprimerie Nationale, 1963).
Mongrédien, Georges, *Recueil des textes et des documents du XVIIe siècle relatifs à Molière*, 2 vols. (Paris: Centre National de la Recherche Scientifique, 1965).
Romero, Laurence, *Molière: Traditions in Criticism, 1900–1970* (Chapel Hill, NC: Studies in Romance Languages and Literature, 1974).
Saintonge, P. and R. W. Christ, *Fifty Years of Molière Studies: A Bibliography, 1892–1941* (Baltimore, MD: Les Belles Lettres, 1942).
Saintonge, P., 'Thirty Years of Molière Studies, 1942–1971', in R. Johnson et al. (eds.), *Molière and the Commonwealth of Letters* (Jackson, MS: University Press of Mississippi, 1975).
Young B. E. and G. P. Young (eds.), *Le Registre de La Grange, 1659–85*, 2 vols. (Paris: Droz, 1948).

Directors and *mise en scène*

Bablet, Denis, *La Mise en scène contemporaine I: 1887–1914* (Brussels: La Renaissance du Livre, 1968).

Les Révolutions scéniques au vingtième siècle (Paris: Société internationale d'art XXe siècle, 1975).

Benhamou, Anne et al., *Antoine Vitez: toutes les mises en scène* (Paris: Godefroy, 1981).

Bibliothèque Nationale, *Don Juan. Catalogue de l'exposition du 25 avril–5 juillet 1991* (Paris: Bibliothèque Nationale, 1991).

Bradby, David and David Williams, *Directors' Theatre* (Basingstoke: Macmillan, 1988).

Braun, Edward, *The Director and the Stage* (London: Methuen, 1982).

Brooks, William, '*Intervalles, Entractes* and *Intermèdes* in the Paris Theatre', *Seventeenth-Century French Studies*, 24 (2002), 107–26.

Carlson, Marvin, *The French Stage in the Nineteenth Century* (Metuchen, NJ: Scarecrow Press, 1972).

Carmody, Jim, *Rereading Molière: Mise en Scène from Antoine to Vitez* (Ann Arbor: University of Michigan Press, 1993).

Clarke, Jan, 'Les Théâtres de Molière à Paris', *Le Nouveau Moliériste*, 2 (1995), 247–72.

The Guénégaud Theatre in Paris (1673–1680), vol. I: *Founding, Design and Production* (Lewiston, NY, Queenston and Lampeter: The Edwin Mellen Press, 1998).

'Illuminating the Guénégaud Stage: Some Seventeenth-Century Lighting Effects', *French Studies*, 53 (1999), 1–15.

Corvin, Michel, *Molière et ses metteurs en scène d'aujourd'hui: Pour une analyse de la représentation* (Lyon: Presses Universitaires de Lyon, 1985).

Daoust, Yvette, *Roger Planchon: Director and Playwright* (Cambridge: Cambridge University Press, 1981).

Dasté, Jean, *Voyage d'un comédien* (Paris: Stock, 1977).

Degaine, André, *Histoire du théâtre dessinée* (Paris: Nizet, 1992).

Deierkauf-Holsboer, S. Wilma, *Le Théâtre du Marais*, 2 vols. (Paris: Nizet, 1954–8).

Delgado, Maria M. and Paul Heritage (eds.), *In Contact with the Gods: Directors Talk Theatre* (Manchester: Manchester University Press, 1996).

Delmas, Christian, 'Sur un décor de *Dom Juan* (III, 5)', *Littératures classiques*, 5 (1983), 45–73.

'*Dom Juan* et le théâtre à machines', *Littératures classiques*, 6 (1984), 125–38.

Descotes, Maurice, *Les Grands Rôles du théâtre de Molière* (Paris: Presses Universitaires de France, 1960).

Dhomme, Sylvain, *La Mise en scène contemporaine d'André Antoine à Bertolt Brecht* (Paris: Nathan, 1959).

Dock, Stephen Varick, *Costume and Fashion in the Plays of J.-B. Poquelin Molière. A Seventeenth-Century Perspective* (Geneva: Slatkine, 1992).

Dusigne, Jean-François, *Le Théâtre d'Art. Aventure européenne du XXe siècle* (Paris: Éditions Théâtrales, 1997).

L'Ère de la mise en scène, *Théâtre Aujourd'hui*, 10 (Paris: Centre National de Documentation Pédagogique, 2005). Contains a detailed analysis of nine productions of *Le Tartuffe*.

Geray, Christine and Christiane Judenne, *Molière, Dom Juan* (Paris: Hatier, 1985).
Green, Amy S., *The Revisionist Stage: American Directors Reinvent the Classics* (New York: Cambridge University Press, 1994).
Herzel, Roger, 'The Décor of Molière's Stage: The Testimony of Brissart and Chauveau', *PMLA*, 93 (1978), 925–54.
'Le Jeu "naturel" de Molière et de sa troupe', *XVIIe siècle*, 132 (1981), 279–83.
The Original Casting of Molière's Plays (Ann Arbor: University of Michigan Press, 1981).
'The Scenery for the Original Production of *Dom Juan*', in David Trott and Nicole Boursier (eds.), *The Age of Theater in France* (Edmonton, Alberta: Edmonton Academic, 1988), 247–55.
Hilgar, Marie-France, *Onze mises en scène parisiennes du théâtre de Molière (1989–1994)* (Tübingen: Biblio 17, 1997).
Jomaron, Jacqueline, *La Mise en scène contemporaine II, 1914–1940* (Brussels: La Renaissance du Livre, 1981).
(ed.), *Le Théâtre en France*, 2 vols. (Paris: Armand Colin, 1989).
Jouvet, Louis, *Molière et la comédie classique* (Paris: Gallimard, 1965).
Lecoq, Jacques, *Le Corps poétique* (Arles: Actes Sud, 1997); trans. David Bradby as *The Moving Body* (rev. edn, London: Methuen, 2002).
Lough, John, *Paris Theatre Audiences in the Seventeenth and Eighteenth Centuries* (Oxford: Oxford University Press, 1957).
McCarthy, Gerry, *The Theatres of Molière* (London and New York: Routledge, 2002).
McGrath, John, *A Good Night Out: Popular Theatre: Audience, Class and Form* (London: Methuen, 1981; rev. edns 1984 and London: Nick Hern Books, 1996).
Miller, Jonathan, *Subsequent Performances* (London: Faber, 1986).
Miller, Judith Graves, 'Vitez's Molière', *Theater*, 11, 3 (1980), 74–81.
Naugrette, Catherine, *L'Esthétique théâtrale* (Paris: Nathan, 2000).
Obliques, 4 (1974?): special 'Don Juan' issue.
Peacock, Noël, *Molière in Scotland* (Glasgow: University of Glasgow French and German Publications, 1993).
Planchon, Roger, Preface to Molière, *L'Avare* (Paris: Livre de Poche, 1980).
Prest, Julia, 'The Problem of Praise and the First Prologue to *Le Malade imaginaire*', *Seventeenth-Century French Studies*, 23 (2001), 139–49.
Reinelt, Janelle and Joseph Roach (eds.), *Critical Theory and Performance* (Ann Arbor: University of Michigan Press, 1992).
Roubine, Jean-Jacques, *Théâtre et mise en scène, 1880–1980* (Paris: Presses Universitaires de France, 1980).
Rudlin, John, *Jacques Copeau* (Cambridge: Cambridge University Press, 1986).
Scherer, Jacques, *La Dramaturgie classique en France* (Paris: Nizet, 1950; new edn 2001).
Taylor, Samuel S., 'Le Geste chez les "Maîtres italiens de Molière"', *XVIIe siècle*, 132 (1981), 285–301.
Trott, David and Nicole Boursier (eds.), *The Age of Theater in France* (Edmonton, Alberta: Edmonton Academic, 1988).
Ubersfeld, Anne, *Antoine Vitez, metteur en scène et poète* (Paris: Éditions des Quatre-Vents, 1994).

Vitez, Antoine, *Le Théâtre des idées* (Paris: Gallimard, 1991).
Écrits sur le théâtre, 4 vols. (Paris: POL, 1994–8).
Whitton, David, *Stage Directors in Modern France* (Manchester: Manchester University Press, 1987).
Don Juan (Cambridge: Cambridge University Press, 1995).
Wilk, John R., *The Creation of an Ensemble: The First Years of the American Conservatory Theatre* (Carbondale: Southern Illinois University Press, 1986).
Williams, David, *Collaborative Theatre: The Théâtre du Soleil Sourcebook* (London: Routledge, 1999).

Comédies-ballets

For further material on music and *comédie-ballet*, see the bibliographies in Charles Mazouer, *Molière et ses comédies-ballets*, pp. 238–58, and John S. Powell, *Music and Theatre in France, 1600–1680*, pp. 539–58.
Abraham, Claude, *On the Structure of Molière's Comédies-Ballets* (Paris, Seattle, Tübingen: Biblio 17, 1984).
Apostolidès, Jean-Marie, *Le Roi-machine: spectacle et politique au temps de Louis XIV* (Paris: Minuit, 1981).
Auld, Louis E., 'Une rivalité sournoise: Molière contre Pierre Perrin', in Volker Kapp (ed.), *Le Bourgeois gentilhomme: Problèmes de la comédie-ballet* (Paris, Seattle, Tübingen: Biblio 17, 1995), 123–37.
Barnwell, H. T., *Molière: Le Malade imaginaire* (London: Grant and Cutler, 1982).
Canova-Green, Marie-Claude, *La Politique-spectacle au grand siècle: les rapports franco-anglais* (Paris, Seattle, Tübingen: Biblio 17, 1993).
(ed.), *Benserade: Ballets pour Louis XIV*, 2 vols. (Toulouse: Société de Littérature Classique, 1997).
Charpentier, Marc-Antoine, *Music for Molière's Comedies*, ed. John Powell (Madison: A-R Editions, 1990).
Christout, Marie-France, *Le Ballet occidental. Naissance et métamorphoses, XVIe–XXe siècle* (Paris: Desjonquères, 1995).
Couvreur, Manuel, *Jean-Baptiste Lully, musique et dramaturgie au service du Prince* (Brussels: M. Vokar, 1992).
Durosoir, Georgie, *Les Ballets de la cour de France. Les fantaisies et les splendeurs du Baroque* (Geneva: Éditions Papillon, 2004).
Fleck, Stephen H., *Music, Dance and Laughter. Comic Creation in Molière's Comedy-Ballets* (Tübingen: Biblio 17, 1995).
Franco, Marek, *Dance as Text: Ideologies of the Baroque Body* (Cambridge: Cambridge University Press, 1993).
Hilgar, Marie-France, *Onze mises en scène parisiennes du théâtre de Molière (1989–1994)* (Tübingen: Biblio 17, 1997).
Kapp, Volker (ed.), *Le Bourgeois gentilhomme: problèmes de la comédie-ballet* (Paris, Seattle, Tübingen: Biblio 17, 1991).
La Gorce, Jérôme de, *L'Opéra à Paris au temps du théâtre de Molière (1989–1994)* (Paris: Desjonquères, 1992).
Jean-Baptiste Lully (Paris: Fayard, 2002).
Lully, Jean-Baptiste, *Œuvres complètes*, ed. Henry Prunières (New York: Broude Brothers, 1966–72).

Œuvres complètes (new edn, Hildesheim: Olms, 2001–)

Mazouer, Charles, *Molière et ses comédies-ballets* (Paris: Klincksieck, 1993).

and Martine Mazouer, *Étude sur Molière: 'Le Bourgeois gentilhomme'* (Paris: Ellipses Édition Marketing, 1999).

Powell, John S., *Music and Theatre in France, 1600–1680* (Oxford: Oxford University Press, 2000).

Rubin, David Lee (ed.), *Sun King. Ascendancy of French Culture during the Reign of Louis XIV* (Washington, London, Toronto: Folger Books, 1992).

Schneider, Herbert, 'Zu den Fassungen und musikalischen Quellen des *Bourgeois gentilhomme* von J.-B. Lully', *Quellenstudien zu Jean-Baptiste Lully / L'Œuvre de Lully: Études des sources*, actes publiés par J. de La Gorce et H. Schneider (Hildesheim: Georg Olms Verlag, 1999), 175–99.

Serroy, Jean, 'Aux sources de la comédie-ballet moliéresque. Structure des Fâcheux', *Recherches et Travaux*, Université de Grenoble III, 39 (1990), 45–52.

Thoinan, Ernest, *Les Origines de l'Opéra français* (Paris, 1866).

Weiss, Allen S., *Miroirs de l'infini. Le Jardin à la française et la métaphysique au XVIIe siècle* (Paris: Seuil, 1992).

Whaples, Miriam K., 'Early Exoticism Revisited', in Jonathan Bellman (ed.), *The Exotic in Western Music* (Boston: Northeastern University Press, 1998), 3–25.

Discography

Charpentier, Marc-Antoine, *Le Malade imaginaire*, Les Arts Florissants, William Christie (Harmonia Mundi, 1990).

Le Malade imaginaire, Les Musiciens du Louvre, Marc Minkowski (Erato, 1990).

Les Fous divertissants (Raymond Poisson) and *Le Mariage forcé* (Molière), New Chamber Opera/Band of Instruments, Gary Cooper (ASV Living Era, 1997).

Lully, Jean-Baptiste, *Les Comédies-ballets. Phaëton*, Les Musiciens du Louvre, Marc Minkowski (Erato, 1999).

Lully ou le musicien du Soleil, vol. 4: *Le Bourgeois gentilhomme*, La Symphonie du Marais, Hugo Reyne (Accord, 2002).

Critical works

Adam, Antoine, *Histoire de la littérature française*, 5 vols. (Paris: Domat, 1948–56), vol. III: *L'Apogée du siècle* (1952).

Albanese, Ralph, Jr, *Le Dynamisme de la peur chez Molière: une analyse socio-culturelle de Dom Juan, Tartuffe et L'École des femmes* (University, MS: Romance Monographs, 1976).

'Images de la femme dans le discours scolaire républicain (1880–1914)', *French Review*, 62 (1989), 740–8.

Molière à l'École républicaine. De la critique universitaire aux manuels scolaires (1870–1914) (Saratoga, CA: Anma Libri, 1992).

Aubignac, Abbé d', *Dissertation sur la condamnation des théâtres* (Paris, 1666).

Baader, Renate, *Molière* (Darmstadt: Wissenschaftliche Buchgesellschaft, 1980).

Bénichou, Paul, *Morales du grand siècle* (Paris: Gallimard, 1948).

Bergson, Henri, *Le Rire* (Paris: Presses Universitaires de France, 1940) (originally *Revue de Paris*, 1899).

Bloch, Olivier, *Molière/Philosophie* (Paris: Albin Michel, 2000).

Borgerhoff, E.B.O., *The Freedom of French Classicism* (Princeton, NJ: Princeton University Press, 1950).

Bourqui, Claude, *La Commedia dell'arte* (Paris: SEDES, 1999).

  Les Sources de Molière (Paris: SEDES, 1999).

Bray, René, *Molière, homme de théâtre* (Paris: Mercure de France, 1954).

Brody, Jules, *Lectures classiques* (Charlottesville: Rookwood Press, 1996).

Cairncross, John, *Molière, bourgeois et libertin* (Paris: Nizet, 1963).

Calder, Andrew, *Molière: The Theory and Practice of Comedy* (London and Atlantic Highlands, NJ: Athlone Press, 1993).

  'From Epic and Tragic to Comic and Satiric: Reversed Perspectives in Painting and Writing from the Renaissance to the Seventeenth Century', *Seventeenth-Century French Studies*, 21 (1999), 261–75.

  'On humour and wit in Molière's *Le Misanthrope* and Congreve's *The Way of the World*', in Sarah Alyn Stacey and Véronique Desnain (eds.), *Culture and Conflict in Seventeenth-Century France and Ireland* (Dublin: Four Courts Press, 2004), 151–62.

Calder, Ruth, 'Molière, Misanthropy and Forbearance: Éliante's "Lucretian" Diatribe', *French Studies*, 50, 2 (1996), 138–43.

Caldicott, C. E. J., *La Carrière de Molière entre protecteurs et éditeurs* (Amsterdam and Atlanta: Rodopi, 1998).

Chasseguet-Smirgel, Janine, *Sexuality and the Mind: The Role of the Father and the Mother in the Psyche* (New York: New York University Press, 1986).

Collinet, Jean-Pierre, *Lectures de Molière* (Paris: Colin, 1974).

Conesa, Gabriel, *Le Dialogue moliéresque: étude stylistique et dramaturgique* (Paris: Presses Universitaires de France, 1992).

  La Comédie à l'âge classique (Paris: Seuil, 1995).

Dandrey, Patrick, *Molière ou l'esthétique du ridicule* (Paris: Klincksieck, 1992).

  Dom Juan ou la critique de la raison comique (Paris: Champion, 1993).

  La Médecine et la maladie dans le théâtre de Molière, 2 vols. (Paris: Klincksieck, 1998).

Defaux, Gérard, *Molière, ou les métamorphoses du comique: de la comédie morale au triomphe de la folie* (Lexington, KY: French Forum, 1980).

Descotes, Maurice, *Molière et sa fortune littéraire* (Bordeaux: Éditions Ducros, 1970).

Dosmond, S., '*Les Femmes savantes*: Comédie ou drame bourgeois?', *L'Information littéraire*, 44 (1992), 12–22.

Doubrovsky, Serge, 'Arnolphe, ou la chute du héros', *Mercure de France*, 343 (1961), 111–18.

Duchêne, Roger, *Molière* (Paris: Fayard, 1998).

Elias, Norbert, *The Civilising Process*, trans. Edmund Jephcott (Oxford: Blackwell, 1994).

Emelina, Jean, *Les Valets et les servantes dans le théâtre comique en France de 1610 à 1700* (Aix-en-Provence: La Pensée Universitaire, 1958).

  (ed.), *Actes de la première 'Biennale Molière'* (2001) (Ville de Pézenas, 2003).

and Gabriel Conesa (eds.), *Actes de la 2ème biennale internationale de Pézenas* (2003) (Pézenas: Édition Domens, 2005).

Eustis, Alvin, *Molière as Ironic Contemplator* (The Hague and Paris: Mouton, 1973).

Fernandez, Ramon, *La Vie de Molière* (Paris: Gallimard, 1929); reprinted as *Molière ou l'essence du génie comique* (Paris: Grasset, 1979).

Forestier, Georges, *Molière en toutes lettres* (Paris: Bordas, 1990).

Gaillard, P., *Les Précieuses ridicules et Les Femmes savantes* (Paris: Hatier, 1978).

Gaines, James F., 'Ménage versus Salon in *Les Femmes savantes*', *L'Esprit Créateur*, 21 (1981), 51–9.

Social Structures in Molière's Theatre (Columbus: Ohio State University Press, 1984).

and Michael S. Koppish, *Approaches to Teaching Molière's 'Tartuffe' and Other Plays* (New York: MLA, 1995).

Gallop, Jane, *Thinking Through the Body* (New York: Columbia University Press, 1988).

Gilot, Michel and Jean Serroy, *La Comédie à l'âge classique* (Paris: Belin, 1997).

Gossman, Lionel, *Men and Masks. A Study of Molière* (Baltimore, MD: Johns Hopkins Press, 1963).

Greenberg, Mitchell, *Corneille, Classicism, and the Rules of Symmetry* (Cambridge: Cambridge University Press, 1986).

Grimarest, Jean, *La Vie de Monsieur de Molière* (1705), ed. Georges Mongrédien (Paris: M. Brient, 1955).

Gross, Nathan, *From Gesture to Idea: Esthetics and Ethics in Molière's Comedy* (New York: Columbia University Press, 1982).

Guicharnaud, Jacques, *Molière, une aventure théâtrale* (Paris: Gallimard, 1963).

Guichemerre, Roger, *La Comédie avant Molière, 1640–1660* (Paris: Armand Colin, 1972).

Gutwirth, Marcel, *Molière ou l'invention comique* (Paris: Minard, 1966).

Hall, H. Gaston, *Comedy in Context: Essays on Molière* (Jackson: University Press of Mississippi, 1984).

Horville, Robert, *Dom Juan de Molière: Une dramaturgie de rupture* (Paris: Larousse, 1972).

Howarth, W. D. (ed.), *Comic Drama: the European Heritage* (London: Methuen, 1978).

Molière: A Playwright and His Audience (Cambridge: Cambridge University Press, 1982).

and Thomas Merlin (eds.), *Molière: Stage and Study. Essays in Honour of W. G. Moore* (Oxford: Clarendon Press, 1973).

Hubert, Judd D., *Molière and the Comedy of Intellect* (Berkeley and Los Angeles: University of California Press, 1982).

Irigaray, Luce, *This Sex Which Is Not One*, trans. Catherine Porter (Ithaca: Cornell University Press, 1985).

Jasinski, René, *Molière et le Misanthrope* (Paris: Armand Colin, 1951).

Kintzler, C., 'Les Femmes savantes de Molière et la question des fonctions du savoir', *XVIIe siècle*, 211 (2001), 243–56.

Knutson, Harold, *Molière: An Archetypal Approach* (Toronto: University of Toronto Press, 1976).

The Triumph of Wit: Molière and Restoration Comedy (Columbus: Ohio State University Press, 1988).

Lalande, Roxanne, *Intruders in the Play World: The Dynamics of Gender in Molière's Comedies* (Teaneck, NJ: Fairleigh Dickinson Press; London: Associated University Presses, 1996).

Lancaster, Henry C., *A History of French Dramatic Literature in the Seventeenth Century*, 9 vols. (Baltimore, MD: Johns Hopkins Press, 1929–42).

Lanson, Gustave, 'Molière et la farce', *Revue de Paris* (1901), 129–53.

Lawrence, Francis L., *Molière: The Comedy of Unreason* (New Orleans: Tulane University Press, 1968).

Longino, Michèle, *Orientalism in French Classical Drama* (Cambridge: Cambridge University Press, 2002).

Lougee, C., *Le Paradis des Femmes. Women, Salons, and Social Stratification in Seventeenth-Century France* (Princeton, NJ: Princeton University Press, 1976).

McBride, Robert, *The Sceptical Vision of Molière* (London: Macmillan, 1977).

The Triumph of Ballet in Molière's Theatre (Lewiston, NY, Queenston, Lampeter: Mellen, 1992).

Mallinson, G. J., *Molière: L'Avare* (London: Grant and Cutler, 1988).

Mazouer, Charles, *Le Personnage du naïf dans le théâtre comique du Moyen Âge à Marivaux* (Paris: Klincksieck, 1979).

Trois Comédies de Molière: Étude sur 'Le Misanthrope', 'George Dandin', 'Le Bourgeois gentilhomme' (Paris: SEDES, 1999).

Mélèse, Pierre, *Le Théâtre et le public à Paris sous Louis XIV, 1659–1715* (Paris: Droz, 1934).

Michaut, Gustave, *La Jeunesse de Molière* (Paris: Hachette, 1922).

Les Débuts de Molière à Paris (Paris: Hachette, 1923).

Les Luttes de Molière (Paris: Hachette, 1925).

Mongrédien, Georges, *Dictionnaire biographique des comédiens français au XVIIe siècle* (Paris: Centre National de la Recherche Scientifique, 1961).

Moore, Will G., *Molière. A New Criticism* (Oxford: Clarendon Press, 1949).

Muratore, Mary Jo, *Mimesis and Metatextuality in the French Neo-classical Text: Reflexive Readings of La Fontaine, Molière, Racine* (Geneva: Droz, 1994).

Norman, Larry, *The Public Mirror: Molière and the Social Comedy of Depiction* (Chicago: University of Chicago Press, 1999).

Nottingham French Studies, 33, 1, ed. Stephen Bamforth (Spring, 1994) (number devoted to Molière).

Nouveau Moliériste (Le), ed. Robert McBride and Noël Peacock (from 1994), published by the Universities of Glasgow and Ulster.

Nurse, Peter H., *Molière and the Comic Spirit* (Geneva: Droz, 1991).

Parish, Richard (ed.), *Le Tartuffe* (Bristol: Bristol Classical Press, 1994).

Peacock, Noël, *Molière: Les Femmes savantes* (London and New York: Grant and Cutler, 1990).

Pineau, Joseph, *Le Théâtre de Molière. Une dynamique de la liberté* (Paris: Minard, 2000).

Plantié, Jacqueline, *La Mode du portrait littéraire en France, 1641–81* (Paris: Champion, 1994).

Pommier, René, *Études sur Le Tartuffe* (Paris: SEDES, 1994).

Raynaud, Maurice, *Les Médecins au temps de Molière* (Paris: Didier, 1863).

Rey-Flaud, Bernadette, *Molière et la farce* (Geneva: Droz, 1996).

Riggs, Larry W., *Molière and Plurality: Decomposition of the Classicist Self* (New York: Lang, 1989).

'Reason's Text as Palimpsest: Sensuality Subverts "Sense" in Molière's *Les Femmes savantes*', *Papers on French Seventeenth Century Literature*, 28 (2001), 93–103.

Scott, Virginia, *Molière: A Theatrical Life* (Cambridge: Cambridge University Press, 2000).

Shaw, David, 'Molière and the Doctors', *Nottingham French Studies*, 33, 1 (Spring, 1994), 133–42.

Simon, Alfred, *Molière. Qui êtes-vous?* (Lyon: La Manufacture, 1987).

Tobin, Ronald W., *'Tarte à la crème': Comedy and Gastronomy in Molière's Theatre* (Columbus: Ohio State University Press, 1990).

Tomlinson, Philip (ed.), *French 'Classical' Theatre Today: Teaching, Research, Performance* (Amsterdam: Rodopi, 2001).

Vernet, Max, *Molière. Côté jardin, côté cour* (Paris: Nizet, 1991).

Viala, Alain, *Naissance de l'écrivain* (Paris: Minuit, 1985).

Wadsworth, Philip A., *Molière and the Italian Theatrical Tradition* (n.p.: French Literature Publications Company, 1977).

Wear, Andrew, 'Aspects of Seventeenth-century French Medicine', *Newsletter of the Society for Seventeenth-Century French Studies*, 4 (1982), 118–32.

Zwillenberg, Myrna K., 'Arnolphe, Fate's Fool', *Modern Language Review*, 68 (1973), 292–308.

INDEX

CAMBRIDGE COMPANIONS TO LITERATURE

Authors

Edward Albee *edited by Stephen J. Bottoms*

Margaret Atwood *edited by Coral Ann Howells*

W. H. Auden *edited by Stan Smith*

Jane Austen *edited by Edward Copeland and Juliet McMaster*

Beckett *edited by John Pilling*

Aphra Behn *edited by Derek Hughes and Janet Todd*

Walter Benjamin *edited by David S. Ferris*

William Blake *edited by Morris Eaves*

Brecht *edited by Peter Thomson and Glendyr Sacks* (second edition)

The Brontës *edited by Heather Glen*

Byron *edited by Drummond Bone*

Albert Camus *edited by Edward J. Hughes*

Willa Cather *edited by Marilee Lindemann*

Cervantes *edited by Anthony J. Cascardi*

Chaucer, second edition *edited by Piero Boitani and Jill Mann*

Chekhov *edited by Vera Gottlieb and Paul Allain*

Coleridge *edited by Lucy Newlyn*

Wilkie Collins *edited by Jenny Bourne Taylor*

Joseph Conrad *edited by J. H. Stape*

Dante *edited by Rachel Jacoff* (second edition)

Charles Dickens *edited by John O. Jordan*

Emily Dickinson *edited by Wendy Martin*

John Donne *edited by Achsah Guibbory*

Dostoevskii *edited by W. J. Leatherbarrow*

Theodore Dreiser *edited by Leonard Cassuto and Claire Virginia Eby*

John Dryden *edited by Steven N. Zwicker*

George Eliot *edited by George Levine*

T. S. Eliot *edited by A. David Moody*

Ralph Ellison *edited by Ross Posnock*

Ralph Waldo Emerson *edited by Joel Porte and Saundra Morris*

William Faulkner *edited by Philip M. Weinstein*

Henry Fielding *edited by Claude Rawson*

F. Scott Fitzgerald *edited by Ruth Prigozy*

Flaubert *edited by Timothy Unwin*

E. M. Forster *edited by David Bradshaw*

Brian Friel *edited by Anthony Roche*

Robert Frost *edited by Robert Faggen*

Elizabeth Gaskell *edited by Jill L. Matus*

Henry David Thoreau *edited by Joel Myerson*
Tolstoy *edited by Donna Tussing Orwin*
Mark Twain *edited by Forrest G. Robinson*
Virgil *edited by Charles Martindale*
Edith Wharton *edited by Millicent Bell*
Walt Whitman *edited by Ezra Greenspan*

Oscar Wilde *edited by Peter Raby*
Tennessee Williams *edited by Matthew C. Roudané*
Mary Wollstonecraft *edited by Claudia L. Johnson*
Virginia Woolf *edited by Sue Roe and Susan Sellers*
Wordsworth *edited by Stephen Gill*
W. B. Yeats *edited by Marjorie Howes and John Kelly*
Zola *edited by Brian Nelson*

Topics

The Actress *edited by Maggie B. Gale and John Stokes*
The African American Novel *edited by Maryemma Graham*
The African American Slave Narrative *edited by Audrey A. Fisch*
American Modernism *edited by Walter Kalaidjian*
American Realism and Naturalism *edited by Donald Pizer*
American Women Playwrights *edited by Brenda Murphy*
Australian Literature *edited by Elizabeth Webby*
British Romanticism *edited by Stuart Curran*
Canadian Literature *edited by Eva-Marie Kröller*
The Classic Russian Novel *edited by Malcolm V. Jones and Robin Feuer Miller*
Contemporary Irish Poetry *edited by Matthew Campbell*
Crime Fiction *edited by Martin Priestman*

The Eighteenth-Century Novel *edited by John Richetti*
Eighteenth-Century Poetry *edited by John Sitter*
English Literature, 1500–1600 *edited by Arthur F. Kinney*
English Literature, 1650–1740 *edited by Steven N. Zwicker*
English Literature, 1740–1830 *edited by Thomas Keymer and Jon Mee*
English Poetry, Donne to Marvell *edited by Thomas N. Corns*
English Renaissance Drama, second edition *edited by A. R. Braunmuller and Michael Hattaway*
English Restoration Theatre *edited by Deborah C. Payne Fisk*
Feminist Literary Theory *edited by Ellen Rooney*
The French Novel: from 1800 to the Present *edited by Timothy Unwin*
Gothic Fiction *edited by Jerrold E. Hogle*